TROUT
in
SOUTH AFRICA

TROUT
in
SOUTH AFRICA

Bob Crass

M

ISBN 0 86954 283 4

First edition, first impression 1986

Published by
Macmillan South Africa (Publishers) (Pty) Ltd
P O Box 31487, Braamfontein, 2017
Johannesburg

Associated companies throughout the world

Cover design and illustrations by Rose Crass Strebel
Set in 10 on 12 point Plantin
by Cityset
Printed and bound by Printpak Books, Cape Town

Acknowledgements

Acknowledgement is due first of all, perhaps, to a four-pound brown trout that aroused the intense interest of the eighteen-month-old son of a country doctor, who brought the fish into the nursery at bath-time. In later years my father fostered that interest, while insisting on the discipline without which no one can become a competent fly fisher.

Later still, those fine naturalists, Frank Bush, Keppel Barnard and A. Cecil Harrison, led me to a study of freshwater ecology which qualified me to join the fisheries section of the Natal Parks Board. To the Board, and in particular to Col. Jack Vincent and John T. Geddes-Page, I owe the opportunity of becoming involved not only with trout, but with the broader field of nature conservation. My experience with the Board forms the basis for much of what appears in the following pages, although any opinions may be purely personal.

To my wife, Joan, has fallen the task of supplying material and moral support, as well as demonstrating an ability to bring more fish to net than her husband. Of the innumerable people who have assisted in the provision of information, the following come to mind: John Campbell, Jake Alletson, Leslie Acutt, Mike Coke, Dave Rowe-Rowe, Orty Bourquin and George Hughes; S.S. du Plessis, Ricky Pott, Eric Brewer and Peter Arderne; Stephen McVeigh, C. Ross-Munro and Pieter le Roux.

Charles Barry acted as catalyst for the project, by persuading David Mitchell, managing director of Macmillan in Johannesburg, to commission a book on South African trout fishing. As a result, Eleanor-Mary Cadell pressed me to begin writing. Basil van Rooyen and Marina Pearson have brought the project to completion. For reading and commenting on the typescript, I am grateful to Hugh Huntley, Thelma Anderson and my daughter, Sally Ovendale. Reg Gush made dark-room facilities available for me. Typing was done by Sue Black.

Tom Sutcliffe gave me free access to his collection of books and photographs and arranged for the use of Tom Burgers' study of the Smalblaar River (p.56), as well as donating the illustration on p.79 and the photograph of A.C. Harrison on p. 145. For the other two illustrations on p.145 I am indebted, respectively, to Ethleen Acutt and Jackie King, who enabled me to obtain the photograph of F.C. Braun. Malcolm Meintjes provided the bottom photograph on p.161, while Bob Frean supplied those on pp.77 and 130. Tom Sutcliffe made available colour photographs of stream insects by Neil Hodges and provided the colour picture of the club room of the Cape Piscatorial Society.

Apart from the photographs, all illustrations, drawings, maps, and art work (including the cover) are by my daughter, Rose Crass Strebel.

Contents

Introduction

Trout have only recently become a part of the South African scene. A hundred years ago the nearest trout were to be found in the Atlas Mountains of Morocco. Since the first successful introduction in 1890, these immigrants from the northern hemisphere, brown trout from Europe and rainbow from America, have become firmly established wherever conditions are suitable.

The pioneers who brought trout to South Africa did so for one reason: to enjoy the sport of fly fishing. Trout have a commercial value as food, of course, and today one can walk into a supermarket to buy trout that spent their short lives in a fish farm before being netted out to supply the gourmet trade. But that is an insignificant aspect of the part played by trout in the social culture of South Africa. Most of the trout bred, even by those whose interest in fish culture is purely commercial, are destined to provide sport rather than food.

Ever since their initial introduction, trout have been accorded a privileged position in this country. At a time when indigenous fish received no special consideration, laws were passed imposing penalties on anyone who caught trout by unauthorised means. Nowhere else in the world, except perhaps in New Zealand, have trout received such rigorous protection as here.

The reason for their privileged position is the glamorous image that trout project. To the angler there is no more glamorous object than a golden-flanked brown trout fresh from a sparkling mountain stream. Even an overfed rainbow from a man-made lake excites the admiration of its captor and the jealousy of other less fortunate fishermen. Fly fishing for trout epitomises that special magic which makes angling, in the words of John Buchan, a way of life rather than a mere pastime.

To a biologist, a trout may be no more than a cold-blooded aquatic predator with very limited brain power. In the context of human behaviour, a trout has attributes which enable it to play a central part in an activity that helps to maintain the sanity of modern technological man. The world is becoming increasingly artificial and townsmen, in particular, need an absorbing hobby as a foil to the strains of urban existence. Following a small white ball across a fairway or jogging along city pavements may offer diversion, but angling provides contact with nature.

Diversity of experience is the keynote of an angler's life. Rivers and lakes are endlessly varied in their scenic attractions, while the response of the fish one hopes to tempt is scarcely ever predictable. New developments in tackle and fishing

1

technique attract interest, debate and finally trial at the waterside. Angling should never be dull; trout fishing least of all.

One of the main reasons for the superiority of fly fishing, in the eyes of its devotees, is its potential for innovation and experimentation. The artificial fly is an object on which more attention is lavished than on any other type of bait or lure. New patterns are constantly being evolved and each angler has his own idiosyncrasies which he is free to express in his choice of a fly. Those who tie their own flies enjoy a hobby that often becomes an end in itself. The ostensible reason for dressing a hook in feathers and silk is to deceive a trout, but the real motive may be self expression on the part of the fly tier. The artistic and colourful concoctions that adorn tackle boxes are designed to impress fishermen rather than fish.

Because fly fishing has such a broad appeal it has inspired a flood of articles in journals and magazines as well as a multitude of books on all aspects of the sport. Many kinds of fish, in both fresh and salt waters, feature in angling literature, but trout hold a unique position. More has been written about trout than about any other animal, except man himself. Interest in trout goes much deeper than merely how to catch them. The life history, habits, behaviour and ecology of trout invite study owing to their intrinsic interest as well as the need for scientific knowledge to plan effective management.

Conservation, in the sense of wise use, depends on understanding the key factors that determine the well-being of a fish population, as with any other resource. Without efficient conservation, the sport of fly fishing has no future. Conversely, measures that help to maintain trout populations are good for the environment generally.

Water resources are scarce in South Africa and their conservation is a national priority. A stream suitable for trout has to be clear, unpolluted and reasonably constant in flow. Such a stream must, by its very nature, be well conserved. The needs of trout therefore coincide with the needs of the whole community. At the very least, one may say that trout are a good indicator of the health of a waterway. But, in fact, trout may be regarded as a positive factor in the drive to promote good conservation practice. People are keener to look after things that give them pleasure than they are to attend to matters of less personal interest. It is therefore easier to work up enthusiasm among sportsmen than among ordinary city dwellers for the preservation of a natural river. A stream that is in good order indicates a well-managed catchment. The voice of every enlightened citizen should be raised in support of the people who look after the veld and soil of our country, but anglers have an especially strong incentive to applaud good conservation and condemn practices that destroy our natural resources.

Regrettably, development is bound to have a negative impact on rivers: farmers cannot avoid a certain amount of soil erosion from the effects of grazing animals and the cultivation of crops; road building increases the sediment load in rivers; water is removed for irrigation or urban use; and towns and factories cause pollution in the form of sewage and chemical effluents. Such impacts may be severe in some cases and negligible in others. The more dense the human settlement the more severe are the effects likely to become. The Eerste River in the Cape, for instance, was once famous for its trout. Today, only the upper reaches remain in a reasonably natural condition. From Stellenbosch to the sea industrial and agricultural developments have radically changed the waterway, leaving virtually no place for a trout to hide. Other well-known rivers have deteriorated owing to soil erosion from denuded catchments.

Whereas human activities have downgraded the status of trout streams, man-made lakes have become a new and beneficial feature of the South African countryside. The activities of farmers and engineers have added a whole new dimension to our aquatic resources. Natural lakes are confined almost exclusively to the coastal plains of the southern Cape and north-eastern Natal. The hinterland has only shallow pans and oxbow ponds.

Dam building has created thousands of permanent bodies of water in which indigenous plants and animals thrive. Although dams are generally designed to supply domestic or agricultural water, many are admirably suited to the support of fish. Trout cannot breed in still water, but stocking with hatchery-reared fish often produces excellent results in dams with suitable conditions for trout to live and grow. The part played by dams in the provision of fly fishing increases year by year and this trend is bound to continue. The capacity of our rivers to produce trout cannot be increased to any significant extent. To meet the expanding demand we must look to man-made lakes and ponds.

Much information has appeared in print on various aspects of trout in South Africa. Books by writers such as Bennion, Hilliard, Nuttall, Yates and Hey form a record of the experiences of an earlier generation of anglers, while Salomon, Meintjes, Blackman and Sutcliffe have recent books to their credit.

In the selected bibliography on p.201 I list books which I have found relevant to trout in South Africa, with comments on each.

Innumerable articles in magazines, newspapers and journals have been written by South African anglers and scientists. The pages of *Piscator*, the journal of the Cape Piscatorial Society, are particularly rich in good reading. Official reports, particularly those of earlier vintage, contain much fascinating information. Fiction, with a fly-fishing theme, is represented by Neville Nuttall's *Proud River*, as well as some short pieces by John Beams.

Writings about trout are mainly anecdotal, didactic or technical. Poets seem not to have been inspired to any great extent by trout, but our own Roy Campbell, in his satirical poem about Natal, *The Wayzgoose*, includes the couplet:

Where trouts the size of salmon throng the creeks
And worms the size of magistrates — the beaks.

Such juxtaposition of trout, worms and magistrates conjures up all manner of dark thoughts. Was Campbell suffering from a guilt complex, because he had used a worm to catch a trout and therefore feared he would be brought before the beak? Or was he suggesting that magistrates themselves might fall from grace?

In the following chapters I have tried to present trout in an historical, human and environmental context, under the following headings:

1. **Life history and requirements of trout.** After some basic information on brown and rainbow trout, including an explanation of condition factors, chapters on breeding, growth and longevity and on feeding behaviour are followed by notes on the way in which brown and rainbow trout have responded to the physical conditions in different rivers and still waters, and to the various predators and competitors.

2. **South African trout waters.** This deals with characteristic features of different areas in the Republic, with the object of giving a general statement of what an angler may expect to find in each area, together with details of some of the more productive and interesting waters.

3. **The art of fly fishing.** Despite the vast amount that has been written about catching trout, there is always debate about tackle and how to use it. I have offered my views in the light of my experience as an angler. The section ends with a discussion on angling ethics and legal restrictions in general.

4. **Development of trout fishing in South Africa.** Many people have been involved in the establishment of trout and the organisation of fly fishing. An historical outline includes information on some of the leading personalities from the time of the pioneers up to the present. The part played and the services offered by official bodies and clubs are discussed.

5. **Conservation and management.** After discussing control and responsibility in general, some aspects of the management of rivers and of still waters are considered in the light of what has been done in South Africa.

1 LIFE HISTORY AND REQUIREMENTS OF TROUT

1. Some basic information

Two kinds of trout are established in South Africa — brown and rainbow. Attempts were made to introduce Atlantic salmon, but these migratory fish had no chance of finding suitable conditions. Eggs of American eastern brook trout have been imported several times. This species is a char, not a true trout, and its intolerance of high temperatures has ruled out permanent survival in this country, although breeding occurred in at least one Natal stream. Brook trout were kept for several years in hatcheries, and proved easy to propagate as long as temperatures remained low. At Jonkershoek, hybrid brook-brown were produced for distribution to angling waters. The cross is known as a tiger-trout and fair numbers were caught in Cape waters — notably Steenbras Reservoir — a few years ago.

The first trout to reach this country were brown trout, which are in fact indigenous to the African continent, but only to the northern extremity that borders on the Mediterranean. Their distribution includes Europe and parts of Asia, but unlike their cousins, the Atlantic salmon, they did not cross the Atlantic to America. The eastern United States had only char, no true trout, until the intervention of man. When you read of the brown trout of such famous streams as the Beaverkill or the Neversink, remember the ancestors of those fish were of European origin.

Rainbow trout hail from the Pacific coast of North America and, thanks to human agency, have spread all over the world, wherever suitable waters occur. Although there is little difference between rainbow and brown trout in their ability to colonise and survive in rivers, the rainbow is easier to propagate in fish farms and is the predominant species in most dams and reservoirs.

It is easy to tell the difference between brown and rainbow, although anglers do sometimes make a mistake. Every now and then one hears of a hybrid, but this always proves to be either a brown or a rainbow with somewhat unusual colouration. There is no authentic record of a naturally produced hybrid, and even artificial cross-breeding generally fails to produce viable embryos. Yet production of crosses with the more distantly related char is feasible.

Trout vary in colouration. Those from clear water and a pale background are brighter than those from turbid, dark waters. Pigmentation is affected by the amount of light that the fish's eyes receive. For this reason, a blind trout is almost black. Another factor that affects a trout's colour is the approach of the breeding season.

Both brown and rainbow have spots on the body, in varying quantity. Each spot on a brown trout has a pale area, like a halo, around it. Those on a rainbow are smaller, with no pale areas around them. Red spots often occur on brown trout, but never on rainbows. A brownish yellow or golden colour on the side of the head and on the flanks is characteristic of browns, whereas a flush of pink indicates a rainbow.

As well as being clearly distinguishable on their appearance, there are a number of differences in life history. While growth for the first two years of life tends to be faster in rainbows, brown trout generally live longer. If both species are introduced to a river, they may co-exist for a few years, but after a time one usually disappears. This is to be expected, since their similar requirements for food, shelter and breeding places lead to competition for available resources in the environment. An interesting point is that rainbow do not necessarily oust brown trout, or vice versa. Generally if one species is well established and the other is introduced, the latter may multiply for a few years but in the end will disappear. This has happened in a number of Natal streams, especially brown trout waters that have received rainbows. Such well-known brown trout rivers as the Inzinga and Mooi have had quite a high proportion of rainbows in certain sections for two or three seasons. Then quite suddenly, the rainbows have disappeared. On the other hand, the Polela and Little Tugela, which for a time carried mixed populations, have become pure rainbow waters.

This tendency for the established species to remain in possession of a river makes it unlikely that the entry of rainbows from a dam or fish farm to a brown trout stream will have any permanent effect. Those who enjoy fishing for brown trout may therefore rest assured that the presence of rainbows in the catchment of a brown trout stream does not pose a threat.

The precise mechanism by which one species displaces another remains obscure. Each individual trout competes with its fellows for a feeding station but there is no evidence that brown trout would gang up on an odd rainbow to drive it out. On the contrary, where only a few rainbows occur among a lot of browns the rainbows may grow bigger than browns of similar age. This was noticeable in the Mooi River. The converse was reported by A.C. Harrison in the Berg River, where the few browns were of better size and condition than the numerous rainbows. These observations indicate that the feeding habits of the two species differ enough to give an advantage to members of the less common species. Yet there must be some type of pressure that causes the disappearance of the minority population.

To unravel the social relationships and behaviour patterns of fish is even more difficult than in the case of birds or mammals. Most fish research is based on dead specimens, which can, indeed, tell us a good deal about what is going on in that particular population.

One of the first things we want to know about a fish is whether it is fat or thin. If it is fat, we can assume it is doing well, that it has ample food and has been growing fast. If its condition is below standard, something is wrong.

What do we mean by "below standard"? How do we set the standard, and how can a large fish be compared with a small one? The answer is to determine the condition factor, which is a measure of relative plumpness. Because a fish grows in depth and breadth as well as length, its mass increases in proportion to the cube of its length.

$M=KL^3$, where M is mass, L is length and K a factor that will remain constant as long as the fish's bodily proportions remain constant. This equation may be rewritten: $K=M/L^3$. The units of mass and length may be either grams and centimetres, or pounds and inches. If we take a fish of 20 cm that weighs 80 g, the K-value comes out at 0,010 0. Similarly, a 40 cm trout of 640 g will have exactly the same K-value. In order to eliminate decimals, we can multiply by 10 000: $K=M/L^3$ x 10 000. For either the 80 g or the 640 g fish, the K-value becomes 100. For a 20 cm trout weighing 96 g, the K-value is 120, which is identical to that of a 40 cm trout weighing 768 g. Thus we have a basis for comparison between fish of different sizes. A trout with a metric condition factor (K) of 100 is a bit on the lean side, whereas one with a condition factor of 120 is in excellent shape.

If pounds and inches are used, the condition factor (written CF) works out at 36 for a fish with a metric K of 100. A very thin trout might have a K-value of only 75 (CF 27), whereas an extremely fat one might have a K-value of 150 (CF 54).

Whether one is working with centimetres and grams or with inches and pounds, there is no need to carry out laborious computations to find the condition factor of a trout. Graphs of various sorts have been devised and, of course, a calculator or computer can be programmed to give the required answer. For the fishery manager who wants to assess the well-being of a trout population, the main problem is generally to persuade anglers to provide accurate data. Records of length and weight are often unreliable. Accurate measurement of length is particularly important because calculation of condition factor requires the length to be cubed. Errors are therefore exaggerated. A simple way of measuring a trout is to lay it flat on a piece of paper, mark the paper at the tip of the fish's nose and at the end of the centre of the tail, remove the trout and measure the distance between the two marks. A good quality spring balance is suitable for recording the weight.

Condition factor varies from one fish to another even in the same water. Some individuals may be more stocky than others that are equally well fed, just as one sees thickset men and tall, slender men. The breeding cycle has a considerable effect on condition factor. Trout that are carrying mature eggs usually have high condition factors, since the eggs increase the body mass by up to 20 per cent. A full stomach will also increase the fish's weight, although seldom by more than three per cent. Condition factors must be interpreted with these facts in mind.

River trout generally have a lower condition factor than dam trout, but there is a wide overlap. Although there is likely to be richer feeding in a dam, there are many exceptions. Even a highly fertile dam may be overstocked, in which case the trout will have condition factors below the optimum. Samples of trout, mainly rainbows, from Natal dams have given a consistent average of about 120, although many fish have been fatter than this.

Well-fed river trout often have a K-value of 120, but the average for both brown and rainbow is nearer 110. Where breeding is prolific and growth slow, condition factors may drop below 100.

With experience, one may assess a trout's condition simply by looking at it. Its behaviour when hooked also gives a good indication of its fitness. A healthy, well-nourished fish pulls line off the reel and often jumps, perhaps several times. Rainbows are generally more vigorous than brown trout, but a brown in peak condition will give a good account of itself, making up in dogged persistence for the more spectacular behaviour of the rainbow.

What is technically known as an organoleptic test, in other words tasting the flesh when cooked, is of prime interest to the gourmet. A trout that is undernourished, or has recently spawned, has soft white flesh of poor quality. A well-fed fish has firm, curdy flesh with orange or pink colouration and excellent flavour. Connoisseurs rate trout from a clear, fast-flowing stream more highly than those from a dam. Natural food is supposed to produce trout of better quality than an artificial diet of pelleted meal. Prejudice may, however, play a part in this belief and there is no doubt that fish-farm trout are by no means inferior if produced under the right conditions. Some people claim that a top-class brown trout has a slightly more delicate flavour than a similar rainbow. I would agree with this opinion.

An angler, who is more interested in catching fish than eating them, will probably make a habit of opening up the first trout of the day to see what it has been feeding on. Apart from mere curiosity, the motivation may be to try to match the trout's diet by offering a realistic imitation of the natural insects. To sort out what is generally a heterogeneous collection, it is helpful to separate the stomach contents in a dish of water or merely in the palm of one's hand.

To obtain a clue to the fish's age, the development of the reproductive organs is a useful guide. Small, orange-coloured ovaries or pinkish, stringlike testes tucked away at the top end of the body cavity indicate a juvenile trout. If it is a male, it is probably less than a year old and if a female, less than two years old. Once a female has spawned, generally at the end of its second year, the ovaries remain enlarged, even in spring when the new season's eggs are still small. A male that has spawned has elongate, whitish testes.

A well-known method of ageing trout is by scale reading, as discussed in Chapter 2. Scales for this purpose should be scraped off the fish's flank, below the dorsal fin. About 20 are adequate. They should be spread on a piece of paper and allowed to dry, before being placed in an envelope labelled with the necessary particulars, especially the accurately measured length of the fish.

Parasites and diseases are seldom found in South African trout, except when the fish are being held under crowded conditions on a fish farm. Even then, trouble is generally due not to disease but to high temperature and lack of oxygen. Bacterial infection may become apparent in trout that are being held under poor conditions, but such infections are unlikely to be the primary cause of death.

Parasitic worms have never been reported in South African trout, although indigenous fish are subject to some that form cysts in the skin and others that occur internally.

A final point about dead trout. Unless they are ones that you or your friends have caught, you probably won't find any. Except in hatchery ponds, where large numbers of trout are being kept, it is a rare event to see a dead fish. In open waters, whether man-made lakes or rivers, trout must be dying all the time, but the rarity with which they are seen is remarkable. One can only assume that crabs and other scavengers rapidly dispose of the remains. Now and again a mass mortality is observed. This may be due to natural causes, such as an extreme rise in temperature, or to pollution by toxic effluents. Apart from such infrequent catastrophes, trout usually end their days by quietly disappearing.

2. Breeding, growth and longevity

Trout breed in the cold part of the year, unlike most other freshwater fish, which spawn in late spring or summer. Whereas adult trout can withstand a temperature of more than 25 °C, at least for a short time, their eggs die if the water is warmer than about 16 °C. In South Africa, therefore, successful spawning can take place only between April and August, except in streams at very high altitude or in those that are fed by cold springs.

Once a trout attains sexual maturity it normally spawns every year until it reaches the end of its life, although there is a tendency for old fish to fail to produce eggs or sperm. Another cause of infertility is stress, either through the fish being subjected to a period of critically high temperature or through a severe shortage of food. Temperature stress is aggravated by a poor supply of oxygen under crowded conditions. After a hot summer, a hatchery manager may find that the female fish in his ponds fail to produce fertile ova. The males may also be affected. River trout may fail to show normal sexual development after a prolonged drought, with low water and high temperatures.

In both sexes, development of the gonads takes place over several months. Males normally mature a year earlier than females. In South Africa the great majority of rainbow males mature at the end of their first season. With brown trout there is a lower percentage of yearlings that become sexually active. In both species, if growth is rapid early maturity is likely. An individual that is large for its age generally matures in its first year, whereas a stunted male may be capable of spawning only in its second year.

Similarly, a poorly grown female may not develop eggs until its third winter, although the great majority of South African brown and rainbow trout do spawn at two years old. This tendency towards early maturity is probably associated with the relatively high temperatures found here, compared with parts of Europe or North America where trout may not develop eggs until three, four or even five years of age.

Growth of the reproductive organs involves a severe drain on the bodily resources. In adult fish, little or no increase in length takes place from the time the roe is developing until spawning is over. Condition deteriorates, through mobilisation of stores of fat around the internal organs and in the muscles. The flesh becomes softer and less tasty when cooked. This applies particularly to males, whose appearance undergoes a marked change in the breeding season. The skin darkens and develops a slimy covering, while the jaws elongate. In old males, the lower jaw turns up at the end, giving the fish a pugnacious look. Even in summer, before the onset of the bodily changes that are associated with spawning, a male's grumpy expression is said, by my wife, to distinguish it from a female.

A mature male's body is deeper and narrower than that of a female and its colouration is more accentuated. In the case of rainbow trout there may be a bright pink flush from the gill cover down the flank, while red spots and golden flanks often characterise male brown trout.

As well as using up a great deal of the nourishment that would otherwise go towards maintenance and growth of the fish's body, sexual maturity involves a change in behaviour. Food-seeking gives place to courtship, particularly in males, whose stomachs appear to shrink from disuse over the spawning period. The reproductive urge becomes paramount as both sexes devote their energy to propagating the species. In rivers, the fish seek shallow areas where the water is flowing over a gravel bed, perhaps close to the pool in which they have been living, but sometimes a considerable distance upstream. Trout in a dam move up the feeder stream if it is large enough. Should the dam have too small an inlet the fish may try to spawn on a stony bed in a shallow part of the dam. The eggs have little chance of hatching, but the female may at least get rid of the ova which otherwise remain in the body cavity. Unshed ova are said by some authors to be reabsorbed, but there is no clear evidence of this occurring. On the contrary, eggs that are carried over to the next season often form an unhealthy mass, compressed by the newly developing ovaries. Fish in which this has happened are described as spawn-bound and may die as a result.

A female that has located a suitable gravel bed, preferably where there is a smooth but fairly rapid flow at the tail of a pool, sets about the task of preparing a nest or redd. She does so by turning on her side and making vigorous up-and-down movements of the tail. The currents set up in the water shift the gravel, leaving a hollow into which the eggs are laid. Fertilisation occurs when the male discharges milt over the eggs as they sink into the redd, where they are covered by gravel disturbed by the female as she makes another redd slightly upstream of the first. The process is repeated until the female has exhausted her supply of eggs, whereupon she leaves the spawning area to seek shelter in a pool.

Each male may fertilise the eggs from several females, or attempt to do so, staying for a prolonged period in the spawning area and competing with other males. Thus although the female produces a greater mass of reproductive material and is responsible for nest cutting, the male is subject to a more severe drain on his resources. The stress of spawning leads to debility in both sexes, but perhaps more so in males. Much of the natural mortality that occurs each year is associated, directly or indirectly, with spawning. The fact that males do not, on average, live as long as females seems to be linked to sexual activity. We shall refer to this again in the section on longevity.

The strain to which a trout is subjected by spawning varies considerably. Given a favourable environment and abundant food, the whole process may represent no more than a temporary setback, but if conditions are difficult the weakened fish may die of food shortage or be killed by predators. There are also differences between the two species, brown and rainbow, with the latter showing more adverse effects than the former. Certainly brown trout males live longer than rainbow males. This may be due in part simply to the fact that fewer yearling brown trout reach sexual maturity. But brown trout are also perhaps less inclined to wear themselves out by aggressive behaviour on the spawning grounds. Another point is that the reproductive organs (soft roe) seem relatively smaller in brown trout than in rainbows. Although statistical evidence is lacking, if there is such a difference it would indicate that rainbow males commit a larger amount of their bodily resources to spawning.

Early in the season, both ovaries and testes are inconspicuous, especially in juvenile fish. If spawning has occurred the previous winter, the gonads remain more elongate than in a juvenile although they have little bulk. The ovaries are orange-coloured with a granular appearance due to the eggs, which gradually increase in size until they reach 4 to 5 mm when ripe. The testes are whitish and flattened, filling out to have a smooth creamy appearance when mature. Liquid milt runs freely from a male that is ready to spawn and such fish are often caught late in autumn.

Trout have a high breeding potential, although the number of eggs produced by each female is very much less than that produced by some other fish. A mullet, for instance, may lay six million eggs and even in freshwater species, which tend to have larger eggs than marine fish, the number may exceed a hundred thousand. A large trout may carry as many as five thousand eggs, but five hundred would be a likely figure for the average four-hundred-gram female. Both the number and the size vary considerably from one individual to another, with larger fish having both more and bigger eggs.

The larger trout also tend to spawn earlier in the season, but the actual date of spawning depends on several factors. First is the effect of heredity. There are early, mid-season and late-spawning strains of trout. Browns generally spawn earlier than rainbows and, in Natal, most of the eggs are laid in May and early June. Rainbows have a later peak period of activity, but overall their breeding season is more extended, perhaps because a variety of strains has been introduced to South Africa. Most of our rainbows spawn in June and July, but spent fish have been caught in May and others are ready to spawn only in August. A batch of rainbows imported from Denmark matured for spawning as late as September (see my report in *Piscator* No. 79, 1970). These were evidently from a spring-spawning strain that maintained its hereditary tendency when brought to the southern hemisphere. Another interesting feature of these trout was that some matured at an age of only one and a half years instead of the usual minimum of nearly two years.

The second determinant of spawning time is light. Maturity can be experimentally accelerated or held back by submitting trout to artificially controlled lighting. The third factor is temperature and, under natural conditions, this probably acts in conjunction with changes in daylight periodicity. Normally, fish are subjected to the combined effects of shortening daylight hours and falling temperatures in autumn, when their eggs are maturing. In the Underberg district of Natal, fish in the headwaters tend to mature earlier than those farther downstream. One might speculate on the possibility that this is due to a stronger response to sunshine cycles in the

A spawning stream at the headwaters of the Umgeni River, Natal. Trout are thrashing about in the shallow water.

shallow, clear headwater areas. The more rapid fall in autumn temperatures might also have an influence.

In rivers with suitable spawning places one seldom finds a female that is still carrying ova in spring, apart from a few odd loose eggs. Where a river is slow-flowing, with a silted bed and no clean gravel, one may find trout well after the spawning season has passed with over-ripe eggs in the body cavity. In general, however, the problem of spawn-bound females occurs only in dams without an adequate feeder stream.

Trout eggs are heavier than water, so they sink into the interstices of the gravel after being deposited. The natural spawning process, including external fertilisation as the eggs sink into the redd, appears somewhat haphazard. Nevertheless, under good conditions a very high proportion of the ova do, in fact, hatch into healthy alevins. In the early days of trout propagation, fish culturists thought that the artificial stripping of eggs and careful mixing of milt in a small quantity of water, with subsequent care of the ova in a hatchery, would result in a higher survival rate than nature could provide. But this is not necessarily true. Many years ago, Hobbs in New Zealand found that up to 97 per cent of naturally spawned ova were fertile. In the 1950s Leslie Acutt confirmed this finding in Natal. Much depends, however, on the quality of water flowing in the stream. Trout embryos are highly susceptible to a lack of oxygen. The female instinctively selects a site in which water can percolate through the gravel bed, maintaining a supply of the life-giving gas. Should a freshet bring down water loaded with sediment, the nest may become choked with silt. Normally South African trout streams run clear in the winter, especially those in the summer rainfall area, but I have examined redds in the Polela River after a sudden storm that turned the water brown with soil. Instead of healthy translucent ova, opaque white eggs were in the majority. Sinister, cottonwool-like fungal threads were spreading from the dead eggs to those that were still alive. Hatchery managers know well the danger of infection spreading through closely packed trays of ova and wild eggs face a similar threat in a poor environment.

Newly fertilised eggs are remarkably tolerant of mechanical shock. They may be dropped from a height onto a concrete floor from which they bounce like miniature tennis balls without suffering damage. But within 24 hours the developing embryos are extremely sensitive and remain so until they have reached the stage at which their eyes become visible through the eggshell. The eggs are now known as eyed ova and may be safely handled and packed for transport, provided they are kept moist in a well-aerated container. Eyed ova are shipped by the million from one continent to another, thanks to modern air transport. Nineteenth-century efforts to carry live ova from Britain to the southern hemisphere in ships succeeded only when refrigeration slowed down development sufficiently to prevent premature hatching on the journey.

Rate of embryonic development depends on temperature, with brown trout taking slightly longer to hatch than rainbow. At 4 °C more than 100 days elapse after fertilisation, at 8 °C about 56 days and at 12 °C less than 30 days. Fish farmers may find it convenient to accelerate or hold back the development of artificially stripped eggs by controlling the temperature in the hatchery. It is particularly useful to synchronise the time at which different batches of eggs become eyed, so as to make up a large consignment that will transform into alevins simultaneously. When a large number of young fish are to be reared, management will be easier if all are of similar age. Under natural conditions, of course, there will be a considerable difference in date of hatching of early and late-spawned eggs. The early ones will be at an advantage if competition develops between the young fish.

After breaking out of its egg-membrane, a baby trout is known as an alevin. Still attached to the yolk-sac that provides its nourishment, it can do no more than wriggle. When first hatched, an alevin wriggles away from the light, burrowing into the gravel where it is safe from predators. After about two weeks the supply of yolk becomes depleted, the negative reaction to light becomes positive and the alevin wriggles upwards to the surface of the gravel bed in which it was born. As the yolk-sac disappears, its fins and jaws develop. The helpless alevin becomes an active fry, feeding on minute aquatic creatures and dodging anything that instinct tells it may represent danger. Very soon the baby trout acquires the basic behaviour pattern that will enable it to survive — if it is one of the lucky ones. The fact is that "many are called, but few are chosen". Each fry is normally a member of a family that numbers several hundred. In a well-populated stream, numerous other families of similar size are all emerging into the sunshine of their new world, but it is a world with strictly limited resources.

In a stream with very few adults, nests may be so far apart that their progeny have ample space to find the individual territories that each fry requires. As a rule, however, fierce competition is the order of the day. Those that are first on the scene, or that happen to be slightly superior in physical activity, take up station in shallow water where the current brings them food. If another fry approaches too closely, it is chased away. Young trout very early in life find themselves subject to a prime biological force, a force that shares out the resources of the world among those destined to survive. Robert Ardrey called it the territorial imperative. It is the mechanism by which nature achieves that great Darwinian principle, the survival of the fittest.

As with most species of living organisms, each individual's most severe struggle for existence is with other members of the same population. A trout's worst enemy is another trout. This does not mean that trout cannibalise each other to any great extent. It is true that a 10 cm trout may swallow a 3 cm trout if it gets the chance. But, under natural conditions, small trout keep well clear of their larger relatives. Judging by the thousands of trout stomachs examined from different waters in South Africa, as well as overseas, and the very small number of cases of cannibalism reported, one must conclude that predation by large trout is an insignificant cause of death among fry. Trout express their enmity towards one another through territorial competition.

Enmity is perhaps an inappropriate word, since it implies an emotional state of which a trout's simple brain is incapable. It would be more accurate to say that trout have evolved aggressive behaviour patterns to meet competition from their fellows for limited resources. Apart from the aggression of males towards one another at spawning time, it is feeding that stimulates competitive activity. Trout that are resting or taking refuge from danger show no antagonism towards one another.

If fry are held in the unnaturally crowded conditions of a hatchery, their territorial instinct cannot find expression. Each fish lives and feeds in close proximity to hundreds of others. Even under these conditions, it is noticeable that some individuals assert themselves by remaining at the head of the shoal and grabbing more than their fair share of food. In a natural stream there is seldom enough food for all the young fish, so those that survive are the ones that compete successfully by finding a good feeding place and keeping others out of their chosen territory — small though it may be. A great deal depends, of course, on the native of the stream and the stock of trout that it carries. If there is an extensive area of shallow water with a stony bed that produces an abundance of insect larvae, there will be space and food for a great many fry. If no violent floods occur, and drought does not severely curtail the young trout's living space, a relatively high percentage may survive to become fingerlings. The more that survive, the greater will be the likelihood that the carrying capacity of the stream will be reached when the fish are only a few months old.

Carrying capacity is the maximum mass of fish that a given area can support. Once carrying capacity has been reached, there can be no further increase in biomass. In theory, growth of all the fish comes to a standstill. In practice, there will be individuals that continue to grow, while others fail to maintain themselves. Within a particular group of similar-aged fish some remain in better condition and grow faster than others. The more crowded the fish, the more irregular their growth rate. Hatchery managers, whose aim is to produce evenly grown fingerlings, grade their fish at intervals and separate the smaller individuals from their dominant fellows. In nature, those that fall behind may fail to survive, resulting in an automatic culling process. Among those that do survive in crowded populations there may be a variation in length of 150 to 200 per cent between the smallest and the largest members of the same age group. Since the bigger fish tend to be in better condition, the longest individuals may weigh more than eight times as much as the shortest. Uncrowded individuals also vary, but not to the same extent.

These size differences should not be too readily attributed to differences in the genetic growth-potential of the fish. Artificial selection, over a number of generations, has been proved capable of producing a strain that grows faster than the original trout, under hatchery conditions. Selected strains might be expected to grow faster in dams with ample food supply and there have, indeed, been claims of "super-trout" in Britain and the USA. Regrettably little scientific evidence is available to substantiate these claims, which seem restricted to artificially created still waters. No one has reported any attempts at improving the genetic constitution of naturally reproducing stocks of trout in rivers, although it used to be said that "new blood" was required to revitalise the fish when they became inbred. There are several references to this idea in old Natal records. For instance, the Annual Report of the Natal Fisheries Department for 1923 states that "in the opinion of some fishermen, fishing will never improve until the small fish are eliminated and fresh blood introduced". This referred to the Bushman's River.

Genetically influenced differences in growth rate should, in theory, have a significant effect on the average size of trout found in a stream, but long-term scientific experiments would have to be undertaken to establish whether this is in fact true. So much more than inherited growth potential is involved in determining how fast a fish actually increases in size. The key factor is the quantity and quality of food consumed each day. Merely to maintain itself, a fish requires about one per cent of its body mass per day of high-grade protein food. The quality of natural food is probably adequate in most cases, although such things as hard-bodied insects contain a great deal of indigestible material. There was much truth in the remark by the late Gilbert Simes, of Loteni, that trout were in poor condition in part of the Umkomaas River because their main food supply consisted of grasshoppers and "you can't even fatten chickens on grasshoppers".

Jokes aside, the most important limitation on the growth of fish is the food supply. Anyone who runs a trout farm knows that the provision of an abundant, well-balanced diet is a prime requisite for the success of his enterprise. Trout in a natural stream are seldom in a position where all the nourishment they require is freely available. Furthermore, what is available is not evenly shared out. The work of Robert Bachman and others has shown that trout occupy restricted home ranges within which they tend to remain for long periods. Although each trout tries to make the best possible use of its own home range for obtaining food, some must find themselves in better localities than others. Natural food production differs from place to place. There is also the important question of competition.

An area that provides ample food for one trout may offer a poor living for ten.

Bachman showed that, within a given home range, each trout uses certain favourable feeding stations which are selected because they offer easy access to food drifting in the current. A large, dominant fish takes up the most favoured position. Smaller trout keep clear of the dominant ones, but they must all still compete for available food. Unless the total fish population is so sparse that there is no rivalry in obtaining food, each individual will have to share what the stream provides. Bachman considered that trout competed for feeding stations rather than directly for food, but he did not investigate to what extent fish feeding in the vicinity take drifting insects that would otherwise have become available to a fish waiting in its favourite lie.

Whatever the precise mechanism may be by which trout compete with one another, the effects are obvious in any South African river where successful spawning produces a lot of young trout. As soon as the population exceeds a certain density, the average size becomes smaller. The fact that some individuals continue to grow well might lead to the conclusion that their hereditary growth potential is superior to that of others in the same age group. More probably, a better-grown fish is simply one that got ahead of its rivals, either through hatching earlier or through obtaining a particularly favourable feeding station, or both. Hereditary differences doubtless exist but their effects are liable to be masked by differences in the environment of each trout.

In general , young fish grow faster than older ones, but much depends on the food supply. Fish, unlike many other animals, have the capacity to grow until near the end of their lives, provided they can find enough to eat. An important factor that slows down the growth of adult trout is development of the reproductive organs. If, therefore, a male that normally matures at the end of its first year remains sexually inactive, it will continue to grow unchecked and will become larger than others of the same age that have matured. Similarly, some of the largest three-year-old females are unusual individuals that have not spawned at the end of their second year.

As well as growth rate, longevity obviously plays a part in determining the final size attained. It is of interest, therefore, that well-fed trout have a longer life expectancy than ill-nourished individuals. Where a high population density results in severe competition for food, one seldom finds old trout. Anglers often refer to the numerous small fish in an overstocked water as "stunted", implying that they are old fish which have not grown. In fact, they are mostly yearlings. Although perhaps considerably smaller than fish of that age could be if not overcrowded, the abundant yearlings are not really stunted. They retain the potential for rapid growth if transferred to a water with ample food supplies, or if the number of competing trout is drastically reduced.

In a stream that has numerous young trout, older ones have a thin time unless there is an adequate supply of larger food items for the bigger fish. A good example from my own experience is the Malibamatso River in Lesotho. After a period of good spawning conditions, the river was sampled by means of angling and rotenone fish poison in March 1969. Great numbers of rainbows and some brown trout, hatched in 1968, were present together with a small percentage of second-year fish and very few third-year fish. The older trout showed poor growth owing to competition for food. The Malibamatso was seldom visited by anglers, so the population was unaffected by fishing.

The fact that a river, if left to itself, may develop a trout population that consists mainly of small individuals has important management implications. Whether it is feasible to correct a condition that gives rise to anglers' complaints is another question which we shall discuss later. Fishermen like to be able to catch well-grown trout in fair numbers. The trouble is that where the fish are growing well they will not be numerous. The fewer the trout, the more vulnerable they become to anglers.

Because so many factors affect the growth of trout, it is pointless to take statistics from diverse situations and bring them together to give average figures. One may, however, draw some general conclusions about South African trout, in comparison with those from overseas. In doing so it is necessary to treat with caution some of the published information, especially that derived from scale reading. Calculating the age and growth rate of a trout from a study of its scales is a useful technique, but far from infallible.

Scale reading depends on the fact that as a fish's body grows its scales grow proportionately. The scale tissue is laid down in a series of rings that look, suitably magnified, much like the rings on a sawn-through tree trunk. When the fish is growing fast, the scale rings are widely spaced. When a check in growth occurs, the rings become crowded together. A check results from maturation of the sex organs, which occurs once a year, so that generally the scale shows a pattern of annual checks which give a clue to the trout's age. Often, development of the reproductive organs results in complete cessation of scale growth, or actual reabsorption of the tissue at the scale's edge, leaving a slight scar when growth is resumed. This is known as a spawning mark and indicates development of the gonads, whether or not spawning actually

Magnified scale of a 3,7 kg rainbow trout in its fifth year of life; each year is indicated by a number.

20

occurred. Trout from dams where no spawning takes place may show spawning marks as clearly as those from rivers in which the fish do spawn.

If one can establish the position of the annual check, or annulus, it is possible to calculate the length of the fish at the time the check was formed, assuming that growth in scale radius and in body length are proportional. Interpretation of scale reading must be supported by other evidence, however, such as that from known-age fish or the analysis of population samples collected at frequent intervals. A number of workers in Britain and New Zealand, as well as some in South Africa, have arrived at incorrect conclusions through the use of scale reading in the absence of other data.

The commonest error has been to underestimate the length of one-year-old trout. A change in scale growth pattern often occurs at an age of three or four months, and this may be taken for an annulus, thus making the fish out to be a year older than it really is. On the other hand, old trout that have grown very little for the last two or three years may appear, from their scales, to be younger than they really are. This type of error is less likely to occur in South Africa than in the northern hemisphere, where trout live longer than in our comparatively warm climate.

Because a distinct annulus is formed only when a trout reaches sexual maturity, a female trout may show almost uninterrupted growth up to an age of two years. Males, on the contrary, generally show a well-marked check on their scales at the end of their first year. While sexual maturity produces easily recognised annuli, adverse environmental conditions, such as a severe drought in summer, may temporarily halt a trout's growth. This leads to the formation of what scale readers call a "false annulus".

Despite the pitfalls, scale reading is a useful method of studying the age and growth of trout. In South Africa, numerous scale readings have been published in *Piscator* by A.C. Harrison and myself. Evidence derived from known-age fish indicates that our interpretation generally corresponds with the actual life history of the trout. The results show that South African trout compare favourably with those in most overseas countries with regard to growth rate and average size.

Great variations occur from place to place, as well as from one season to another, depending on the productivity of the water and the number of trout that have to share the available food. Some examples will be given later of typical growth rates of trout in different South African waters.

3. Feeding behaviour

Finding enough to eat occupies a large part of the life of all but the most fortunate of trout. There are some that have ample food readily available and fish-farm trout may actually suffer from overeating. Too lavish a supply of artificial feed may cause excessive accumulation of fat, as well as degenerative changes in the liver, leading to death at a comparatively early age. Overeating is never likely to occur under natural conditions, where food shortage is often the cause of a short life expectancy. Few fish find enough food to grow as fast as their genetic potential would allow.

For maintenance alone a trout requires a fairly substantial amount of food each day, especially at higher temperatures. Winifred Frost found that at 5 °C a food intake of one per cent of body weight per day was enough for a trout to maintain its mass, but at 20 °C about two per cent was required. These figures were for fish held in aquaria and similar results have been reported by other workers. A wild river-trout would probably use more energy swimming against the current and pursuing its prey, so increasing its maintenance requirement. Growth depends on the surplus nutrients which the trout obtains, over and above what is needed for maintenance. A trout cannot afford to be too energetic in hunting its food. Each item is of value to the fish only if the energy devoted to its capture is less than the energy derived from its digestion. An insect of low nutritional content is not worth much effort on the part of a trout, however succulent a morsel it may be. A large object, such as a minnow, is well worth having if easily caught, but an unsuccessful minnow hunt would involve profitless effort. The need to conserve energy plays a large part in the feeding behaviour of trout.

In general, a trout takes whatever food is most readily available. For this reason, we find an enormous variety of objects in the stomachs of the fish we catch. Sometimes a trout may seem to have selected one particular type of insect or other organism to the exclusion of others. Whether this selectivity is due to preference is, however, doubtful. Normally, a trout responds to any stimulus that indicates the presence of something that is edible, but if a succession of, say, iron blue duns enters its field of vision the generalised predatory reflex may become narrowed down. The fish may become temporarily conditioned to respond only to the visual signal received from an iron blue dun. Once this happens, the trout no longer "sees" any other potential food. The result is a fish that may be rising repeatedly, yet shows no interest in a selection of artificial flies that are offered to it.

This is the sort of situation that is welcomed by the angler who enjoys trying to "match the hatch". He presents the trout with an artificial that he hopes will look sufficiently like the real thing to attract the trout's attention. Whether the trout will then actually grab the angler's offering or simply turn away at the last moment is always a matter of uncertainty. What is certain is that a trout that accepts a dressed-up hook cannot really be as selective as the fisherman would like to believe.

The unbiased evidence of our own eyes must provoke profound scepticism about the concept of exact imitation. The truth is that although a trout has well-developed eyesight, it has too simple a brain to be able to integrate a visual image in the same way that we do. Experiments have proved that fish react to some particular element in a visible object, rather than to its detailed structure. Male sticklebacks, for instance, are aggressive towards other males. To excite aggression in a territorial stickleback one merely has to show it a small elongate piece of wood, painted red underneath to simulate the red belly of a rival male. There is no need for the model to have eyes, fins and a lifelike stickleback shape — a red colour is all that is needed.

Similarly, a feeding trout reacts to some significant feature of an object that may enter its field of vision. The size, contour, translucency or colour pattern may trigger the trout's predatory response. Most important of all is movement. I remember watching a trout cruising to and fro in a small pond near Underberg, obviously looking for food. Scattered over the muddy bottom were several large tadpoles of which the trout took no notice until one of them panicked as the trout swam towards it. The tadpole's attempt to escape was short-lived.

Trout may sometimes take a motionless natural or artificial fly on the water surface, but generally there must be some movement to attract the fish's attention. An unnatural movement, of course, evokes a negative response, as the dry-fly fisherman well knows when he guards against "drag". Some items in a trout's diet are immobile, such as snails clinging to weed or blackfly larvae attached to rocks in swift water, and these may be eaten in large numbers. Perhaps, however, they are located by senses other than eyesight, although organs of taste and smell seem to play a much less important part in the life of a trout than do its eyes. Certainly trout are severely handicapped in very turbid water that prevents them from seeing their prey. In any case, the attraction of an artificial fly depends solely on its visibility, so any feeding activities which depend on senses other than sight are of no more than academic interest to the angler.

A trout's feeding strategy is based on intolerance of the close proximity of its fellows. Hatchery trout cannot avoid living in a crowd, and a free-living group of fish may remain together when migrating. In a low river, trout may be visible as a shoal in the deepest part of a pool. But when feeding, a trout normally seeks its own territory. This is not as obvious in still water as in a stream, but trout in dams may select a particular area. John Campbell of Himeville has a four-hectare dam stocked with rainbow trout. One day he noticed a fish moving out of the shallows and, guessing that he had disturbed it from a regular feeding place, told his grandson the next day to creep quietly up and cast his fly in the appropriate spot. Sure enough the trout was waiting to take the youngster's fly.

Alex Behrendt, of Two Lakes in Hampshire, tells the story of a trout that made a habit of lying under a footbridge, where it was regularly observed until an angler, ignorant of the sentimental regard in which the fish was held, ended its career.

In rivers, it has long been known that trout select foraging sites for regular use. Robert Bachman has reported a fascinating study of foraging behaviour of free-ranging brown trout in a stream. Each trout had an average of about six regular feeding stations, in one of which it could be found day after day. Any particular station might be used by more than one fish, but never simultaneously, and if a fish was in residence another could displace it only by a show of aggression. The basis for selection was the physical nature of the stream bed and the rate of flow of the water. All the sites in which Bachman observed trout feeding were such that the fish themselves were lying out of the current, which brought food items within easy reach. Thus minimal energy was required to obtain a regular supply of drifting insects. The wild-bred inhabitants of the stream had a well-ordered social system in which little conflict took place. The bigger fish were dominant and, if a senior trout was feeding, the juniors in the vicinity would occupy a respectful position behind the owner of the foraging site.

When Bachman introduced hatchery trout to his experimental stream, some of them located and used the foraging sites of wild fish. The accuracy with which they occupied the precise lie already identified by another trout proved that such lies have specific physical features that are instinctively recognised by the fish. Another interesting result of introducing hatchery trout was the aggressive reaction of residents, which made vigorous efforts to drive away the newcomers. Such efforts were unsuccessful if a hatchery fish was larger than the resident, but victory in an initial encounter did not mean that a hatchery fish became permanently established. On the contrary, the introduced trout failed to settle down, spent less time feeding than the wild trout and, after a relatively short time, they all disappeared.

Bachman's trout lived in a stream with more constant flow than one finds in South Africa and with conditions that favoured drift feeding. A downstream drift of both nymphs and insects trapped in the surface film is characteristic of any trout stream and, when plentiful, this drift is the main source of food utilised by the fish. Intercepting objects carried to it by the current provides an easy living for a trout and involves little expenditure of energy. Fish that live in still pools, however, have to keep on the move when feeding, even if the area they patrol is quite small.

In a river, most of the insects, crabs and tadpoles on which trout feed are to be found on the bottom, where a trout has to search them out if it cannot rely on a current to carry edible objects to where it is waiting. There are some river-dwelling organisms that regularly swim in mid-water, especially minnows, but the great majority crawl among stones and gravel or cling to vegetation. Shallow water is generally more productive than deep pools and feeding trout therefore move into the shallows, particularly after sunset. Many nymphs are concealed beneath the surface and some have burrows where they are safe from trout or other predators until they come out into the open. All nymphs have, eventually, to swim to the surface to hatch into adult insects and trout make good use of the vulnerability of hatching mayflies, caddisflies and midges.

The water of a dam is likely to offer more opportunities for mid-water feeding than a river. Fertile reservoirs support dense blooms of small crustaceans and insect larvae, known collectively as plankton. Daphnia, commonly called water fleas because of their size and shape, may occur in such quantities that trout are able to strain them out by the thousand and pack their stomachs with the tiny crustaceans. Daphnia are well known as nutritious food for trout fry and fingerlings, but it may come as a surprise to find the stomach of a fish of a kilogram or more stuffed with objects of such insignificant size.

Other forms of plankton that trout may swallow in abundance are the immature stages of various species of midges, including the phantom larva, so called because it is almost completely transparent, except for its eyes. More familiar are the worm-like midge larvae that live in weed or on muddy bottoms in still water. Trout often seek out and eat these larvae and at least one angler has expressed concern at finding what he thought were parasitic worms in a trout's stomach. The larvae may, for a time, remain alive in a fish's stomach, leading to the conclusion that they are parasites, but they are in fact nutritious food. Midge larvae that live on the bottom may be bright red in colour. They are known as blood worms, an apt description since they contain the same red pigment, haemoglobin, as occurs in the blood of vertebrate animals. Daphnia may also contain haemoglobin, which aids survival in water that is low in oxygen.

Various groups of insects make their home in still water and proliferate in man-made ponds and lakes. Anyone interested in learning about the insect life of still waters could do no better than acquire a copy of John Goddard's *Trout Flies of Still Water*. Although his book deals with British conditions, there is a close similarity between the insects Goddard describes and those found in South Africa. There is a greater variety of aquatic insects here than in Britain, but some, such as stoneflies, that feature in overseas literature are not well represented in South Africa.

Dragonflies and damselflies are among the most conspicuous of waterside insects. Goddard regards them as unattractive to English trout, but I have found up to a dozen damselflies in the stomach of a trout that had taken them as they fluttered enticingly among overhanging vegetation. A splashy rise under a bank on a warm January day is likely to mark the demise of an unwary damselfly. Dragonflies fall victim to trout occasionally, despite the swift power of their flight as they lord it over the lesser insects of pond and stream.

Dragonfly nymphs are robust creatures that live in a variety of habitats in running and still water. They normally remain quiescent, concealed in gravel or sand, ready to seize their prey. Reaching a length of 50 mm or more, they provide a fine mouthful for a trout. Damselfly nymphs live mainly among submerged plants. If forced to swim, they progress by means of lateral movements of their slender bodies, whereas dragonfly nymphs have a jet propulsion system that gives them quite a turn of speed.

A quickly retrieved Walker's Killer is likely to attract a trout that is feeding on dragonfly nymphs. A lightly dressed hair streamer, such as Louis van der Westhuizen's Green Mamba, or Hugh Huntley's specially designed imitation, may give the impression of a damsel nymph.

In contrast to the sun-loving dragonflies, caddisflies are on the wing mainly at dusk. These small, mothlike insects are also known as sedgeflies. Their rapid, uncertain flight may give an impression of inebriation to the imaginative observer. This led K.H. Barnard to name a Cape caddisfly *Schoenobates potes*, which means "drunken acrobat" — in recognition, so he said, of its erratic flight and black-and-white colouration, reminiscent of a well-known brand of scotch.

However far such flights of fancy may be from a fisherman's thoughts, sundown is the time to watch for the slashing rise of a trout in pursuit of a caddisfly as it skims the water surface. Easier for the trout to catch are the females as they return to the stream to lay their eggs, or the pupae that swim upwards to hatch. Caddisflies have a comparatively short adult life, but live for about a year as larvae and then as pupae in both running and still water. The larvae generally make protective cases for themselves, either from sand grains or from pieces of grass cemented together. Those with vegetable cases may be seen propelling themselves through the water, like swimming sticks. Despite their disguise they are often swallowed, case and all, by trout. So are those with sand-grain cases that live on the stream-bed where trout can pick them up.

Less subject to predation are the caddis larvae that live concealed under stones. They make no case, but build a shelter of pebbles and silk, and in some instances spin miniature nets to trap particles of edible material. If you turn over a few stones in running water, caddis larvae will probably be among the insects visible. There may also be some mayfly nymphs that scuttle away or swim off as the stone is disturbed.

Mayfly nymphs are plentiful in South African streams and are the most frequent items to be found in the stomachs of river trout. Some 50 different species of mayflies are described in the publications of Barnard and myself. The adults are, of course, the models for traditional artificial dry flies, while hackled wet flies imitate mayfly nymphs. Known as Ephemeroptera, signifying short-lived winged creatures, mayflies are unique in having two flying stages. The underwater nymph emerges as a dun, which then sheds a delicate skin from body and wings to become a spinner.

The name "spinner" may have originated from the habit of male mayflies of indulging in a nuptial dance. The insects collect in swarms, their delicate wings appearing to spin as they rise and fall in constant movement. There is no sight more inspiring for a fly fisherman than hundreds of dancing mayflies glistening in the rays of the setting sun. Soon the trout will be rising as spent spinners fall on the water and drift down to the waiting fish.

Good hatches of mayflies are somewhat erratic in South Africa, although fine autumn evenings generally see considerable activity on the part of dancing males and egg-laying females. Duns commonly hatch throughout the day, giving trout an opportunity to feed on both the emerging nymphs and the flies before they have a chance to leave the water.

Three types of large mayfly, which are similar to the well-known Ephemera of Europe, are to be found in Natal, but fishermen seldom see them. This is due partly to their sporadic occurrence and partly to their habit of hatching late, just before dark, when it is difficult to see what is provoking the intense activity that trout display in pursuit of the succulent insects. The nymphs live in burrows in the river-bed for two years, where they are fairly safe from predators, although trout do manage to find a certain number.

More familiar to anglers are the numerous smaller nymphs that occupy a wide variety of habitats in running and still water. Some live under stones in rapids, such as the hump-backed nymph of the smoky-winged mayfly known erroneously as the Mooi Moth. Others live in trailing herbage or on exposed rock surfaces. A large and interesting nymph that may be seen clinging to rocks in swift water rejoices in the name *Oligoneuriopsis lawrencei*. When full-grown, in autumn, this nymph is about the size of an artificial tied on a No. 8 hook. It has hairy forelegs, which it holds out as if in greeting, a habit shared by an American relative known as the Howdy, in recognition of its apparently friendly salutation. The nymph's attitude is, in fact, purely utilitarian. The legs are held at an appropriate angle to strain minute particles of food out of the current.

Nymphs are of immense importance to trout and hence to fishermen. Indeed, it was the presence of such a bounteous supply of aquatic insects, including many types similar to those of the northern hemisphere, that made South African streams pre-adapted to the acclimatisation of trout.

One inhabitant of our streams that is not found in the northern hemisphere is the freshwater crab. This formidable crustacean was considered by some of the earlier trout enthusiasts to constitute a threat to the introduced fish. Crabs are, indeed, carnivorous, but their main interaction with trout is to provide food. In rocky sections of river, where crabs are plentiful, they form an important part of the diet of both brown and rainbow trout. This applies particularly to the larger fish. A three or four pounder has no difficulty in swallowing a crab the size of a baby's hand. The smaller the fish, the smaller the crab it can tackle, but even a fingerling will eagerly snap up a pea-sized crab newly released from its mother's brood pouch.

Crabs are adept at concealment, living under stones or in burrows in the bank, and it is something of a mystery how trout manage to catch so many of them. Fortunately there is no indication that they are in any danger of extermination. As with other aquatic creatures, a large proportion live in places that are inaccessible to trout, so the breeding stock is not endangered.

The same applies to frog tadpoles, which are relished by trout. The common river frog frequently falls victim to big fish, even when it has grown to a size that renders it safe from attack by younger trout. In dams, platannas are common, but the adult frogs are rarely eaten by trout despite their remaining permanently in the water, unlike other frogs which spend a lot of time ashore. Platanna tadpoles form large shoals, hanging in midwater where trout gorge on them in late spring and summer. They are often mistaken by anglers for small fish, but close examination reveals the widely set eyes and an absence of ribs that characterise the tadpoles.

Tadpoles are slower-moving than minnows, which probably accounts for the fact that, in general, tadpoles are more often found in trout stomachs than are small fish. The only type of tadpole avoided by trout is that of the toad. Anyone clever enough to make an exact imitation of a toad tadpole will go home empty-handed.

Small fish are eaten when available, and trout have been blamed for exterminating local populations of indigenous minnows in some river systems. The interaction of trout with other organisms will be discussed in Chapter 5. At this point, it may be noted that examination of thousands of trout stomachs in Natal has revealed comparatively few cases where trout have eaten other fish. Chubby-head minnows (*Barbus anoplus*) are the most frequently eaten and it is interesting that instances in which trout have made a meal of the minnows have been mainly in winter, when the minnows are less active than in warm weather. This is in accordance with the generalisation that trout take what is most easily caught.

While the major part of the trout's food comes from aquatic organisms, terrestrial insects are important at times. Almost anything that appears edible is likely to be swallowed, although indigestible objects may be rejected. I once dropped two large hard-bodied beetles in front of a brown trout that promptly rose and took them one after the other. A few moments later, however, both the beetles floated to the surface.

The brown cockchafer beetles that commonly fall into streams from overhanging trees are eagerly taken and one may find a couple of dozen in a trout's stomach. The popular artificial, Coch-y-bondhu, is said to represent a beetle, although not our South African cockchafer.

Grasshoppers are, of course, attractive to trout that are on the lookout for surface food, while moths and even butterflies provide an occasional mouthful. Brightly coloured bees and wasps appear to be acceptable, providing an excuse for the fisherman who likes to try gaudy creations that bear no resemblance to the usual prey of trout.

By far the most abundant of terrestrial insects that fall onto rivers and dams are winged ants. On fine autumn days, vast swarms of flying ants leave their nests and a surprising number end up drifting helplessly on the water surface. They vary in size, but all are less than 10 mm in length, with blackish bodies, apart from chestnut brown on the abdomen, and shining transparent wings. A trout that is rising persistently to objects that are invisible to the angler is likely to be taking ants. Hundreds are often swallowed in the course of a few hours.

Whereas one may well question the nutritive value of hard-bodied ants, flying termites provide a more digestible meal. These characteristic inhabitants of Africa are a welcome addition to the diet of all sorts of animals, from men and lions to frogs and fish. Their hatches are more sporadic than those of ants, with which they are often confused, but if ever you want to see precisely how many trout there are in a pool, stand on the bank when there is a good fall of flying termites. Every fish in the vicinity will be breaking the surface to grab the trapped insects as they struggle to free their outstretched quivering wings.

To see the water boiling with fish may be exciting, but you will be lucky to catch anything. To simulate the quiver of a termite's wings is the ultimate challenge for the disciple of the school of exact imitation.

4. Reaction to physical conditions

Trout can tolerate a fairly wide range of environmental conditions. The ideal range is, however, quite narrow and each fish tends to seek the most favourable situation available. It does so through inherited behaviour patterns that have evolved in response to the pressures of various physical factors. These instinctive behaviour patterns, fixed by natural selection over many generations in the trout's home in the northern hemisphere, are generally appropriate for survival in South Africa. An exception is the instinct to migrate downstream in search of the sea.

Both brown and rainbow trout have this atavistic tendency, inherited from ancestors that made use of salt water for part of their lives long before the first man speared a trout for his supper. Migratory brown trout are known as sea trout, while rainbow with similar habits are referred to as steelhead. Early scientific studies of trout led to the conclusion that migratory and non-migratory forms were separate species. Thus sea trout were called *Salmo trutta* and their river-dwelling relatives *Salmo fario,* with a corresponding separation of *Salmo gairdneri* and *Salmo irideus.* Later all European trout were amalgamated under the name *Salmo trutta,* and all rainbow trout became *Salmo gairdneri.* Linguistically this was a pity, as *fario* and *irideus* are nicer names. Charles Ritz perpetuated the old name for the brown trout in his famous Fario Club.

The fact is, however, that there is no clear distinction between migratory and non-migratory trout, although it has been widely held that hereditary differences account for the behaviour of sea-going and resident individuals. With rainbow trout, in particular, some strains have been regarded as migratory and others as sedentary. European sea trout were also regarded as breeding true to type, only going to sea if their parents did. Recently, doubt has been thrown on this idea by workers at the Salmon Research Trust of Ireland. From studies of the blood proteins of sea trout and brown trout it has been established that no evidence exists of hereditary differences between the two. If this is so, *any* trout may develop migratory behaviour, given the right stimulus, irrespective of its ancestry.

Whereas in Europe or North America a trout that goes downstream is likely to find suitable temperature conditions and rich feeding in the sea, a trout headed for the lower waters of almost any South African river is doomed to perish. The only exception is the Eerste River, whose story I shall tell in Chapter 6, and possibly its neighbour, the Lourens. Behaviour that is beneficial in one area may therefore be fatal in another.

Migratory behaviour appears to be of two types: first, movements such as those to and from the sea or upstream in response to the spawning urge; and second, movements to escape deteriorating water conditions. The second type of behaviour occurs in times of drought, when the flow of a river shrinks to a fraction of its normal volume. Actually to observe fish deserting a stretch of river is difficult, but circumstantial evidence is often strong. On many occasions a well-populated stretch of river has ceased, quite suddenly, to hold trout. This has happened both in Natal and the Cape. In the absence of anything that could have killed the fish, such as a rapid rise in temperature, one can only assume that there has been a mass exodus due to instinctive reaction to dangerously low water. This sort of response, to avoid a deteriorating environment, differs from the normal migratory movements of sea trout, or of fish seeking spawning grounds, although it may sometimes be difficult to make the distinction in practice.

Whatever may be the nature of the stimulus that impels trout to desert their home water, the results are highly significant. Three possibilities exist: first, the fish may move away only temporarily, returning later to their original place of residence; second, they may become permanently established in their new environment; and third, they may meet with disaster. In South Africa, disaster is the most likely outcome. I know of little evidence for successful migrations of either brown or rainbow trout in the rivers of the Republic.

When the shallow upper waters of a river are deserted by trout, one might expect to find pools lower down well populated. Generally, however, in times of drought fish seem to vanish from the whole river, apart from a few survivors in the most favourable areas. Such survivors are often adequate for breeding once conditions return to normal, since only a few adults are required to re-establish the population, but this takes time as the new generation grows to maturity. If a reserve of adult fish is available, their migration into vacant water is obviously the most rapid way of restoring the position. Movement of trout upstream, after the first spring rains, does occur in some Natal rivers. This has been proved by trapping experiments. Anglers have reported finding trout in hitherto deserted stretches, and Peter Root, who spent much of his life on the upper Loteni River, firmly believed that brown trout, which had moved downstream in winter, returned in spring if there was adequate rainfall.

In the Cape, rainbow trout that left the lower Eerste River as it dried up in summer were apparently able to find sanctuary in the estuary, whence they returned once the streamflow was restored by winter rains. As a rule, however, successful migrations of South African trout are confined to local movements associated with breeding and growth. At spawning time mature fish seek shallow, gravelly stretches to deposit their eggs, before returning to water of adequate depth and volume. Fry and fingerlings remain in the nursery areas until reduced streamflow prompts their retreat to the pools.

Individual variability in the way trout respond to physical conditions is clearly shown by young fish living in a stream that has been dammed. Instead of all the fingerlings moving out of the stream into the lake or pond simultaneously, some may migrate when two or three months old and others not until they are a full year old. Since feeding is generally richer in the dam, those that migrate early grow much more rapidly than the stay-at-homes. Once a trout has settled down in a particular place, it is likely to remain there indefinitely. Experienced anglers know that once a big trout, whether brown or rainbow, has been located it is likely to be found in the same place on a future occasion. Angling folklore is full of tales of well-known fish that took up residence in certain pools and remained there for two, three or more seasons.

Robert Bachman, in his study of brown trout in Spruce Creek, found that most individuals established a home range in their first or second year of life and remained in the same locality thereafter. Older fish seemed to reduce the size of their home range, of which the average area was only about 16 square metres. Such an extremely small home range is unlikely to apply to South African trout. Our rivers fluctuate more than Spruce Creek, in which the same feeding and resting places could be used for months on end. Nevertheless, a favourable habitat attracts and holds trout wherever they occur.

Two aspects of its physical surroundings attract a trout: shelter and a good feeding station. Submerged rocks, undercut banks or overhanging bushes provide shelter. So does depth of water, although trout generally seek sanctuary under a rock or bank if these are available. A featureless river bed, even in a deep pool, is seldom populated by large fish. Indeed, one often comes across water that is too deep.

The hole excavated by a plunging waterfall is seldom a profitable place to fish and the same applies to a place where the stream runs deep between walls of rock. Trout prefer water less than 2 m in depth, with an uneven bed that offers a habitat for insects, crabs and tadpoles. A mixture of rock, gravel, sand and loam provides for a diversity of bottom-living organisms on which the trout feed.

Brown trout seem willing to remain in shallower water than rainbow, although a pool no more than a metre in depth may be occupied by a large rainbow if there is adequate cover.

Where severe fluctuations in water level occur, as in most South African rivers, a trout will have to seek different feeding and resting places according to the state of the stream. An example was a big brown trout that lived in a pool on the Little Mooi River. The pool was some 60 m long and my father hooked and lost the fish twice, once near the middle of the pool and once near the lower end. The third and final encounter took place when the river was flowing strongly. The fish had moved into a small pocket between two boulders in the rapid above the pool. By that time it was a portly four pounder.

Assuming that a pool of, say, 600 square metres may be the home range of a Natal trout, this is considerably more extensive than the area occupied by Bachman's trout, but it would still indicate a strong tendency to remain in familiar territory. Trout that have been recaptured after being marked and returned in Natal rivers have remained close to the point of original capture in most cases — both browns in the Mooi River and rainbows in the Umzimkulu. In the Cape, Robin Fick of the Fly Fishers' Association has reported the recapture of rainbows in the Liesbeek and browns in the Witte River in precisely the same spot as they were caught the first time.

Trout tend to select and remain in an area with physical features that satisfy their needs. On the other hand, there is a latent migratory instinct which may be brought into play by a change in the environment or by physiological changes in the fish itself. Reproductive maturity causes movement, generally upstream, at spawning time. Sea trout in Europe undergo a hormonal change that gives them a silvery appearance before they leave their native stream for salt water. A year or two later they return to that same stream to breed. So even migratory trout retain an attachment to their home.

Volume of flow and water temperature are two factors that vitally affect the lives of river trout. They are interrelated, since the effect of hot weather is accentuated by a low river, while a particularly traumatic change in temperature is that caused by flood waters following a hailstorm. A third significant factor is turbidity, which is also related to stream flow.

The most productive trout streams are those that have a relatively constant flow, no great fluctuations in temperature and clear water. These conditions are fully met only by spring-fed rivers, such as the chalk streams of southern England. Elsewhere in Europe and America, where extensive aquifers occur in limestone formations, similar streams are found. Not only do such rivers provide superb physical conditions for trout, but they are also rich in calcium which is favourable for aquatic plants and animals, including trout.

Dolomitic springs occur in the Transvaal, and help to stabilise the flow of some of the trout streams. but in the rest of South Africa the mountain catchments have a relatively small capacity for storing and releasing underground water. River flow is dependent on rainfall. The result is that the dry season discharge is a minute fraction of that occurring after heavy precipitation. Animals that live on land or in the sea are subject to various environmental pressures but not to the drastic changes in living space that afflict the inhabitants of a rain-fed river.

Flood waters present trout with three problems: the sheer force of the current, a change in temperature and poor visibility. A swift current might be expected to sweep trout downstream, but in fact trout seem well able to take shelter in the quieter marginal areas and backwaters. On many occasions severe spates have had no apparent effect on the number of trout occupying a stream. There are records of trout, as well as indigenous fish, being found stranded after a river had overflowed its banks, but such loss of life is usually on a small scale. Major losses may occur following a hailstorm that produces a rush of ice-cold water. On 10 October 1972, for instance, a thermograph in the Bushman's River at Giant's Castle Game Reserve registered a drop in temperature from 21 °C to 1 °C within minutes. On the following day the banks of the river were strewn with dead trout. Generally, however, trout survive summer floods remarkably well.

Unseasonal floods seem to have the worst effect. In May 1959, all the rivers in southern Natal suffered a heavy spate, with disastrous consequences for the trout populations. So severe was the effect that the local conservancy and fishing club committees called for a special investigation to assess the position. Fortunately eggs already laid in the gravel produced substantial numbers of young trout but many stretches were devoid of older trout.

Cold, clear water from a dolomitic spring feeds the concrete raceway in which Richard Pott rears trout. Indigenous tree-ferns are to be supplemented with other native vegetation to replace pine trees: Maggsleigh Conservation area, Eastern Transvaal.

Poor visibility during a period of high water handicaps a trout in its search for food, to an extent that depends on the degree of discolouration. If silt is washed off eroded hillsides, fields or roads, a river may remain dirty for weeks in rainy weather and the trout suffer in consequence. A flooded river always reduces the food supply, even if discolouration is insufficient to prevent the fish from seeing their food. It is a common misconception that a spate brings an abundance of worms and other creatures to the waiting trout. In fact, trout that I have examined from flooded rivers have invariably contained little nutritious material, but mainly quantities of grass

33

stems, leaf fragments, pieces of stick and other debris. If you want to know how I obtained the fish, that is a question which, as Kipling suggested in another context, you would be well advised not to ask.

Even when the flood has passed, and the fish can see an artificial fly, one finds that much of the trout's stomach content consists of land insects instead of the usual underwater creatures. Severe reduction in the bottom fauna of a stream as a result of a torrential flow of water has been documented on several occasions. Jackie King, a biologist who has worked on Cape rivers, mentions that this removal of bottom fauna may be only temporary in situations where deep gravel beds occur, since larvae survive below the surface and work their way up again when the flood has subsided. Nevertheless, for a time at least, trout are likely to suffer from food shortage in an abnormally full river. The only bonanza that a season of exceptionally high rainfall is likely to provide is that frogs, which breed prolifically in the flooded areas alongside a river, are likely to find their way into the main stream in greater numbers than usual.

In contrast to the problems associated with too much water are the stresses of drought conditions. An obvious effect of compressed living space is increased competition for food. If, however, the trout population is sparse, a low river generally offers good opportunities for growth. Fish desert the shallow places, except for forays after dark in search of food, but they continue to do well as long as the weather remains cool. Summer droughts are particularly lethal. Dry periods are normal in the Western Cape summer season and the lower, more open stretches of river often become too warm for trout, especially where water abstraction produces unnaturally poor flows. In the mountain kloofs, however, dry summer weather has less impact, especially if the streams are left with a good flow after abundant winter rains.

In the Eastern Cape, Natal and the Transvaal, little rain can be expected between April and September. This is good for breeding and all goes well if the spring is "normal". When the heat of October brings no significant rainfall, however, trout find life increasingly precarious. Even in a "normal" spring, which might be defined as one in which precipitation approximates to the seasonal average, periods of hot, dry weather occur. Once the water temperature exceeds 25 °C, trout are under stress. Prolonged exposure to a temperature of 26 to 28 °C is fatal and at 30 °C death is rapid. The main effect of high temperature is to reduce the amount of oxygen available, while at the same time accelerating the fish's rate of metabolism and thereby increasing its oxygen demand.

Rainbow trout are said to be slightly more tolerant of high temperatures than brown, but much depends on the overall conditions and the duration of exposure. Age has a definite influence. Very young trout will die sooner than those that are a few months old, while adults again become more vulnerable. Large trout have a lower ratio of gill surface to body mass, so they are less adaptable to poorly oxygenated water than younger fish. It has been noticed, both in Australia and South Africa, that after a period of critically high temperatures most of the survivors are yearlings.

Within their normal range of tolerance trout become less active in both cold and warm water. Little feeding or growth takes place as the temperature approaches freezing point. South African trout waters seldom fall below 4 °C, however, especially in man-made lakes, so the fish continue to feed throughout the winter. Most favourable are temperatures of 12 to 18 °C, although feeding continues above 25 °C in well-aerated waters. The behaviour of trout is affected by fairly minor fluctuations in temperature, as well as changes in light intensity and in the weather. Cloud cover, wind direction and barometric pressure all seem to have an effect, either independently or in combination.

Since trout are cold-blooded animals that do not need energy to maintain their body temperature above that of their surroundings, they can go without food for extended periods. Fish may simply sink to the river-bed and cease their feeding activity if environmental signals are unfavourable. Some of those signals clearly convey an important message. An approaching thunderstorm may threaten to convert the trout's quiet pool into a raging torrent that will tax the fish's ability to survive. Nevertheless it seems strange to the human observer that trout may go off the feed when the storm is still far away. No more than a few seconds are required to leave a feeding station and seek cover. Yet we have all had the experience of trout becoming uncatchable as soon as a summer day turns muggy, cumulus clouds build up on the mountains and thunder rumbles ominously.

When trout no longer respond to our flies, it may be difficult to prove that they have, in fact, stopped feeding. But the inference is clear. The fish have reacted to the threatening storm at a time when we may feel ample time still remains for us to walk back to the shelter of our car. Why should the trout stop feeding so soon?

If we think there is going to be no more than a light shower it may be worthwhile remaining on the river bank. As the first raindrops hit the water there is often a burst of activity that continues after the cloud has passed. In a heavy downpour, on the other hand, I have never caught trout. They seem to have an uncanny knowledge of what is going to happen.

Light, continuous rain is good for fly fishing — as anyone knows who has braved a chilly spring day in Natal, with a southerly wind pushing the clouds across the tops of the Drakensberg foothills. On either dam or river a limit bag is almost a certainty under such conditions, with fine raindrops dimpling the clear water to conceal the angler from his quarry.

Whether there is a cloud or not, a cool day with a breeze from any quarter between south, through west to north, is likely to bring trout on the feed. But "when the wind is in the east, 'tis good for neither man nor beast" — an English adage which applies to Natal and possibly other parts of South Africa, as far as the fly fisherman is concerned. Many a day has been spoilt by a chilly wind creeping up the valleys of east-flowing rivers, with a fluffy mist collecting on the hills in the afternoon. If the wind dies down at sunset, there may be something of an evening rise, but it seems to consist mainly of half-hearted splashes at hatching duns, with little response to the angler's fly. Air that is colder than the water puts the fish off. This applies less to the deep water of a dam than to a river.

Why trout should respond so negatively to an east wind is a mystery. There may be a correlation between an easterly wind and a falling barometer, which is regarded by many authorities as an unfavourable sign. A rising barometer, on the other hand, lifts the spirits of both fish and angler. Again it is difficult to know why this should be so.

A lower barometric pressure means slightly less oxygen in the water, but the difference is insignificant compared with differences due to temperature or to altitude. Increasing height above sea-level has a substantial effect on the amount of oxygen in solution, but high-altitude trout seem just as lively as those lower down, unless the temperature reaches a critical level.

Whatever the mechanism, in terms of fish physiology, the fact remains that atmospheric changes are not only detectable, but of proven importance to trout. On a cool, crisp morning with a north-west wind the fish will be in as cheerful a mood as you are. A Berg wind, they say, blows the fly into the fish's mouth.

Trout share with most living creatures a daily activity rhythm, subject to modification by other factors. In hot weather, early morning sees the fish actively filling their bellies, before the water warms up. Ken Pennington and Romyn Every made a practice of starting at dawn on the Bushman's River and their efforts earned them some big brown trout of up to more than four pounds. In cool weather, however, I have found no great advantage in departing from my own diurnal activity rhythm. I have caught more trout between 10 and 12 o'clock than either earlier or later.

A mid-morning rise generally indicates a fish that is feeding seriously and is likely to accept a well-presented artificial fly. In the hectic half hour at sundown the trout often seem bent on enjoying themselves, rather than co-operating with the angler. Fish may be showing all over the place, but to catch them is another matter.

There is evidence from observations on both wild trout and those held under artificial conditions that small fish are more active, over a longer period, than big ones; yet one hears of heavy trout taking a fly early in the afternoon, at a time when the general level of feeding activity is at its lowest. It is seldom safe to predict the behaviour of fish.

As darkness falls, trout tend to move into shallow water. This seems to apply particularly to brown trout. In the Maletsunyane River I once took two of 700 g each that were making bow waves as they chased tadpoles in water barely deep enough to cover their backs. Rainbows also take advantage of failing light to feed in shallow riffles, glides and backwaters. Trout that remain in deep water are likely to approach the surface after sunset.

Once dusk has given place to night, activity becomes reduced, although moonlight may keep fish on the move. This may explain the anglers' belief that daytime feeding activity is curtailed over the full-moon period. Even in the absence of moonlight, after a quiet spell in the late evening, trout are likely to be on the hunt soon after midnight. Some years ago, when camping was permitted on the shores of Highmoor Dam in the Natal Drakensberg, a number of big trout were caught between one and four in the morning.

Trout have eyes that are adapted to seeing under conditions of low light intensity. In addition, surface objects are silhouetted against a starlit sky. It is seldom that darkness is so total as to prevent fish from feeding.

Behaviour may be based on instinctive reactions to the environment, but on occasion trout can show remarkable determination. A.C. Harrison records how rainbows surmounted a seemingly impassable chute on the Malibamatso River in Lesotho to colonise the stream above. Another example of co-ordinated agility occurred when Leslie Acutt was in charge of the Underberg Hatchery. One morning he found a three-pound rainbow missing from a pond. He located it in a water furrow that the fish could have reached only by jumping up a pipe, 100 mm in diameter, that discharged water half a metre above the surface of the pond.

5. Predators and competitors

"Greater fleas have lesser fleas upon their backs to bite 'em, And lesser fleas have littler fleas, and so *ad infinitum.*" That describes a food-chain of a sort, and expresses the principle that one animal preys on another.

Trout are placed well up towards the top of the food-chain: they eat crabs that eat dragonfly nymphs that eat midge larvae that eat minute plankton. In their turn, trout are preyed on by birds, otters and men.

The concept of a food-chain is, in fact, not really accurate. Modern biologists prefer the term food-web, which is a better description of the complex relationships that exist in any natural community. Trout, for instance, may feed directly on midge larvae or dragonfly nymphs, while either a dragonfly nymph or a crab is quite capable of catching a baby trout if the opportunity arises. Normally, a crab has to be content to scavenge plant material off the rocks, but even a large trout will be eaten alive by crabs if it is trapped in a confined space. Thus the tables may be turned on the predator.

The role each organism plays in the food-web may vary according to circumstances, except for the primary producers, the plants that provide the basic source of energy for the whole community. In rivers, two types of plant material form the food of herbivorous animals: primitive algae and more complex, rooted plants. The latter may be growing either in the water or on the bank. Few South African trout rivers have significant amounts of submerged aquatic plants, commonly called water weeds, and most of the food derived from rooted vegetation consists of leaves that enter the stream from grasses, shrubs and trees that grow on the banks. As these leaves are broken down by the running water, or by bacterial action, they are reduced to small fragments, known as detritus, which many insect larvae and other animals make use of. Detritus is regarded as a major contributor to the food-web of streams in Europe and America, while the work of Jackie King and others has shown the significance of detritus in some South African rivers. Many insect larvae feed directly on whole leaves, but the importance of leaves and leaf detritus is subject to two limiting factors: lack of vegetation and severe flooding that scours the river bed.

In areas where detritus is scarce, the basic source of nutrition for the aquatic community consists of the growths of primitive plants, consisting of bacteria, fungi and single-celled algae that give submerged rocks a slimy feel. Although each cell is microscopic, a prolific growth of algae is visible as a greenish or brown layer. These minute green plants, like the more familiar grasses, shrubs and trees, require sunlight for maintenance and growth. Therefore, if silt smothers the river-bed, primary production ceases.

Shading by tall trees may also reduce production. Too many riparian trees are liable to cut down the food of invertebrate animals on which the trout depend. This applies especially to trees such as wattles, which have tannin-filled leaves that do not break down into edible detritus.

Any piece of water, whether a running stream or a pond, has a basic productivity that depends on its physical and chemical properties. It is this productivity that ultimately determines the total mass of trout that can be supported. What anglers want is to have as many fish as possible, of a size that they consider large enough. They will be dissatisfied with either a lot of small fish or with so few large ones that sport is poor.

Even if fishermen realise there must be a compromise, and that a particular water has a limited carrying capacity, the actual yield of fish is seldom regarded as being up to the expected standard. If things are not as they should be, there must be a cause. A popular explanation for poor fishing is the presence of predators. Any predator that kills trout is, *ipso facto,* regarded with enmity. Traditional enemies are eels, cormorants, otters and, especially, human poachers. A poacher may be defined as anyone fishing without permission and/or using methods of which fly fishermen disapprove.

Going back through the records of the various acclimatisation societies, con-servancies, angling clubs and provincial fisheries departments, one finds innumer-able debates on methods to control the depredations of the various finned, feathered, furred and two-legged destroyers of trout. There was even a proposal by an honourable member of the Natal Parliament, soon after trout had been established in the Colony (as it then was), that members of a certain immigrant group should be repatriated to the Asiatic continent from whence they came, on the grounds that their fishing expertise was such that they represented a dire threat to the existence of trout!

Action against poachers has tended to decline in severity with the passing of time. There has also been a growing realisation that the impact of authorised, legally approved angling is often more significant than any other type of predation. This has led to stricter controls on fishermen and efforts to spare the stock by catch-and-release angling.

While the effects of predation within the natural aquatic community are generally limited to the removal of individuals that are, for one reason or another, surplus, there are exceptions, especially where man has interfered. An otter that visits a fish farm in which large numbers of trout are concentrated may indulge in wholesale destruction. Similarly the stocking of a dam with artificially reared trout may give cormorants an opportunity to catch a high proportion of the fish. Even a kingfisher that would have no impact on the trout population of a river, may sit on the edge of a hatchery pond and fling several dozen small fish onto the grass, apparently for sheer sport.

Whereas in the past official bounties were offered for the killing of "vermin", there is now a commendable reluctance to indulge in campaigns to destroy natural predators. Of the two species of otters that occur in South Africa, the larger and commoner Cape clawless otter is not normally a fish-eater. Studies by D.T. Rowe-Rowe and others have shown that the main diet of the clawless otter consists of crabs, with frogs, birds, fish and other miscellaneous food being taken when the opportunity occurs.

The smaller, web-footed, spotted-necked otter is a more active swimmer than the Cape clawless otter and is able to pursue and capture fish. An interesting point is, however, that most of the fish it catches are small, contrary to the opinion of many anglers who believe that an otter takes mainly large trout. The reason for the predominance of small fish in their diet is simply that they are less swift than large ones, and are therefore easier to secure. Small fish are also generally more plentiful than large ones and an otter, like any predator, will take whatever is most easily available. Either species of otter will kill big trout if the opportunity occurs, especially at spawning time. Trout that have entered a small feeder stream from a dam are easy for otters to catch and more may be killed than the animals can eat. I have seen several trout lying dead along a short section of stream, each with only a small portion of the throat and belly eaten. Such a sight is likely to upset the owner of the dam from which the trout came but it is an exceptional occurrence.

Otters have been said to have an indirect effect on trout by consuming large numbers of crabs. Oddly enough this has been used as an argument both for and against otters. On the one hand, it has been said that crabs are predators on trout eggs, alevins and fry and therefore otters should be encouraged, while on the other it has been said that crabs are valuable food for big trout and therefore otters should be destroyed. Both arguments appeared in reports of the Natal Fisheries Department in the 1920s.

While predation by crabs on the early stages of trout must occur, the fact that large, even excessive numbers of young trout survive wherever suitable spawning conditions exist is a clear indication that crabs are not a problem. The counter argument, that crabs are a source of food, is much better based.

That does not mean, however, that otters are necessarily bad for trout. This would be true only if the otters ate so many crabs that the share available for trout was significantly reduced. No one has tried to estimate the impact of otters on the crab population, but the two have co-existed for many thousands of years. It seems safe to apply the principle that the numbers of prey and predator are in a state of balance, subject to normal fluctuations.

Crabs might be considered more under threat from the introduced trout than from the indigenous otter, but there is no evidence for this either. As with the stream-dwelling insects on which trout also feed, no more than a small part of the crab population is subject to attack by trout. Crabs live under rocks, in holes in the bank and in small sidestreams or shallows that are inaccessible to fish. In addition, adults are too big for any but the largest trout to tackle. Whereas otters probably take mainly big crabs, it is the small ones that are cropped by trout. One may safely assume that a large percentage of the young that leave the brood pouch of a female crab are doomed to perish in one way or another. The trout merely represent an alternative source of mortality.

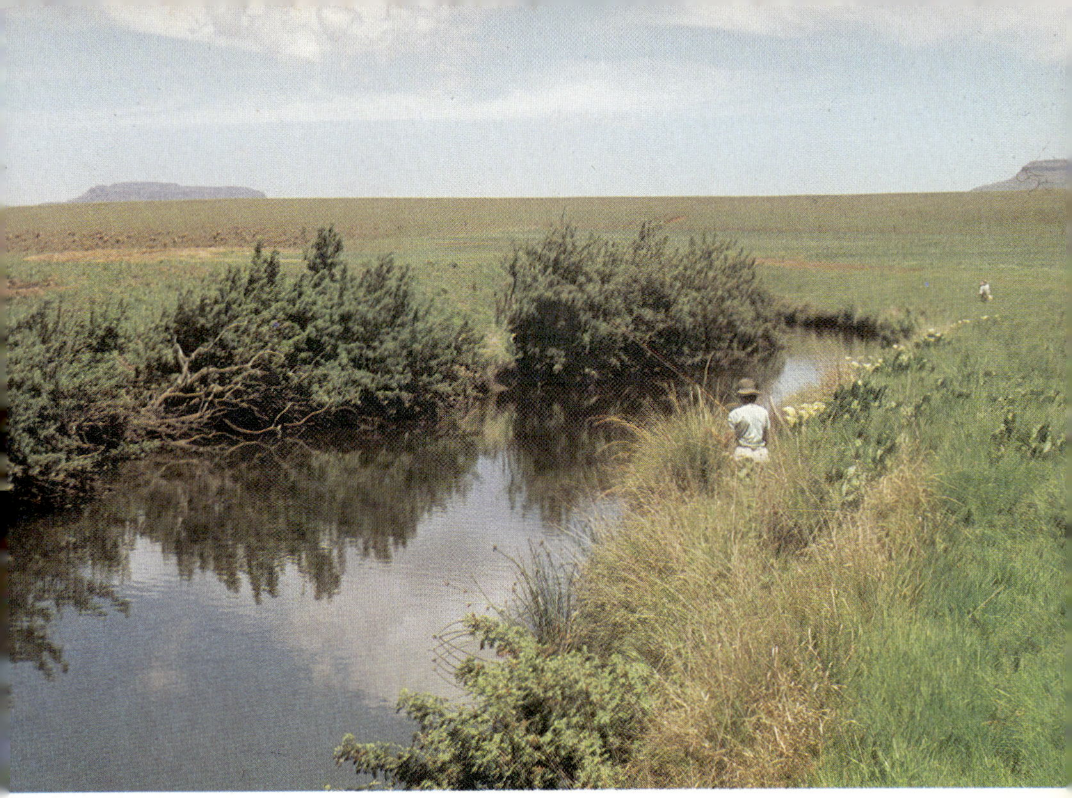

ɔper Mooi River, Natal

ɔb Frean on the Little Mooi River, Natal

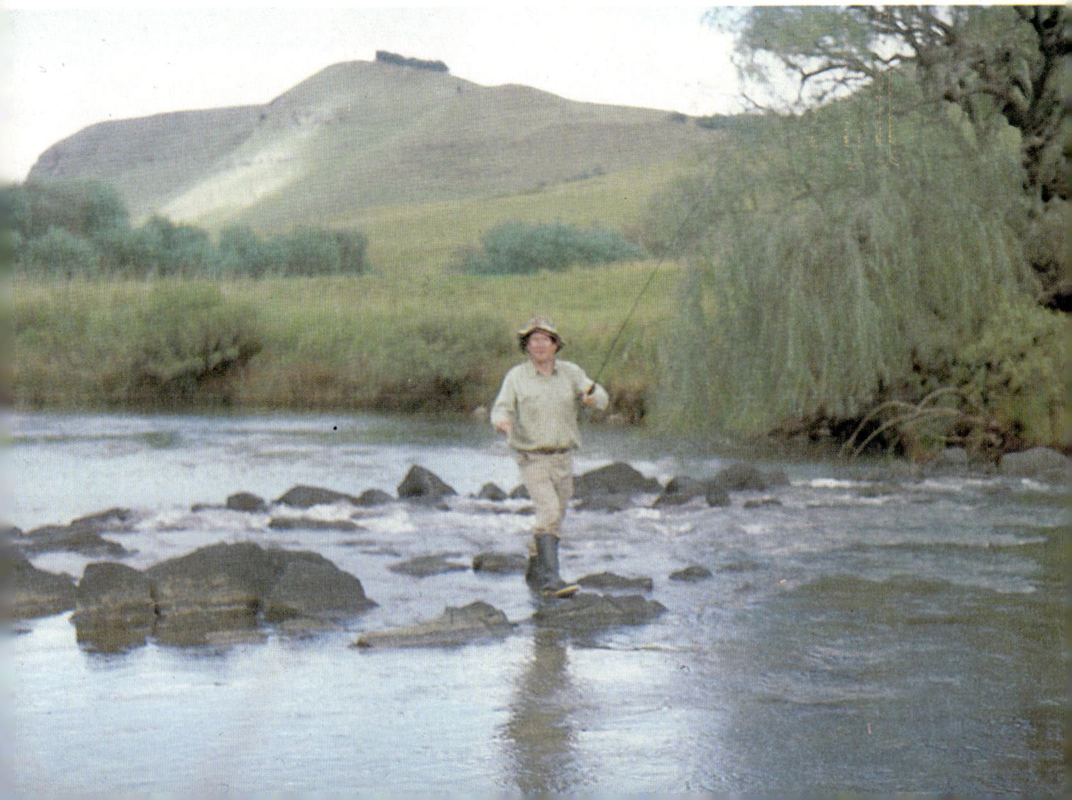

Insects that occur in trout streams

Mayfly nymph

Damselfly nymph

Burrowing mayfly nymph

Dragonfly nymph

Adult mayfly

Stonefly nymph

eenbras Reservoir, Cape

trout dam, Himeville, Natal

Sally Ovendale with a 750 g rainbow from the Umzimkulu

A brown trout at home in the Witte River, Cape

Far more significant than predation, is the effect of changes in the environment. All aquatic organisms are under pressure when drought shrinks their living space. Conversely, a severe flood may displace all but the most stable types of stream-bed. Banks, in which crabs have their holes, may be sliced away by the force of the floodwater, and food in the form of algae and detritus may be swept downstream. Where silting and degradation of the stream habitat occurs, crabs will suffer, together with all other aquatic organisms.

Disease cannot be ruled out as a factor in natural population fluctuations. I have, on occasion, seen numbers of dead crabs, not merely the empty shells which live crabs have to shed periodically as they grow. In general, however, there seems to be no cause for concern about the welfare of crabs. Few may be seen in the course of a day's fishing, but sit down comfortably on a flat rock to clean your catch, and as you drop the trout guts into the water, one after another the sly crustaceans will emerge from cover and converge on the unaccustomed feast. After a few minutes, a mass of legs and nippers will surround each piece of offal.

As well as occupying their natural habitat in and around rivers, and moving across country in wet weather in search of new homes, crabs make use of dams and irrigation furrows. Their habit of tunnelling for considerable distances is apt to render them unpopular with farmers, when leaks appear in earth embankments.

No other inhabitant of the South African freshwater ecosystem occupies a position in the food-web comparable to that of the crab. It provides food for otters, water mongooses, kingfishers and other birds, eels, yellowfish and, of course, trout. In its turn, it preys on whatever it can catch, although generally existing as an opportunistic scavenger.

There are, in fact, two distinct species of crab belonging to the genus *Potamonautes* in Natal. One, known as *depressus,* is seldom seen out of the water and favours rocky mountain streams. The other, *sidneyi,* is inclined to burrow in sandy banks and is more of a land crab. The Cape *perlatus* is closely related to *sidneyi.* But whatever its scientific name, the crab deserves respect for the major part it plays in the stream community.

While trout prey on a great many of the indigenous aquatic animals and are, in their turn, preyed upon, there is a remarkably harmonious relationship between the original inhabitants and the newcomers. Trout have fitted into their new environment and form an integral part of the community, wherever physical conditions are suitable.

Translocating plants or animals from one continent to another may be dangerous. Alien plant invaders pose a dire threat to indigenous vegetation in many parts of South Africa and a number of animal pests have also originated overseas. On the other hand, attempts to acclimatise desirable importations have often met with failure.

The main preoccupation of the trout pioneers was to overcome what they saw as hazards to the establishment of their fish. They underestimated the ability of the trout to adapt to our conditions. Arthur H. Reid, whose *Trout and Angling in South Africa* appeared in 1921, paints a gloomy picture of young trout becoming "the wholesale victims of every predatory creature that exists".

Over the years, salmonophiles (if one may coin a word) have come to realise that

41

their protégés are not as delicate as was feared. Now, one hears more from the salmonophobes, who fear that trout constitute a threat to the indigenous fauna, in particular certain species of fish. Unfortunately, it is very difficult to arrive at either an accurate assessment of the problem or an effective solution. The reason is that whatever impact trout had on the indigenous fish is now a matter of history. If local populations of minnows were exterminated by trout, this happened many years ago, at a time when virtually all suitable pieces of water, as well as a great many that were not suitable, were being stocked.

There seems no doubt that minnows have disappeared from certain places where they used to occur, but clear evidence is often hard to come by. Take the case of *Oreodaimon quathlambae*, a unique little fish from the Drakensberg, first described by K.H. Barnard in 1938. The original specimens were sent to the Natal Museum and from there to the South African Museum, but there was always some doubt as to the precise locality from which they were collected. The locality given by Barnard was Mkomazana River, "a tributary of the Umzimkulu". But the Mkomazana is actually part of the Umkomaas system.

Repeated efforts were made to find more of the minnows in the rivers on the Natal side of the Drakensberg escarpment. I consulted Ivor Vaughan of Underberg, one of those responsible for submitting the original collection to the museum, but he was vague about where the fish had been found. Since they were supposed to have come from the Mkomazana, and brown trout had become established in this river, the trout were blamed for exterminating the *Oreodaimon*.

Then came a surprise. Tom Pike and Alistair Tedder rediscovered the minnows at Sehlabathebe in Lesotho on 20 November 1970. Other streams on the western side of the Drakensberg were also found to harbour *Oreodaimon*. At Sehlabathebe rainbow trout had been stocked some years before, and Pike found a minnow in the stomach of one of the trout he caught. There was no doubt that the trout would eat *Oreodaimon* if a chance occurred, but they had not exterminated them.

Why then were none of the minnows to be found in the Mkomazana River? That is a question to which there are two possible answers. The first is that the minnows did, indeed, occur there and that after 1938 they disappeared as a result of predation by trout or deterioration of their habitat, or both. The second possibility is that they never occurred there. This may seem to contradict the fact that Barnard believed the fish came from the Mkomazana River. There is nothing unique, however, about a mix-up in localities. In this case it could have happened so easily. The road between Himeville in Natal and Mokhotlong in Lesotho traverses the Sani Pass. Anyone travelling along that road might have stopped to net minnows either before ascending the pass, in the upper Mkomazana valley, or over the top of the pass in one of the westward-flowing streams that form part of the Orange River system.

Thus we have two hypotheses, neither of which can be proved. In such a dilemma we may turn to Occam's razor. William of Occam stated that if there are two ways of accounting for an observation, the simpler hypothesis should be accepted.

In this case, the fact that no Natal *Oreodaimon* have been found since 1938 can be explained by making two improbable assumptions: that the minnows lived on both sides of a major watershed and that they subsequently disappeared from one side of the escarpment. On the other hand, we may set up the hypothesis that there was a simple error in recording where the original specimens were collected. There seems little doubt where Occam's razor must fall. In my opinion, *Oreodaimon* has always been confined to the Orange River system and was never indigenous to Natal.

Authentic cases of minnows disappearing from waters in which they used to occur are generally associated with deterioration of the habitat due to man-made changes in the catchment, although the predatory activities of trout and other fish, especially bass, may have a severe impact in some situations. Even predators that are indigenous may wipe out vulnerable populations.

Peter Jackson studied the fishes of the Middle Zambezi River before Kariba Dam was built and he became convinced that the absence of minnows from the main channel was due to the ferocious tigerfish. The river's open sandy bed gave small fish no place to hide, whereas the same species might be plentiful in sheltered side streams.

The effect of cover is apparent in many situations. A report by J.G. Visser (*Piscator*, Spring 1969) describes how the minnow, *Barbus trevelyani*, co-existed with trout in stony stretches of the Tyumie River in the Hogsback. One may presume they are there to this day.

While the effect of a predator that kills and eats its victims may catch the imagination, competitors are often of greater significance in their ecological impact.

Competition has to do with either food or living space, or both. Often, competition is most severe between members of the same species, or between individuals of different species with similar requirements. Thus trout and grass carp may be stocked together in a dam without any likelihood of competition. Trout go about their business of hunting daphnia, insects, tadpoles and, perhaps, minnows; grass carp concentrate on consuming rooted plants. The grass carp probably increase the food supply of trout by breaking up the plant material and passing considerable quantities through their guts, so putting nutrients back into circulation. Bass, on the other hand, have similar feeding habits to trout. Competition will therefore develop if more than a minimum number are present. In a dam trout cannot breed, whereas largemouth bass breed prolifically. Big trout may eat small bass, although there is little evidence for this. In a dam belonging to the Transvaal Fly Fishers' Club Barry Bradley showed me what looked like a mass of tiny bass fry in the stomach of a rainbow trout. They were, in fact, young platanna tadpoles.

Even if bass fry may be considered a source of trout food, as the bass grow they rapidly become competitors. It is well known that hatchery trout of less than 20 cm suffer so severely from competition where bass are numerous that the trout fail to survive.

Much depends on the environment. If a habitat is marginal for one fish but favourable for another, the latter will have a competitive advantage. Bass prefer warmer water than trout, so a cold, high-altitude dam will favour the survival of trout, whereas a warmer dam may be taken over completely by bass.

Interactions between trout and indigenous members of the yellowfish or minnow families involve mainly competition for food, although predation does play a part. Adult trout eat small fish and it is possible that young trout may, in turn, suffer predation. Lionel Day, the first Natal Inland Fisheries Officer, believed that scalies (Natal yellowfish) ate trout eggs and alevins. This was the reason, in his view, for the failure of rainbows to become established in rivers populated by scalies, which moved upstream in spring onto the trout spawning grounds. Whereas brown trout laid their eggs in early winter and the fry had already become sufficiently advanced to take care of themselves by the time of the upstream scaly migration, the later-spawning rainbows were, according to Day, in danger of being destroyed.

Like many interesting theories, there was little factual basis for the Day hypothesis. It so happened that the best rainbow rivers, the Ngwangwana and Umzimkulu, had no scalies, whereas other streams where rainbows failed, such as the Hlatikulu, offered a poor habitat for trout of any sort.

Where indigenous fish are present in large numbers, they may compete with small trout for food, reducing the latter's survival rate. Both the Little Mooi and the Polela River at one time had large populations of scalies and comparatively few trout — browns in the Little Mooi and rainbows in the Polela. In each river the scalies had been introduced artificially, above falls which prevented their natural occurrence in the upper reaches. In the 1950s traps were placed in the Polela to reduce the number of scalies, although it is doubtful whether this had any effect.

Later, the balance shifted, apparently due to an epidemic disease that affects scalies in Natal rivers. In recent years few scalies have been seen in either the Little Mooi or the Polela. Once the scaly population became reduced, the falls on each river prevented any recruitment from downstream.

On rivers such as the Loteni and Umkomaas, where no falls restrict upstream movement, the scalies appear to be as numerous as ever, swimming towards the headwaters in spring and returning downstream in autumn.

In the Eastern Transvaal, both the Sabie and Blyde Rivers have indigenous *Varicorhinus,* a type of yellowfish, co-existing with trout. Some years ago attempts were made to reduce the numbers of yellowfish by dynamiting pools on the Sabie River. Such action to destroy indigenous fish in favour of trout would not be looked on with favour by the new generation of wildlife conservationists!

In any event, attempts to adjust the balance between members of a community are generally pointless. Any temporary reduction in numbers is soon made good by new recruits, unless really drastic action is taken.

Provided the environment remains stable, predation and competition between individuals are not undesirable. They are a natural part of community interactions. Even the introduction of a new predator, such as the trout, is likely to cause no more than minor adjustments. Exceptions do occur, but there is little ground for fears, on the one hand, that trout will be decimated by otters and cormorants, or on the other hand, that indigenous aquatic life will be destroyed by trout.

II SOUTH AFRICAN TROUT WATERS

6. Cape Province

Each of the trout areas in South Africa has its own special features. If you find yourself looking into water the colour of weak black tea flowing over white sandstone pebbles, you will know that you are in the south-western Cape. The river will probably be swift-flowing with heavily bushed banks in a narrow valley surrounded by spectacular peaks. These steep-sided mountains, together with their unique vegetation, are unlike anything else to be seen in South Africa. The rivers to which they give birth are therefore notably different from the streams of the north-eastern Cape, Transkei, Lesotho, Natal and the Transvaal.

An especially desirable feature of south-western Cape waters, from an angler's viewpoint, is their clarity. Some carry a brown stain, while others are crystal clear, but all are remarkably free of silt, in contrast to more northerly waters that are often heavily discoloured by soil washed off eroded hillsides in the rainy season. Where sediments do appear they consist mainly of sand, derived from the sandstone peaks. Table Mountain Sandstone is the predominant geological formation, not only on the mountain that stands above Cape Town, but throughout the Hottentots Holland, Franschhoek, Wemmershoek and other ranges that give birth to rivers of the Eerste, Berg and Breede systems.

Because of their origin in sandstone formations, Cape rivers are low in chemical nutrients and therefore relatively infertile compared with waters draining volcanic rocks or limestone deposits. Even those streams that have no visible peat stain have a pH slightly below 7; that is, they are on the acid side. Waters draining peat bogs have a brown stain and a pH considerably below the neutral point. Acid water is less favourable for most aquatic life than neutral or alkaline water.

Western Cape streams are not as acid as those of the coastal ranges farther east. Along the Tsitsikama coast attractive-looking rivers flow down from the Outeniqua Mountains, but their extreme acidity has precluded the establishment of trout. Associated with humic acid is a dark stain, giving deep pools an almost black appearance. Such waters contain few fish of any description, apart from a rather sparse population of eels.

The main rivers of the Western Cape rise in the mountainous belt running northwards from the eastern shores of False Bay. This complex system of steep-sided mountains reaches an altitude of over 2 000 m to the north of Worcester. The high massifs trap rain clouds moving in from the Atlantic, to produce an abundant winter

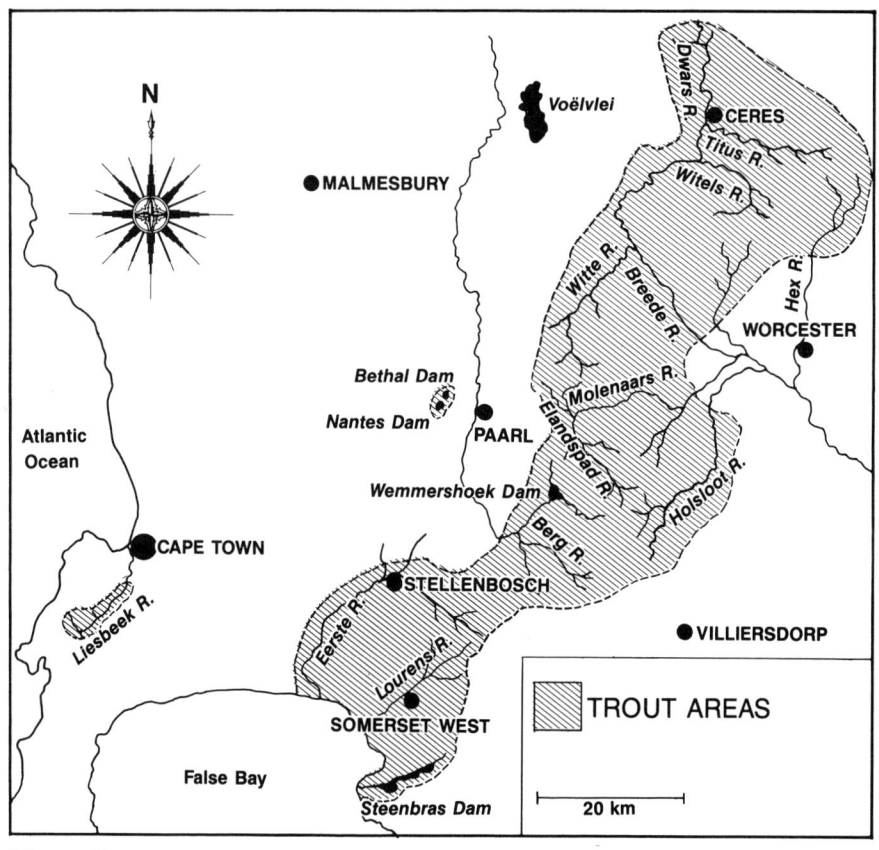

Western Cape trout areas.

precipitation, with a heavy seasonal runoff and adequate seepage throughout the dry summer to maintain streamflow. All the headwaters of the Cape rivers from the Breede in the east to the Berg River in the west, rise within a comparatively small area of less than 2 000 square kilometres. Whereas the majority of South African mountain ranges are in the form of escarpments with one side steep and the other falling gradually to a plateau, many Cape mountains have high peaks towering over deep valleys on all sides. Access to the more remote kloofs presents a challenge for the angler who enjoys wild country.

One large species of the yellowfish family occurs in the western Cape rivers to which trout have become acclimatised, as well as five species of indigenous redfin minnows. In contrast to the paucity of fish life, a wide variety of insects and crustaceans occurs. The underwater stages of insect life provide the bulk of the food of trout in Cape rivers, as in most other streams where trout are to be found, whether in South Africa or overseas. Crabs and tadpoles may supply substantial items for the larger trout, which also take small fish when these are available. Land insects, such as flies, beetles and ants, give trout an additional source of nourishment and tempt them to rise. Anglers make use of the free-rising tendency of Cape trout to enjoy dry-fly fishing on the sparkling clear mountain streams, most of which remain in their pristine condition in the high kloofs. Dams and road construction have affected some of the rivers, even in their upper reaches, while severe deterioration has taken place in water courses in the lower valleys where intensive agriculture is practised.

The eyes of a trout fisherman living in Cape Town will turn east and north to the mountains of the hinterland. But an unassuming little river, the Liesbeek, which flows through the southern suburbs of the city, has a remarkable history as a producer of trout. The story of the Liesbeek and its trout has been told by A.C. Harrison and Dale Lewis in *Piscator* No. 74, 1968/69, with further documentation in later issues of the same journal.

The Liesbeek's headwaters tumble off the south-western escarpment of Table Mountain, uniting to form the main stream in the National Botanic Gardens at Kirstenbosch, at about 120 m above sea-level. From there the Liesbeek flows northeast then north, through Bishopscourt, Claremont, Newlands, Rondebosch and Rosebank to join the Swartrivier near the Observatory and enters Table Bay east of the docks. The distance from Kirstenbosch to the tidal reaches is only about 7 km in a straight line.

Historically, the river was of some significance to the early settlers, although the origin of the name Liesbeek remains obscure. Perhaps it was derived from *lies* (flank) and *beek* (a stream), in recognition of the course of the waterway along the flank of the mountain. For the trout fisherman, its earliest claim to fame was the use made of water from the Albion Springs for the first successful hatching, in the Cape, of imported brown trout ova in 1892. Albion Springs form part of the water supply to the Liesbeek — indeed a very significant part — during periods of drought when the mountain streams dry up. These springs provided water for the famous Ohlsson's Brewery. The brewing of beer made no difference to the Liesbeek, but water was also abstracted for domestic use. The resultant diminution in flow, together with various forms of pollution, rendered the river little more than a stormwater drain for many years.

A campaign to restore the Liesbeek was put into effect in the 1930s. Not only was pollution stopped, but the springs were once again allowed to flow unhindered. In 1945 a dam in the lower reaches created a lake of five hectares that looked so attractive as to suggest an experimental stocking with trout. Five hundred rainbow fingerlings were therefore purchased by the Cape Town City Council from the Jonkershoek Hatchery and introduced to the lake on 20 December 1946. Fourteen months later the proprietor of the Vineyard Hotel, Newlands, put another 150 fingerlings into the Liesbeek next to his hotel.

After reported sightings of trout, fly fishermen began to visit the river in September 1948. Of 16 fish recorded, 14 were from the first stocking in the lake, whence some had moved upstream to Rosebank. Their weights ranged from 1 lb to 3 lb 6 oz. (1,52 kg), showing a remarkably fast rate of growth. Members of the Cape Piscatorial

Society were excited at the prospect of trout on their doorstep and further action was taken to develop and stock the Liesbeek. The watercourse was cleared of obstructions and a fish pass built to allow upstream movement past a concrete chute under a road bridge.

Conditions in the lower Liesbeek, near the dam, began to deteriorate as a result of silting and weed growth, as well as the appearance of shoals of goldfish and, later, carp. The stream itself, however, continued to provide sport. As much of its course lay through land controlled by the City Council, anyone in possession of a trout licence could fish. Some of the most attractive pools, near Bishopscourt, could be reached only by violating the privacy of episcopal property. That such violations occurred has been admitted by young anglers who have since become mature citizens.

On 14 December 1950 a rainbow of 4 lb 2 oz. (1,87 kg) was caught at the head of the lake, the largest trout to be recorded from the Liesbeek system. A number of other fish of up to 3 lb were taken by licensed anglers over the next year or two and poachers using illegal tackle were said to be active. Successful spawning took place in the headwaters and the Liesbeek became established as a producer of good trout. Some fat rainbows were caught in the lake in January 1952, but several were found to be inedible, probably owing to tainting of the flesh by oil pollution, although the fish were healthy and vigorous.

No other mention is made of possible pollution in the period up to 1968, except for the suggestion that poisonous weed-killers may have contributed to the ill-effects of low water conditions in 1966. Catches fluctuated from year to year, but each season well-grown rainbows and the odd brown trout continued to feature in reports from anglers who frequented this unique suburban fishery, in which naturally occurring galaxias minnows provided a staple diet for the introduced predators.

A four-pound male rainbow was the largest of a number of good fish landed in the spring of 1969 and in the wet spring of 1970 the little suburban stream gave members of the Cape Piscatorial Society better sport than any of their other rivers. This lent weight to the concern expressed by members at their annual general meeting in August 1970 with regard to planned canalisation of the watercourse, as well as deterioration of the Liesbeek lake. The City Council responded favourably to the society's representations and the following year some good fishing was enjoyed, notably by Robin Fick, who made a practice of releasing fish after clipping a fin for future recognition. One fish was recaptured three times.

After several droughty periods that reduced catches to a low level, the opening day on 1 September 1975 saw anglers out in force, following good winter rains. Many of the fish caught were large male rainbows recently released from Jonkershoek Hatchery. Despite reservations about the quality of these adult hatchery fish, annual releases continued for several years. Natural breeding added its quota of wild fish when river conditions were favourable. In 1980, however, no trout fingerlings were to be seen, although large shoals of galaxias minnows were present, and in recent seasons there have been few reports of fish being caught. With increasingly dense urban development, the future of the Liesbeek River as an angling water seems uncertain.

Another Cape river that has been radically altered by development is the Eerste, noted as the only river in sub-Saharan Africa to have migratory, sea-run trout. The name refers to its position as the first river to be crossed on the journey eastwards from the Cape Flats towards the Hottentots Holland mountains. The Eerste has its sources high up among the peaks of the Jonkershoek range, which exceeds 1 500 m above sea-level. The headstreams descend rapidly, uniting to form the Jonkershoek River, which is, in fact, the upper Eerste. It is a typical torrential Cape mountain stream making its way down a boulder-strewn bed in a series of miniature waterfalls and runs, with rocky pools at intervals. The banks are heavily overgrown with bush, the indigenous fynbos so beloved by botanists who delight in the immense variety of plant species that have evolved at the southern tip of Africa. An angler is likely to regard fynbos in a less favourable light. With tough, resilient branches and harsh leaves, the dense shrubbery that grows along the stream makes progress difficult for anyone armed with a fly rod. As in other Cape mountain kloofs, the line of least resistance is to wade and boulder-hop in the bed of the river.

As the stream's course becomes less precipitous, the valley opens out, pine forests cover large areas of hillside and other non-indigenous trees make their appearance. A short distance above the Government forestry station, a concrete wall has dammed the river to hold water for industrial and domestic use. A pipeline introduces water from another catchment. This foreign water is more heavily peat-stained than that of the Eerste, or Jonkershoek River, as it is still designated on the map.

The upper Eerste River, above Stellenbosch, is well shaded by fynbos.

At an altitude of slightly over 200 m above sea-level the river passes the historic Jonkershoek Hatchery and continues its north-westerly course towards Stellenbosch. It is fast-flowing, with an average gradient of 15 m per kilometre and a predominantly stony bed. The banks are overgrown with a mixture of indigenous and exotic shrubs and trees, including oaks which are so characteristic of the town precincts. On the water's edge beside some of the pools grow clumps of palmiet, a curious indigenous plant that might be described as a cross between a rush and a palm.

From Stellenbosch, the river — now officially recognised as the Eerste — swings west, then south of west, as it heads towards the sea over 20 km away, its gradient flattening to less than 5 m per kilometre. The bed becomes increasingly sandy as the river flows across an open plain to Lynedoch, then south past Faure and Sandvlei, where its course becomes easterly, to the Kramat and Macassar. After an abrupt turn, the direction of the final 2 km is due south to the coast at Macassar Beach. During the dry season, the Eerste River ends in a blind lagoon cut off from the sea by a substantial sandbar. Periodically, the bar is breached when the river comes down in spate, forming an open channel through which fish are able to migrate.

Despite the sandy nature of the plain across which the lower Eerste flows, adequate pools to shelter trout used to occur even in dry summers. In recent years, however, soil erosion from cultivated fields has resulted in pools being filled with sediment, while abstraction of water for irrigation has left no more than a trickle for months at a time. When the mouth is closed, a considerable body of water builds up behind the sandbar, although evaporation may raise salinity to a level above that of the sea. Salinity does not render the lagoon uninhabitable for trout, and the most fascinating feature of the Eerste is the manner in which its rainbow trout population has made use of salt water, not merely for survival but to produce fish of exceptional quality.

Successful breeding in the headwaters above Stellenbosch keeps the river well supplied with small trout, some of which move downstream as they grow. There conditions have become progressively worse over the years, with pollution adding to the problems created by water abstraction and silting. Recent anti-pollution moves may improve matters, however, at least in the area near Stellenbosch. Perhaps one cannot expect a return to the days when Mary Chaplin, the young daughter of the Curator of Jonkershoek Hatchery in the 1920s, showed Colonel Henry Birch-Reynardson how to catch South African trout. Certainly no future angler can look forward to the sport enjoyed by Fred Bowker and his companions on the lower Eerste. His semi-fictional account of the lives of two rainbows, *Shiny and Shiness* (written under the pen-name "Kingfisher"), includes actual records of fish that he caught. For a number of years Bowker regularly landed rainbows of three to five pounds, although catches varied according to the condition of the river in wet or dry seasons. A drought brought the likelihood of poor sport. Sometimes trout actually died when the river was low and hot weather raised water temperature to a lethal level.

Bowker was one of those who did not believe trout migrated from the river into the open sea and back into fresh water, although he admitted that they might take refuge in the saline lagoon when the river became uninhabitable. He noted a marked deterioration in the lower Eerste during the early 1940s. By 1946, pools that had always been reasonably deep in earlier years were now filled with sand. Despite progressively poorer summer conditions in the river, anglers continued to catch fine silvery rainbows when autumn and winter rains restored the flow.

A.C. Harrison (*Piscator* No. 87, 1973) takes up the story of how he proved that these fast-growing, silvery fish not only looked like the sea-run steelheads of the American Pacific coast, but had indeed reverted to the migratory pattern of their ancestors.

After unconfirmed reports of professional seine netters taking rainbow trout in the open sea of False Bay, as well as in the saline lagoon behind the coastal sand dunes, a team from Jonkershoek Hatchery took nets to the lower Eerste in March 1947. Five trout were caught in the lagoon, together with numerous mullet and other saltwater fish. The trout were less than two years old and their scales showed rapid growth, owing no doubt to the availability of ample quantities of small fish. Later that year, and in 1949 and 1952, more trout were netted near the river mouth. One of 29 cm was caught in the channel close to the surf of the open sea, when the river mouth was open. At the end of July 1958 a fat rainbow of 1,05 kg, 41 cm, was caught on bait in the tidal water at the bottom of the estuary. Five months later, when the river was no longer flowing, another of 44 cm was netted in the closed lagoon, which was more saline than the open sea.

Between 1958 and 1960 several reports were received of rainbow trout being netted off the beaches of False Bay and three specimens were actually examined, two from Muizenberg, about 25 km from the Eerste River mouth, and one from Melkbaai, only 4 km from the Eerste. There was no doubt, therefore, that trout were able to live in the sea within False Bay.

As well as this direct evidence of the ability of rainbows to exist in salt water, records of fish from the Eerste River are strongly in support of the anadromous tendency of its trout. Anadromy, that is migration from fresh to salt water and back again up the river to spawn, is a natural part of the life cycle of the salmon and trout family. While it may be impossible to prove that a particular individual has migrated, there is ample circumstantial evidence that Eerste River rainbows made use of the sea.

In October 1945, a landowner on the stony part of the river, below Stellenbosch, found that his section of river had become occupied by numerous silvery rainbows that were easily distinguished from the usual dark, well-spotted individuals resident in the area. The silvery fish soon disappeared again. Farther downstream, in 1949, when the flow was starting to fail in the lower river, about 50 trout from 30 to 60 cm in length were seen making their way downstream. The following day the shallow pools were devoid of fish. Yet in April 1950 rainbows of up to 1,5 kg were caught in places that had dried up completely during the summer.

After good rainy seasons in 1950, 1951 and 1952, in which the river produced an excellent harvest of trout up to 2 kg, there was a "calamitous mortality" amongst trout in the lower river in December 1953. Yet the following spring fishing was again good. February 1955 saw the death of many trout from winery pollution. Once again, plenty of silvery rainbows were taken near Faure in the late spring of that year. More fish were caught in 1956, including one of four pounds, and angling was good in both spring and autumn of 1957/58. In February 1959, all fish, including thousands of mullet, were killed in the Eerste estuary by gross pollution from a fruit-processing plant, followed by a distillery discharge. Surprisingly, eight sea-run rainbows were caught by angling in June 1959, presumably from recruitment from inshore water in False Bay. Within three years, however, in A.C. Harrison's words, "the final deterioration of this renowned fishery seemed to be at hand".

Most of the reports appearing in *Piscator* between the spring of 1973 and 1982 were gloomy with respect to conditions in the lower Eerste, where pollution and water abstraction made life difficult for the trout. An additional factor was the appearance of parrots-feather weed, which choked much of the river down to the estuary. The first optimistic note for many years was struck in Seymour Wilmot's report in August 1983 (*Piscator* No. 112, p. 35) that "not since the good old days of 1932 onwards have I seen such improvement in the quality of the water and the fighting quality of our Eerste River rainbow trout". This accords with Stephen McVeigh's report (*Piscator* No. 114, 1984) of the efforts being made to improve conditions in the main river and its tributary, the Plankenbrug, by the Stellenbosch Freshwater Fishing Club.

However little hope there may be for the lower Eerste, from the town stretch upstream into the Forest Reserve good quality fly fishing should remain available. As recently as 1975 some excellent sport was enjoyed by local anglers who knew how to tempt the trout of the Stellenbosch town water. From a single pool, no more than 15 m long and 5 m wide, Albert van Reenen took over 50 sizeable rainbows in two seasons.

Whatever the future holds, the Eerste will always retain the honour of being the only river in the southern hemisphere to have developed a population of sea-going rainbow trout. G.B. Hobbs, in his book *Fisherman's Country*, describes the sport of fishing for saltwater trout at the mouths of some of the rivers in the South Island of New Zealand, but these are brown trout, not rainbows.

With regard to the migratory habits of Eerste River trout, Harrison mentions the mixed ancestry of the rainbows that were brought to South Africa, some originating from the supposedly resident population of the McCloud River in California, while others came from areas inhabited by migratory steelheads. Originally, scientists thought that migratory and non-migratory trout belonged to distinct species. Thus the brown trout of European rivers was named *Salmo fario*, while the sea trout was identified as *Salmo trutta*. Similarly, the rainbow of the American west was named *Salmo irideus* and the sea-run steelhead was called *Salmo gairdneri*. Further research showed that all European trout should be considered one species and that the same applied to the American rainbow and steelhead. Although brown trout and sea trout became recognised as one species, it was still thought that probably some strains were migratory and others resident, with heredity determining how a particular population would behave. Recently, however, the Salmon Research Trust of Ireland has presented evidence, based on electrophoretic studies of blood samples, that there are no genetic differences between brown trout and sea trout on the west coast of Eire. If this applies elsewhere in Europe, and also to American rainbow/steelhead populations, it may be true to say that heredity is not a factor in determining whether an individual fish will tend to migrate. In that case, there may be no significance in the mixed origin of our South African rainbow trout. Rainbows in general are considered to be more inclined than brown trout to wander from the place in which they were hatched. In South Africa, any tendency to move off downstream is disastrous if the lower waters are unsuitable for the survival of trout. Only in the Cape is it possible for trout to live anywhere near the sea and, even there, the Eerste is unique. No other river has trout which give evidence of anadromy, that is spending part of their life in salt water before returning to fresh water to spawn.

The Lourens River enters False Bay only a few kilometres east of the Eerste estuary and trout used to be found within a short distance of the sea. It is a smaller stream than the Eerste and is subject to severe water shortage in its lower reaches. Half a century ago many rainbows were caught by Fred Bowker and others near the estuary of the Lourens, but there has been no published record of any silvery trout that might be suspected of being sea-run fish.

In addition to abstraction of water through dams in the upper catchment and pumping for irrigation farther downstream, pollution from agricultural fertilisers and domestic waste rendered the lower river completely uninhabitable by trout in the late summer. The poor state of the river prompted the formation, in 1982, of the Lourens River Advisory Board. In a report by S.A. Krohn and B. Coldicott (*Piscator* No. 112, Dec. 1983) some improvement was already evident a year later, with good catches of trout being taken in the municipal area of Somerset West. On the private farms farther upstream natural breeding has always maintained a population of rainbow trout.

Apart from the Liesbeek, Eerste and Lourens, Cape trout streams are all situated in the mountainous hinterland and belong to either the Berg River system or the Breede system. Headwaters of the Olifants River were stocked with trout in the 1890s and some heavy bags were taken a few years later, but little was heard of trout subsequently and the whole of the Olifants catchment is now treated as an area for the conservation of indigenous fish, with no stocking of bass or trout permitted.

The Berg River rises close to the headwaters of the Eerste, but flows first east then north through the fruit-farming district of Groot Drakenstein. Clear mountain streams come tumbling off the sandstone formations of the Drakenstein, Franschhoek and Wemmershoek ranges to unite in an upland valley at about 150 m above sealevel. The junction pool of the upper Berg and its tributary, the Dwars, was a famous fishing spot from which many large brown trout were taken until a great flood in 1941 filled the pool with rubble. A.C. Harrison made a particular study of the Dwars (see *Piscator* No. 69, p.20), which contained numerous small rainbows as well as a smaller number of brown trout of better size and condition than the rainbows. The heaviest brown trout recorded was caught by Donald Swan in 1932 and weighed 8 lb 8 oz. (3,85 kg).

With more intensive development of the Groot Drakenstein area, the best holding water for trout became degraded and even as early as 1958 much of the former glory of the Berg River system had departed. Below the confluence of the Berg and Dwars, the Wemmer River joins the main stream from the east. A radical change to this once-famous trout water followed the construction of the Wemmershoek Dam. On the positive side, a fine stillwater fishery has been created by the dam.

From the north-east side of the Wemmershoek range, which forms the divide between the Berg River system and the Breede River system, flow the Elandspad and Smalblaar. The Elandspad is regarded as a tributary of the Smalblaar, although the former is the larger stream. The main road from Paarl to Worcester crosses the Elandspad a short distance above the confluence, with the site of the new bridge at the exit from the 3,913 km road tunnel slightly downstream of the old bridge. From the confluence, the Smalblaar runs at the bottom of a deep kloof on the north side of the road.

After a few kilometres, the river is renamed the Molenaars. It passes the Protea Park Hotel and is bridged by the main road 11 km farther on. This section includes the well-known Molenaars fishery, controlled by the Cape Piscatorial Society.

The waters of the Smalblaar-Elandspad-Molenaars offer the most productive rainbow trout fishing in the Western Cape. Many glowing reports of the sport to be enjoyed, especially by dry-fly fishermen, have appeared in the pages of *Piscator*. Details of the rivers, and access to different parts of their wild and beautiful kloofs, will be found in the Cape Piscatorial Society's publication *Trout in the Kloofs*. Regrettably, threats to the natural condition of the area have developed since the book appeared in 1962. In July 1985, the society's Fishing Development Group reported that the Smalblaar-Elandspad-Molenaars complex was under heavy pressure from the new road tunnel and the widening of the road between the tunnel and Worcester, as well as a proposal for a major dam and a recreation area.

A dam was built some years ago in the neighbouring Stettyn's Kloof, on the Holsloot River, and since the situation stabilised both river and dam have provided sport. Jack Blackman gives a lively account of fishing the river in his *Flies and Fly Fishing in South Africa*. From the southern end of the Hex River Mountains flows another tributary of the Breede River, the spectacular Jan du Toit, which epitomises the magnificence of an untamed Cape kloof according to John Beams. It was stocked only in 1968 and remains inaccessible to all but the most energetic anglers.

In contrast to the rainbow waters, which predominate in the Cape, is the Witte River in Bain's Kloof to the north-west of Du Toit's Kloof. The mountain block Oostenberg has a famous stretch of the river that is controlled by the Cape Piscatorial Society. First stocked in the 1890s, it has always been a brown trout fishery. The cover picture on Tom Sutcliffe's *My Way with a Trout* shows the author looking at a two-pound brown trout in the clear amber water of the Witte.

The society has introduced a "no-kill" rule on the Witte to conserve the rather sparse trout population. Robin Fick has described how he caught and returned a large trout and repeated his exploit on the next visit, recatching the same fish in the same place.

Opposite: The Smalblaar River, Du Toit's Kloof, Cape.

Conditions are much the same on the Witte in its isolated kloof as they were in 1939 when A.C. Harrison studied the trout and their food supply. An unusual feature is the abundance of caddis larvae that form a considerable proportion of the food of the brown trout. The only attempt to introduce rainbows proved unsuccessful, perhaps fortunately, since rainbows in the Cape mountain streams tend to breed more prolifically than the brown and remain small, whereas the Witte River browns, although lean, grow to a considerable size.

The headwaters of the Breede River rise in the Witzenberg range and flow through the Koekoedoukloof to the town of Ceres, where the river is known as the Dwars. The town water has several pools that have produced fish well in excess of 2 kg. John Beams was particularly successful in the Belmont Pool, from which his best rainbow scaled 2,7 kg. Possibly this pool owes some of its productivity to a pipeline that conveys hotel kitchen waste into the river.

Other sources of unnatural nourishment also originate in the town and, when the river is low, may constitute pollution instead of enrichment. Periods of drought cause conditions to deteriorate, but seasons of good rainfall restore the situation. Both brown and rainbow trout are to be found, as well as smallmouth bass and bluegills. The trout are usually in excellent condition and Stephen McVeigh (*Piscator* No. 109) mentions that angling returns indicate that a successful angler might expect to catch an average of 1,8 kg of trout per visit. That is good fishing.

Steenbras Reservoir, Cape; the Coffer Dam is exposed at low lake level.

Below the town section, with its often heavily bushed pools, the river plunges down into Michell's Pass, where it is joined by the Witels, which is a brown trout stream that flows through a wild and inaccessible kloof. A graphic account of the exploration of the Witels is to be found in *Trout in the Kloofs*. Although the fish are rather slow-growing, they provide enjoyable dry-fly fishing for anyone with the skill and energy to negotiate the watercourse.

River fishing in the mountains of the Western Cape is, with local exceptions, a strenuous business. Several well-known still waters offer less arduous conditions.

Within easy reach of Cape Town is Steenbras Reservoir, set in picturesque scenery overlooking Gordon's Bay, at an altitude of 330 m above sea-level. The original dam was completed in 1920, the retaining wall was raised in 1954 and the storage capacity further increased by creating an upper lake in 1974. The water area is now 380 hectares, with a capacity of 34 million cubic metres and an average depth, when full, of 9 m. This large area of water, 10 km in total length, calls for local knowledge to select productive fishing areas.

Many fine brown trout, some good-sized brook trout and a few rainbows have been taken by members of the Cape Piscatorial Society over the years. No breeding takes place of either brown or rainbow although smallmouth bass do breed in the dam.

The water at Steenbras is stained brown by peat, which reduces the pH to a level of acidity that has proved less suitable for rainbow trout than for brown. Tiger trout, produced by using brook trout males for the artificial fertilisation of brown trout eggs, were introduced for several years and their growth was good. So was that of most of the brown trout which supplemented their diet by feeding on small Cape kurper (*Sandelia*) and galaxias minnows. Of recent years a shortage of brown trout at Jonkershoek Hatchery, and the cessation of production of tiger trout, has led to the stocking of more rainbows. Although percentage survival of the rainbows has always been low, growth and condition of those caught has been good. Blustery weather, characteristic of the Cape coast, may make fishing unattractive, but a sheltered picnic spot is always to be found among the surrounding pine woods.

Another large reservoir, also part of Cape Town's water supply, is Wemmershoek Dam. It has clear water, in contrast to the dark stain of Steenbras, and is fed by two tributaries of the Berg River, the Olifants and the Drakenstein. With maximum dimensions of 4,5 by 2 km, the lake is set in magnificent surroundings of pine-clad slopes and towering peaks. When full its area is 300 hectares, with an average depth of nearly 20 m.

Wemmershoek was first opened for fishing in 1960 and natural breeding in the feeder streams has maintained a large population of rainbow trout, without any artificial stocking. Despite the numbers of trout present, the fishing is not always easy and, as at Steenbras, spinning is allowed in addition to fly fishing. During hot summer weather the trout retreat to deep water and seldom enter the marginal shallows until March.

Despite the presence of numerous phantom midge larvae and the availability of red-fin minnows, growth of trout has generally not been rapid and the average size of those caught has seldom exceeded a pound. Conditions may improve after good rains and the autumn of 1985 produced some of the best results for years, with some rainbows of up to four pounds being caught.

Two fascinating man-made lakes are the Paarl reservoirs, Bethal and Nantes. As one approaches the town, Paarl mountain looms up out of the plain with three rounded masses of bare granite at the top. One would never suspect that there would be any opportunity to fish in such apparently waterless terrain. But a road, Jan Phillips Drive, takes one up to an undulating plateau, dominated by the three granite outcrops. Built across valleys lying in folds of the plateau at an altitude of 500 m are the walls of the two reservoirs, fed by clear springs and surrounded by indigenous fynbos. The bush provides a habitat for coveys of Cape francolin and other wildlife, while rameron pigeons clatter out of scattered pines along the roadside.

Bethal, the more northerly of the reservoirs, is the more attractive, with two arms, one nearly a kilometre in length, running back from the wall. Fishing is probably best in autumn when the water may be 4 m or more below spillway level, leaving an open space, clear of the fynbos thicket that is almost impenetrable for the would-be angler. Bass breed in the reservoirs, but are not numerous enough to prevent the trout, which are stocked annually, from growing reasonably well. If fly fishing proves unprofitable, spinning tackle may be used.

Whether or not the fish are co-operative, no one can fail to be moved by the superb panorama across the Berg River valley to the barrier of the Groot Drakenstein and Klein Drakenstein mountains, through which the new Du Toit's Kloof road tunnel passes.

Before departing from the Western Cape, a visitor might do well to try Lakenvlei Dam in the Bokkeveld near Ceres. A gold reef was reputed to exist in that area, which Thomas Bain investigated in 1873. There has been no talk of gold since that time, but for permit-holders of the Cape Piscatorial Society the dam was the most profitable fishing place of any of their still waters in 1984, with anglers landing an average of six rainbows each, up to four pounds.

Beyond the Bokkeveld stretches the vast Karroo, with the nearest trout far to the east, near Port Elizabeth and East London. Even when one reaches these main centres of the Eastern Province there is little encouragement for the trout lover.

Fair-sized streams flow from the Outeniqua Mountains, but their waters are too peat-stained and acid for trout. A few minor rivers inland from Humansdorp and Port Elizabeth have been stocked repeatedly and the trout have grown in favourable seasons, but have not become established. The only regular fishing is provided by a two-hectare dam that is controlled by the Eastern Province Freshwater Fish Conservancy.

North-eastwards, the Amatola Range from the Hogsback to Stutterheim attracts sufficient rainfall to maintain upland streams with adequate volume for trout to survive, except in times of drought.

The enthusiasm of fly fishers is not dampened by limitations of the environment and, more than 100 years after the Frontier Acclimatisation Society was formed, members of the angling fraternity still showed enough faith in the future of trout to form the Federation of East Cape Trout Angling Clubs, on 4 September 1982.

Evening light on Bethal Reservoir, Paarl.

Six organisations, including the veteran Frontier Acclimatisation Society, were represented at the inaugural meeting. Of the clubs in the Federation, the only one with river fishing (apart from the Barkly East and Lady Grey clubs from the area close to the Lesotho highlands) is the Hogsback Club.

The Hogsback is a well-watered escarpment, by Eastern Cape standards, with the Klipplaat River winding away westwards across the plateau and the Tyumie plunging off the eastern edge and meandering down a broad valley towards Alice. Trout breed at the foot of the escarpment but seldom grow to more than a pound or so in weight. I once enjoyed an excursion down the torrential stream where it flows through indigenous forest at the foot of the mountain. Despite pouring rain I returned triumphant with enough fat little rainbows for the family supper.

The Klipplaat is an entirely different sort of stream, with a slight gradient and long pools paved with the flat stones that give the stream its name. Breeding is at best sporadic, but ample food supplies have produced trout of 3 kg and more. With regular stocking, over 100 km has been made available for fishing, from the headwaters down to the extensive Waterdown Dam.

Southeast, along the Amatola Range near King William's Town, is the historic Pirie Hatchery. Farther down the same valley are the Maden Dam (10 ha) and the Rooikrantz Dam (85 ha), both well-known producers of trout, some of large size. In the adjacent Keiskammahoek district several minor trout streams occur, including the Wolf, described by S.A. Hey in his book *The Rapture of the River*.

Near Stutterheim, east of Keiskammahoek, is the 120-hectare Gubu Dam, situated at more than 940 m above sea-level in a picturesque setting with pine trees growing close to the water's edge along the northern and eastern sides, which are within a State Forest. With a long axis of more than 2 km, the dam has an irregular shoreline, giving an attractively natural appearance.

When full the dam is nearly 24 m deep, but for several recent seasons the level has been considerably below the spillway. The first stocking was carried out in 1968 and by the end of the 1971 season a rainbow of 4,85 kg had been taken. This excellent growth rate has declined somewhat. Fish of an average size of 400 to 700 g have commonly been taken, with fair numbers of over 1 kg and a few of 3 to 4 kg.

In the early years, brown trout were stocked, as well as rainbows, but none have been introduced since 1980. By 1985 difficulties were experienced with restocking owing to unavailability of trout from the Pirie Hatchery. Rainbow fingerlings and, more recently, fry have been transported from Jonkershoek Hatchery near Stellenbosch. Whether the introduction of these small fish will maintain an adequate population of catchable-sized trout remains to be seen. The 1985 annual competition on Gubu Dam yielded barely one fish per rod, compared with two or three in previous years, but this poor return may have been due to bad weather.

Nearly 200 km to the north of Stutterheim are the Lady Grey and Barkly East districts, close to the Lesotho border. This is high, cold country intersected by rivers that have produced some of the most spectacular rainbow trout fishing in South Africa. Barkly East is the only place in the Republic where there is a chance of catching an eight-pound trout in a river.

An eight pounder from a river seems no more than a dream to most fly fishermen but it was a dream that came true for two Natal anglers in 1983. On Thursday, 31 March, Clive Hatton was fishing the Langkloof River at Barkly East when he hooked and landed a female rainbow of 4,058 kg, 67,5 cm long, condition factor 125, just before dark, with a sinking line and No. 2 Walker's Killer. Two days later his friend Sean Larkan, using a floating line and No. 4 Taddy, took another rainbow female, 3,760 kg, 65 cm long, condition factor 137. These two fish of 8 lb 15 oz. and 8 lb 4½ oz. easily broke the previous record for the district of 7 lb 4 oz., established the year before.

The first stocking of Barkly East rivers took place in 1910 and since then all the streams, including Langkloof, Kraai, Sterkspruit, Bokspruit, Riflespruit, Bell, Vaalhoek and Saalboom, have had trout introduced, as well as the Karringmelkspruit near Lady Grey.

Opposite: Trout areas in Eastern Cape, Natal and Transvaal.

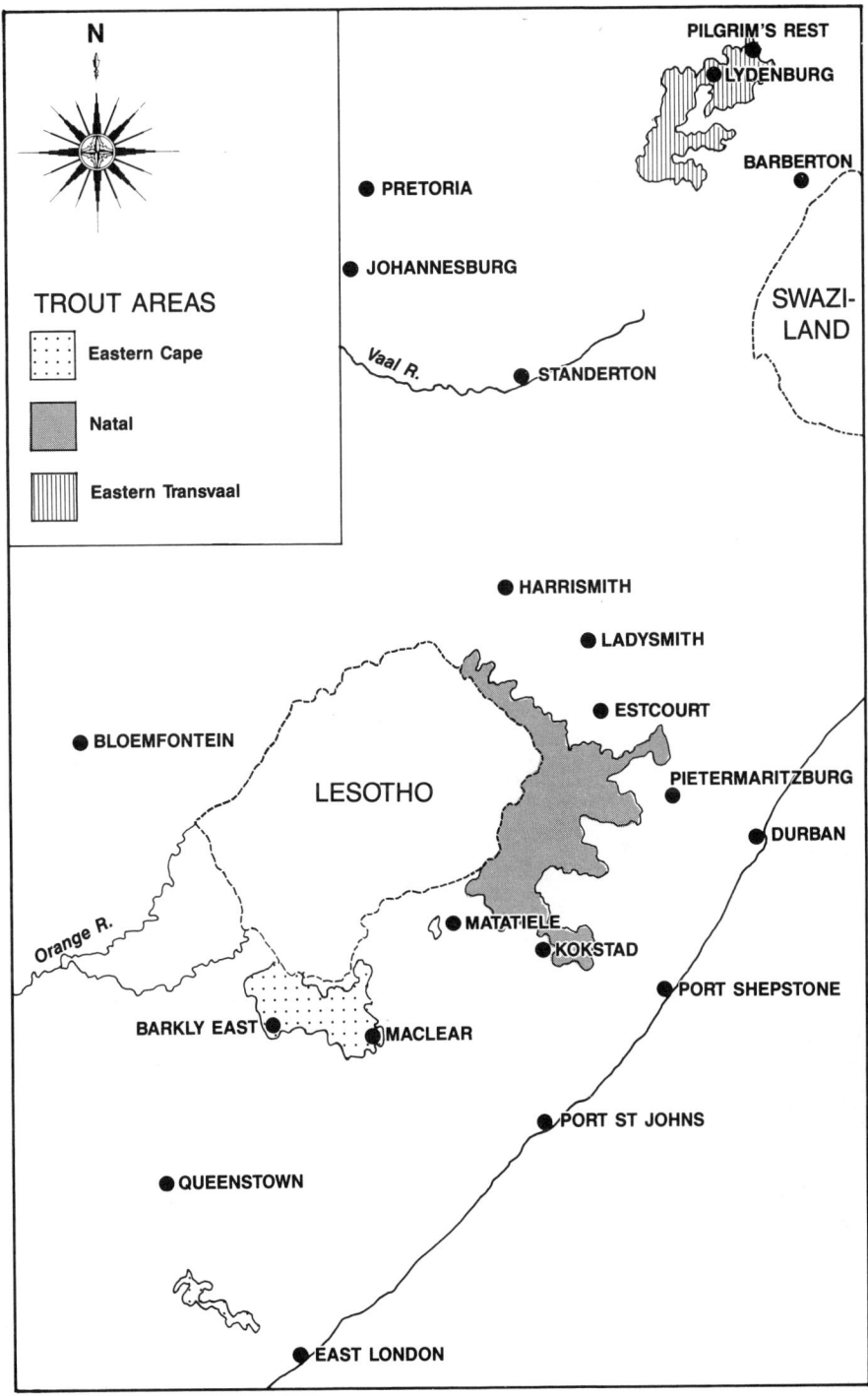

N

TROUT AREAS

Eastern Cape

Natal

Eastern Transvaal

PILGRIM'S REST
LYDENBURG
BARBERTON
PRETORIA
JOHANNESBURG
SWAZI-
LAND
Vaal R.
STANDERTON
HARRISMITH
LADYSMITH
BLOEMFONTEIN
ESTCOURT
LESOTHO
PIETERMARITZBURG
DURBAN
Orange R.
MATATIELE
KOKSTAD
PORT SHEPSTONE
BARKLY EAST
MACLEAR
PORT ST JOHNS
QUEENSTOWN
EAST LONDON

In general, the Barkly East rivers have a moderate to flat gradient with excellent production of aquatic insects and other trout food, as the water originates in nutrient-rich basalt rock formations.

The great shortcoming is irregularity of rainfall, with as little as 327 mm in exceptionally dry years compared with a maximum of 942 mm. After a succession of good years, breeding builds up excessive numbers of trout, with a consequent reduction in size. In 1968, for instance, Fred Birch of the Department of Nature Conservation poisoned one small pool and removed 534 trout, all small. In the Bokspruit he used an electric shocker to remove over 3 000 rainbow trout, which were transferred to other waters. On the other hand, several poor seasons, such as those of 1982-84, reduce the rivers to mere trickles and the trout suffer in consequence, although the survivors in the deep pools may grow out exceptionally well.

As well as the rivers, several dams have become known as producers of big trout. The Barkly East municipal dam was a popular fishing water until it dried up in the 1984 drought.

Whereas the rivers of the Barkly East district are incised into a high plateau and make their way into the westward-flowing Orange River system, the headwaters on the eastern side of the continental divide flow down a steep escarpment on their way to the Indian Ocean. East of Barkly Pass are the tributaries of the Tsitsa River, part of the Umzimvubu system that drains a 200 km arc of the main Drakensberg

Flat-topped sandstone bluffs, characteristic of the Maclear district, rise above the Tsitsa River, lined with exotic wattles and weeping willows.

The silt-laden waters of the Tina River; a once-famous trout stream now ruined by soil erosion in its catchment.

range. This large river basin is remarkable for the fact that the only indigenous fish found in the whole system are eels and the chubby-head minnow, *Barbus anoplus*.

Many of the tributaries of the Umzimvubu system became famous trout streams, including the Wildebeest, or Inxu, at Ugie; the Little Mooi, Mooi, Little Pot, Big Pot and the Tsitsa itself in the Maclear district; the Luzie and the Tina near Mount Fletcher.

In his classic, *The Rapture of the River*, Sidney Hey gives mouth-watering descriptions of the fishing he enjoyed around Maclear soon after the streams were stocked. He himself put trout into some of the more remote streams that had never been stocked. For many years the district was regarded as one of the finest rainbow trout areas. But as long ago as 1956, Hey remarked on the degradation of some of the catchments, with consequent silting and deterioration of the rivers. By 1970, the famous Gemfana stretch of the lower Tsitsa was no longer productive. In 1984, when I was advised to leave the drought-stricken rivers of Barkly East in favour of Maclear, I was greeted with the encouraging news that several keen trout fishermen were still resident in the town and that they would be on the water that weekend. And where would they be fishing? At Matatiele, in Natal.

River conditions and the resilient trout may perhaps return to something of their former glory in Maclear, but there was a ghostly feel about the Royal Hotel, that once-famous fishing hostelry where today's staff seem to know nothing of the angler or his needs.

At the end of his book Hey expressed the hope that he would join up once again with his good companions "in those Elysian fields, to explore the rivers of our dreams". Dreams of the past seem more real than hopes of the future, in Maclear.

7. Natal

Western Cape mountain streams have a special appeal for those who can reach them; the Transvaal has intensively managed and highly productive trout waters; but Natal provides a wider range of accessible and inexpensive fly fishing than any other part of the Republic.

Once known primarily for its rivers, Natal now has so many dams that more trout, and bigger ones, are taken from man-made lakes and ponds than from the rivers. This applies particularly during periods of below average rainfall, as in the years 1981 to 1984. There is also a lot more interest in stillwater fishing than there used to be. In former times, there was a tendency to look down on dams as a poor substitute for running water. Today a great many trout anglers are content with the less strenuous option of casting a fly on a dam, where there is a reasonable chance of hooking a heavy fish, rather than scrambling along the overgrown banks of a river.

The majority of trout waters in Natal are on private farmland. A substantial proportion are not fully utilised, either because the owner has no interest in fishing or because the water is strictly preserved for the use of only a few people. An increasingly active part is being played by fishing clubs in making water available to members of the angling public.

Trout occur mainly in the Drakensberg foothills at an altitude of about 1 200 to 1 800 m above sea-level. Above 1 800 m the streams are generally too small and precipitous, while below 1 200 m rivers become too silted or sluggish and dams tend to be too warm for trout. Suitable conditions exist in the uplands, from the south-western corner of the province northwards, throughout the Swartberg and Underberg-Himeville districts, past Impendle to the Nottingham Road-Mooi River area. Farther north, beyond the valley of the Bushman's River, the landscape falls rapidly to a level that is too low for trout, so there is only a narrow strip habitable by trout along the foot of the escarpment from Cathkin to Mont-aux-Sources.

Away from the high Drakensberg, small enclaves of trout country are to be found here and there. In the south, near Harding, tributaries of the Umtamvuna that rise on the Ingeli range are well-wooded streams that remain cool down to an altitude of less than 1 000 m. Trout do well in these clear mountain rivulets, as well as in dams. In the midlands trout streams and dams occupy valleys in the Karkloof range

Opposite: Main trout areas in Natal

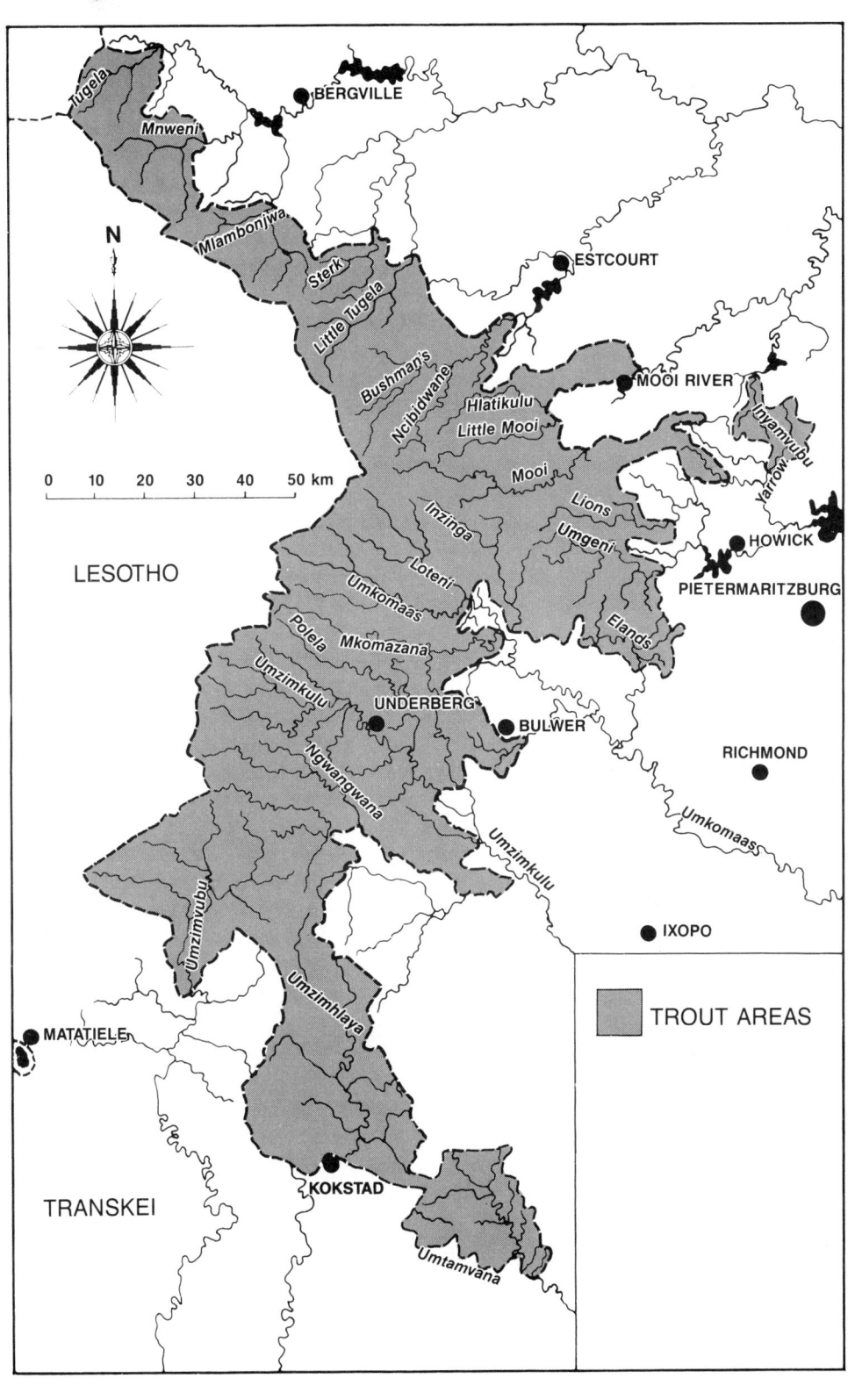

N

LESOTHO

TRANSKEI

BERGVILLE

ESTCOURT

MOOI RIVER

HOWICK

PIETERMARITZBURG

RICHMOND

IXOPO

MATATIELE

UNDERBERG

BULWER

KOKSTAD

Tugela

Mnweni

Mlamboniwa

Sterk

Little Tugela

Bushman's

Ncibidwane

Hlatikulu

Little Mooi

Mooi

Inzinga

Lions

Umgeni

Loteni

Umkomaas

Elands

Polela

Mkomazana

Umzimkulu

Ngwangwana

Umzimvubu

Umzimhlava

Umzimkulu

Umkomaas

Inyamvubu

Yarrow

Umtamvana

0   10   20   30   40   50 km

TROUT AREAS

and also near Greytown, while northern Natal has trout waters west of Newcastle and north of Utrecht.

In all, about 7 000 square kilometres, or roughly eight per cent of Natal-KwaZulu, may be considered suitable for trout. Temporary success has been achieved in growing trout in ponds fed by spring water close to the subtropical Natal coast at Kloof, west of Durban, and near Eshowe. But such experiments are of little practical significance. Fly fishermen seek their sport within sight of the high hills.

Trout everywhere are subject to the vagaries of the weather, and in Natal there is an especially strong correlation between rainfall patterns and the welfare of fish populations. Ever since trout first became established, there have been cycles of good and bad seasons, depending on the quantity of rain.

Two or three seasons of abundant, well-distributed precipitation are followed by good angling. A prolonged drought, on the other hand, has a severely negative impact. Short-term fluctuations in the weather have a profound influence on fishing prospects. Generally, conditions are most stable in autumn and winter. The autumn is therefore a popular time for fly fishermen to visit the rivers, while the availability of dams that are open throughout the year has done away with the need to pack trout tackle into storage for the winter.

The spring months of September and October often give excellent sport in Natal, before the heat and thunderstorms of summer discourage fishing expeditions. An uncle of mine could not be persuaded to take out his rod between 10 November and early March. However, while the weather may certainly disrupt one's plans, fishing can be good at any time. A spell of cool, cloudy weather, without any heavy downpours, will allow rivers to run clear and the water in stream or dam to drop to a temperature at which trout feed freely. As a river fines down after a spate, the fish will be hungry. Conditions in December or January may well be more favourable than during a hot spell in spring, when water levels are at their lowest and dust devils dance across the scorched landscape.

Spring in Natal is delightful if early rains bring a green flush to the burnt veld and life to drought-shrunken streams, but it is not always like that. In high summer the countryside can be relied on to look its best and, with luck, the fishing may be good too. There is an ever-present risk of thunderstorms and it is inadvisable for anyone who dislikes being caught in a downpour to venture far from shelter when the Drakensberg peaks are buried in menacing cumulo-nimbus cloud formations.

The roar of an approaching hailstorm may tempt one to take cover under a tree, but this increases the chance of being struck by lightning. An overhanging bank is safer, although I know from personal experience that an avalanche of ice-cold water may pour down one's neck in such a situation. To reduce the risk from lightning, one should avoid rocky ridges, especially those containing dolerite, and it may be as well to remember that a graphite rod is an electrical conductor.

Despite its vagaries, Natal weather may seem preferable to some of the extremes one experiences in the Cape, with its buffeting south-easters or the wild storms that blow in from the Atlantic in autumn and spring.

Natal trout streams belong to several major river systems. In the south-west, the

Umzimvubu River system drains a long segment of the Drakensberg escarpment. About 100 km, from the Transkei border to north of Swartberg, lies within the Umzimvubu basin. Most of the streams come tumbling down very steep valleys before joining the upper Umzimvubu, which has at times produced excellent catches of rainbow trout in the area north of New Amalfi.

Lower down, on the plains between New Amalfi and Cedarville, the river has too low a gradient to be suitable for trout to breed. Large rainbows were caught for some years after the initial stocking in 1911, but sediment deposition from soil erosion farther upstream has affected the well-being of trout. In addition, carp became established, with deleterious effects.

Fortunately for anglers in the Matatiele district, the Matatiele Nature Reserve Mountain Dam, above the town, is an excellent producer of large trout and should remain so, provided it can be kept adequately stocked. In 1977, Ray Wade of Maclear caught a rainbow in the lake of 4,15 kg.

The upper Umzimvubu rises in inaccessible country on the Lesotho border and flows southwards, to be joined by the Little Umzimvubu below New Amalfi. From the eastern side of the catchment comes the Krom, which rises on an outlying buttress of the main Drakensberg and flows south, then west, meandering on an elevated plateau.

The catchment of the Krom River has suitable terrain for the construction of dams, some of which are among the most productive man-made trout waters in South Africa. Dorning's Dam produced John Rorich's famous rainbow of 12 lb 3,6 oz. (5,55 kg) in May 1958, and many other fine fish have been caught there over the years.

Near Kokstad, the most easterly tributary of the Umzimvubu is the Umzimhlava, which rises to the north on Swartberg Mountain. It was stocked as early as 1903 and has had to be restocked at intervals ever since. It is mostly shallow and has a limited catchment area, so it becomes extremely low in times of drought. In addition, breeding places for trout are scarce, and carp are established in parts of the stream. Therefore, despite having a reputation for producing trout in excellent condition in years of good rainfall, the Umzimhlava is not a notable angling water. Its chief claim to fame is the 7 kg brown trout that was killed with a knobkerrie in a shallow ford near Franklin in 1913.

If one travels on the road from Kokstad through Swartberg towards Underberg, one crosses the watershed between the southward-flowing Umzimvubu system and the eastward-flowing Umzimkulu system. The first sizeable stream is the Ndowana River, which used to form the border between the Cape Province and Natal before East Griqualand was transferred to Natal.

Within a few hundred metres of the Ndowana bridge, a 20 m high dam has impounded the river to create a 150-hectare lake that fills the valley far upstream. It is to be hoped that this lake will remain free of bass, which occur in many of the dams in the Swartberg district and, more recently, have appeared in some of the well-known Underberg trout dams. Fortunately the dam, which is privately owned, should always be populated by trout which breed in the Ndowana River. Although the lower part of the stream has a bed of mud or sheet rock, with little breeding potential, the upper waters produce good numbers of young trout in favourable seasons.

Some of the fish from the headwaters probably used to move downstream into the deeper pools of the lower reaches, near the confluence with the Ngwangwana, at the eastern boundary of Coleford Nature Reserve. Now construction of the dam across the Ndowana has changed the natural waterway, but perhaps large trout will leave the lake in time of flood. If any should take up residence in the river below, there might be a pleasant surprise in store for some angler.

Production from the new sheet of water will depend on the extent to which it remains discoloured from silt washed in after heavy rain. Both the Ndowana and Ngwangwana have a greyish opacity due to clay deposits in their valleys, but this colloidal material is not harmful, as is suspended sediment.

The Ngwangwana is the most southerly of the major Natal trout rivers. Its sources lie on each side of Bushman's Nek Pass, on the Natal-Lesotho border, and the headstreams unite to form two major tributaries that join a short distance from the Bushman's Nek Forest Station.

Trout are to be found for several kilometres up each of these main tributaries, especially on the larger north fork, which is the main Ngwangwana River. From the foot of the pass, trout have been caught for nearly 90 km downstream, to a point not far above the river's confluence with the Umzimkulu near Creighton. For a South African river to provide a habitat suitable for trout over so long a stretch is unusual, indeed probably unique.

The reason for the length of trout water is that the Ngwangwana remains at a relatively high altitude above sea-level and that the gradient of the valley is neither too flat nor too steep. For the first 15 km the stream flows fairly rapidly, with a gradient of 10 m per kilometre. Grassy banks, with nchichi and heather bushes, give easy access to attractive runs and pools. In summer or early autumn, when the river is full, the small rainbows that are generally numerous in this section give good sport on light tackle.

Near the boundary of State Forest land is a picturesque cascade, where the river plunges over a dolerite sill into a deep pool. Several more attractive pools take one to the first private farm, New England, which holds good trout after a period of high rainfall, but whose rather shallow, open pools become almost devoid of fish in times of drought.

On the next farm, Bergview, a rocky gorge produces a turbulent section with deep pools and an attractive variety of water. For many years, this property has been owned by the Michaux family, who were among the pioneers responsible for establishing trout in the Underberg district. Many a lively descendant of the trout originally introduced to the river, three-quarters of a century ago, has been taken from Bergview and from the adjoining stretch on Gowrie, a retreat much beloved by Doctor George and Archie Campbell, brothers of the poet Roy, whose reference to "trouts the size of salmon" may have been inspired by Ngwangwana rainbows.

From the road bridge at the boundary of Gowrie and Elton, the tumbling waters of the upper Ngwangwana become more sedate, flowing across a broad valley, with many twists and turns as the river meanders for 25 km, with a gradient of only 4 m per kilometre, to the farm Lammermoor, below the bridge on the main Swartberg-Underberg road. This long meandering portion is mostly fairly shallow, which is ideal for trout as long as there is a good flow of water. But in severe droughts such as those of 1984 and 1985, the river shrinks and most of the trout disappear, until the weather cycle changes. Depopulation of the river has occurred several times in its history as a trout water. My first introduction to the Ngwangwana was in May 1945, when few fish were present. But those that had survived were magnificent specimens. One might find no trace of a fish in several pools and then see a portly two pounder cruising in the clear water, rising every now and then to take an insect off the surface.

Within a few years, the Ngwangwana was again full of trout and the river remained for many seasons the most reliable provider of sport in the Underberg district. Then came the flood of May 1959, which decimated the upper river. Recovery was followed by the drastic effects of the drought of 1984-85.

The lower part, from Lammermoor downwards, is also affected by droughts and floods, but perhaps not quite so severely as farther upstream. On Lammermoor, the river enters a long gorge where it cuts its way through a mass of dolerite. Deep runs and rocky pools make attractive fishing water for several kilometres. The river finally emerges into an open valley at Coleford, where two farms were purchased in 1945 to create a nature reserve, with 8 km of river.

Although some well-known pools are to be found on Coleford Nature Reserve, long stretches are shallow, with a bed of flat rock that offers little shelter for fish when the river is low. An attempt was made to rectify this deficiency by discharging explosives, the object of which was to blow holes in the bedrock. Regrettably, however, the employee of the explosives company which donated the experimental material seemed ignorant of the correct technique. Spectacular plumes of water went skywards, and a few minnows were stunned, but the river-bed remained in its natural condition.

Below Coleford, the Ngwangwana, now joined by the Ndowana, continues for a long distance to have an almost ideal gradient of 8 m per kilometre, with excellent holding water for big trout. In summer the river is likely to be too discoloured for fly fishing, but spring and autumn have yielded some impressive baskets of trout up to three pounds and more for those who have had the opportunity to reach this inaccessible stretch of stream.

Finally, trout disappear as the Ngwangwana becomes increasingly silt-laden on its way to join the Umzimkulu.

The upper Umzimkulu occupies a broad catchment, with several tributaries that are worthy trout streams in their own right. Most southerly of these is the Umzimouti, which shares with the Ngwangwana the characteristic feature of flowing across a high plateau in its upper reaches. It then descends through a rocky gorge past the southern shoulder of Garden Castle mountain, continuing as a charming little river to join the Umzimkulu about 1 550 m above sea-level.

The Umzimouti averages no more than 6 or 8 m in width, but it is by nature a stable stream, with well-grassed banks and a succession of good trout-holding pools.

Gravel beds provide abundant spawning places and its clear waters usually swarm with yearling fish, as well as some older ones. The river is little affected by agricultural development or the demands of irrigation, but climatic extremes, especially drought, do take their toll. As with other Natal trout streams, however, a severe reduction in the number of fish has the advantage of improving the growth rate and size until the population builds up again to its usual density.

The main sources of the Umzimkulu are on the Berg, west of Drakensberg Garden Hotel. The upper river comes rushing down a steep, rocky course, without much holding water, until the gradient begins to flatten out near the hotel. The bed remains unstable, on a broad flood-plain across which the river changes course with each big flood, until it emerges onto a wide alluvial peneplain, to be joined by the Tugelana stream, coming in from the north.

The Tugelana has produced some remarkably well-grown trout, up to a kilogram in weight. Five-hundred-gram trout have been taken from the main river in favourable years, although prolific breeding generally keeps the size down. A former owner of the farm Castle End used to make a practice of taking out yearling fish each winter with an electric shocker, to stock a 30-hectare dam on one of the sidestreams. This man-made lake has yielded numerous trout of up to 2,5 kg over the past 35 years. Annual production has on several occasions exceeded 600 fish, averaging about a kilogram each.

After winding across the open valley at about 1 700 m above sea-level, the Umzimkulu is joined by a major tributary of almost the same volume as the main river. This is the Mlambonja, which comes in from the north. Close to the confluence is the road bridge, below which lies The Poort, a great gash carved by the river through a massive dolerite dyke.

For about 10 km a series of fine rocky pools and bubbling runs tempts the angler to cast a fly. Although big fish are seldom caught, numerous vigorous half pounders have been taken in this somewhat inaccessible section. Where the valley opens out on the farm Glenside, the Umzimouti joins the Umzimkulu from the south.

The river has now assumed the stately proportions that make it the premier rainbow trout stream in the Republic. It sweeps grandly from chuckling run to curving pool, as much as 30 m wide, its grassy banks dotted with indigenous nchichi bushes and the not-always-welcome osier willows.

On the farm Rainbow, the Umzimkulwana joins the main river from the north. This beautiful little stream, seldom more than two rod-lengths in width, gave me my first introduction to the rainbow trout of the Underberg district in January 1941. At that time its upper reaches were accessible only on foot or horseback. Today, a homestead stands on the shores of an extensive man-made lake impounded by a wall across the river some 7 km from its junction with the Umzimkulu.

Rainbow farm used to be owned by a well-known resident of the Underberg district. One day he is said to have found an angler on his river. The unwitting trespasser was, in fact, His Honour, the Administrator of Natal, who announced his identity as Gordon Watson. "Well," came the reply, "I am Cliffy Watson and you'd better get to hell off my land!"

...zimkulu River: channels in sandstone rock

...nch Barlow surveys the results of weed clearance in his Natal dam

A trout dam in the Drakensberg

A 2,2 kg rainbow killed by an otter

A 650 g rainbow marked by a cormorant's beak

Although the river down to and including Rainbow farm is still privately controlled, much of the river from there past Underberg is available for fishing through the Underberg-Himeville Trout Fishing Club.

The section down to the main road bridge, 4 km from Underberg, is as close to an ideal trout stream as one can find in South Africa. It was first stocked by John Parker in 1902, according to Sidney Hey, although there is some doubt as to whether this stocking was successful. In 1913, Doctor Croudace was instrumental in obtaining ova from the Cape, which farmers hatched and liberated into the river. For a number of years additional stocking was carried out with fish caught and transported across from the Polela, as well as fry hatched in floating boxes. Probably much of this later stocking was unnecessary, since natural breeding never fails in the most favourable areas, even under adverse weather conditions.

The Umzimkulu, like the Ngwangwana, has always been a rainbow river. Any brown trout that may have been introduced have never become established. Nor are there any large indigenous fish, except eels, above a small fall near the lower limit of trout water. Below that the scaly, *Barbus natalensis,* is present. The chubby-head minnow, *Barbus anoplus,* is quite plentiful above Underberg, but whether this species occurred naturally is open to question. No specimens were recorded until after some minnows were brought, in the 1950s, from the upper Tugela and released in a dam.

From the confluence of the Umzimkulwana at 1 500 m above sea-level, the river has a gradient of less than 5 m per kilometre for the next 35 km. This includes the section known as Thurston's Gorge, into which you look if you park at the roadside picnic spot a mile along the Pietermaritzburg road out of Underberg. As one's eyes move up from the river winding through its rock-bound course far below, past Underberg village to the distant peaks of the high Berg, as fair a prospect unfolds as you are likely to see anywhere in South Africa. The prospect is less fair than it used to be, before buildings intruded, but the river retains its primeval quality.

To the north of the Umzimkulu is the Polela. The two eventually join, far down towards Creighton, but the Polela has an identity notably different from that of the Umzimkulu. To reach it, the road leads from Underberg to Himeville, past an avenue of oaks, each tree planted by a family of the district as a friendly link between the villages. Two kilometres beyond Himeville is the Polela meandering quietly along, minding its own business, through farms with pasturelands spreading far and wide.

Green pastures, dotted with dairy cows, make a pleasant rural scene. But when the rains are late in spring the fields need water, which has to come from the river. Poles carrying electric cables mark the sites of irrigation pumps, each one sucking out a proportion of the streamflow. The total quantity sprayed onto the land is negligible when the river is full, but the effect is obvious if the river is barely flowing, as happened in the spring of 1985.

The Polela, like other Natal rivers, has suffered from droughts in the past and recovery has always followed. Despite the increased demands of irrigation, there is no reason to doubt that the river will return to its former glory in seasons of abundant rainfall.

After an abortive stocking with rainbows in 1902, brown trout were introduced in 1906, and did well, although they eventually disappeared. One of 4,2 kg was taken by W. Hayward in 1918 and it may be seen to this day, reposing in a glass case in the Himeville Hotel. In more recent years, the Polela has yielded more rainbows of over 2 kg than any other Natal river. John Kirkman, when he owned the Beeverstowe stretch, was particularly adept at catching big fish.

Originally, the Polela had no indigenous fish, probably not even minnows. A farmer named Blaikie caught scalies below a waterfall in the lower reaches, to which the fish were confined, and put them into a dam that burst, allowing the scalies to colonise the river. They were so numerous in the early 1950s that a trapping programme was put into effect to thin them out. For the last 20 years or so, few scalies have been seen. Chubby-head minnows, on the other hand, which were introduced to a dam about 30 years ago, are well distributed in the river.

The Polela rises high up in the cleft between Hodgson's Peaks to the south of Sani Pass. Once the stream reaches the foot of the escarpment, it becomes an inviting, clear brook occupied by trout for a distance of 4 or 5 km above the Forest Station of Cobham. The first pools habitable by trout are at about 1 850 m above sea-level. Despite the steep gradient of nearly 25 m per kilometre, the bed is fairly stable with deep pools at intervals. Below the boundary of State Forest, the river winds across an open valley in which the owner has conserved natural growths of nchichi bush and other indigenous vegetation. Two productive dams have been built on a sidestream. The larger, of 30 hectares, has yielded many fish since its construction in 1949. This is the well-known McDougall's Dam, available to members of the Underberg-Himeville Trout Fishing Club.

Another large dam, originally owned by Colonel Holt, is situated on the Polelana, a tributary that joins the main stream from the north. This dam, together with the Polela itself, supplies water to the largest trout farm in Natal, owned by the Tongaat group. Farther up the Polelana is a private dam of nearly 100 hectares in surface area.

More dams are situated in the Polela valley near Himeville, including one of three hectares and another of 12 hectares, on Himeville Nature Reserve. Regrettably, bass have gained entry to most of these dams.

After winding eastwards through farmlands, the Polela plunges over a waterfall at Reichenau Mission, passes under the bridge on the main Bulwer-Underberg road and enters a deep valley, eventually joining the Umzimkulu.

North of the Umzimkulu River system is that of the Umkomaas, with four main constituents: the Mkomazana, the Umkomaas itself, the Loteni and the Inzinga.

The Mkomazana rises a few kilometres south of Thabana Ntlenyana, the highest point in southern Africa, 3 458 m above sea-level. From the road that zigzags to the crest of Sani Pass, at 2 750 m, one looks down on the upper Mkomazana. Sizeable pools occur from an altitude of about 1 800 m, but the stream is extremely torrential. Even the section above Ridgway's Store has a gradient of more than 20 m per kilometre which, combined with an unstable bed of waterworn stones and gravel, gives few places for trout to shelter. The fish that do live among the sandstone boulders are red-spotted and golden-flanked — beautiful examples of the colourful brown trout that live in clear mountain streams.

The first sizeable pool is below the Sani Pass Hotel, on the farm Seaforth, where a waterfall initiates a change to more stable stream conditions. The fall prevents upstream movement of scalies, which are plentiful in the river in summer. Above the falls was the site at which the rare minnow, *Oreodaimon quathlambae*, was supposed to have been collected in 1938. As I mention in Chapter 5, the minnow has not been found by anyone on the Natal side of the Drakensberg escarpment since 1938, and it may well be that the original specimens came, in fact, from over the top of Sani Pass.

Rainbow trout were introduced to the Mkomazana on several occasions, but only browns have been seen in recent years. A rather sparse population lives in the section from Seaforth down to the bridge on the main Himeville-Nottingham Road road, where gravel beds are available for breeding.

Farther downstream, the gradient decreases to less than 4 m per kilometre, with considerable accumulations of fine sediment choking the river-bed. Therefore, despite good holding pools inhabited by a few well-conditioned trout, little breeding takes place. In the past trout were to be found for nearly 40 km below the main road bridge.

To the north of the Mkomazana lies the valley of the upper Umkomaas, with Vergelegen Nature Reserve offering access to the wilderness area that is under the control of the Directorate of Forestry.

The Umkomaas rises on the high Drakensberg midway between Sani Pass in the south and Giant's Castle in the north. As the stream reaches the foot of the main escarpment it cascades down a valley hemmed in by high sandstone bluffs. Pools begin to appear as the gradient eases, generally where the torrent has scooped a hole behind one of the boulders fallen from the cliffs above.

If one explores the river above Vergelegen Nature Reserve more time will be spent scrambling up the rock-strewn floor of the valley, with its thickets of nchichi and heather bushes, than casting a fly. When a likely place does appear a careful approach and accurate delivery of a small nymph may produce a tug from a lively brown trout of superb beauty. Whether one decides to liberate it or to take it home for supper, carefully wrapped in damp newspaper, a trout from the topmost reaches of the Umkomaas has a special quality that fits the beauty of its surroundings.

Below the confluence of the Vergelegen stream, access is easy as river and road run close together. Pools are infrequent for several kilometres but wherever an undercut bank or a hole behind a boulder gives cover, a trout may be waiting. Sometimes a surprisingly large fish may appear; big brown trout are more often found in shallow water than rainbows of similar size. Farther down, the Umkomaas has produced more trophy-sized brown trout than any other Natal river with the exception of the Bushman's. This is probably due to the physical nature of the river, with its rather unstable bed and tendency for sediment to clog the gravel in which trout spawn. The Umkomaas never has as dense a population of small fish as, for instance, the Mooi. The growth rate therefore tends to be more rapid and the older fish have less competition from the yearlings.

Ten kilometres from the Vergelegen stream the Mcatsheni tributary comes in from the south and 8 km below that is the bridge on the main Himeville-Nottingham

Road road. This part of the river flows down several minor gorges cut through black dolerite rock, with big pools at intervals. The gradient is about 12 m per kilometre, considerably flatter than farther upstream. Except where silver wattles have become established, the banks are open, offering easy access to the angler.

Below the bridge, the river winds away eastwards through a rocky valley to pick up the Loteni and Inzinga Rivers coming in from the north and the Mkomazana from the south. Although trout become fewer the farther down one goes and the habitat deteriorates owing to siltation from eroded hillsides, fishing in early spring or late autumn may produce browns of impressive size. Fritz Hoch landed one of 2,4 kg in 1981 at the confluence with the Mkomazana.

Rainbow trout were introduced as early as 1904 but this stocking was recorded as "above Impendle", which indicates that the young fish were released too far down the river. Whatever the reason, this introduction was unsuccessful. Credit for establishing trout in the Umkomaas goes to the Root brothers, Willie and Bert, who caught brown trout in the Loteni River in 1917 and carried them across the mountains, on horseback, and liberated them near the present Vergelegen Nature Reserve.

The Loteni, on which the Roots owned one of the farms that now form part of Loteni Nature Reserve, had been stocked by John Parker and Donald McKenzie in 1907. It is similar to the upper Umkomaas, with its sources extending onto the southern flank of Giant's Castle. It has two main branches which unite at 1 500 m above sea-level not far above the nature reserve hutted camp. Trout have been caught for some distance above the confluence, but the streams are small, with a precipitous gradient of 45 m per kilometre.

Through the nature reserve the river flows merrily over a bed of sandstone rocks and gravel and through a short gorge section that includes several large, deep pools, before being joined by the Mbodhla Stream, which is itself large enough to hold trout. The gradient of the Loteni in this area is about 18 m per kilometre, which means it is still a rapidly flowing river.

When carrying a good volume of water, say two cubic metres a second, the Loteni is as delightful a stream to fish as one can find anywhere, with a vigorous stock of colourful brown trout. Its upper catchment is well conserved, so the water clears rapidly, even after heavy rain. The sparkling shallows and swirling pools are ideal for upstream nymph or dry-fly fishing. Peter Root, son of Willie, is an expert at the use of a dry fly in the rough water of his old home stretch of the Loteni.

Like any other quick-running shallow stream in South Africa, drought reduces the Loteni watercourse to a mass of exposed stones with no more than a trickle finding its way from one isolated pool to another. On the other hand, one can hear the rumble of rocks churning over one another when the river is in violent spate. Changes in course may occur in a flood, and the Bush Pool, which produced several five pounders in its time, was left completely isolated after a big storm in 1951.

Despite the extremes that its fish have to face, the Loteni offers good habitat and abundant feeding on insect larvae and crabs in years of bountiful rainfall. Indigenous scalies move upstream in early summer, as they do on the Mkomazana and Umkomaas, and there is always the chance that one will take a fly, although none of the yellowfish family is as keen on artificial lures as are trout. Underneath rocks, the little rock catlet, *Amphilius natalensis*, is occasionally to be found.

Below the nature reserve, two sizeable tributaries join the river which meanders through a narrow valley, its comparatively flat gradient of 8 m per kilometre allowing more silted conditions to develop. Earth off eroded hillsides keeps the water turbid in summer, but in spring and autumn good fishing has been enjoyed near the main road bridge and farther downstream, even as far as the confluence with the Umkomaas.

Rainbow trout have been introduced to the Loteni on several occasions, but have never become established. In the Inzinga (which occupies the next valley to the north), on the other hand, rainbows have at times been more numerous than browns.

The Elands, a Natal midlands brown trout stream.

The Inzinga is a fascinating little river that rises short of the main Berg, at about 1 800 m above sea-level, and has no holding water for trout until it is within 3 km of the main road between Himeville and Nottingham Road. Below the road there is a 10 m waterfall into a deep pool which, like most waterfall pools, is not as productive as shallower places with a better food supply.

The waterfall marks the river's entry into a remarkable sunken basin in which the once horizontal rock strata dip at a crazy angle. The river leaves the basin through a narrow defile and flows through a deep valley that looks almost unchanged since the day in 1930 when I caught eight brown trout of up to a pound in weight. There were no rainbows in the Inzinga at that time, although 200 had been introduced in 1904.

Farther downstream the valley opens out, with the river winding through cultivated fields. Above the bridge on the road to Impendle long, deep pools occur with rather heavily silted beds. The final section of the river is rocky, as the valley deepens to join that of the Umkomaas.

The most easterly trout-holding tributary of the Umkomaas is the Elands, which rises on the Inhluzane range and flows southwards to cross the main Underberg-Pietermaritzburg road at Boston. Above the road, the Elands flows across a broad, flat valley. It is a narrow stream with banks heavily overgrown by long grass and shrubs. Brown trout have been established in the stream for many years, probably since the first recorded stocking in 1905, but owing to its small size and shortage of water in drought years, it is not a notable angling water.

Of the midland rivers that rise away from the main Drakensberg, the Umgeni, together with its tributaries the Lions and Yarrow, is the most important for trout fishing. The Umgeni shares with the Bushman's River the honour of being the first to be stocked successfully in Africa south of the Sahara.

The Umgeni catchment is particularly notable for the many dams that provide an excellent habitat for trout. Whereas the Umkomaas system is characterised by valleys deeply incised into the landscape with few sites suitable for dam construction on feeder streams, the Umgeni catchment has a large number of minor valleys that lend themselves to the creation of man-made lakes. Many of these are more than 1 200 m above sea-level and have become productive trout waters. With minor exceptions, the higher parts of the Umgeni catchment are all in private ownership and almost every farmer has built one or more dams on his property.

Two of the largest of these dams are situated on the lofty plateau east of Spioenkop mountain at nearly 1 800 m above sea-level. Each has a surface area of about 80 hectares and both have provided excellent fishing, with rainbow trout of up to more than 5 kg. Lake Lyndhurst has had runs of spawning fish going up a feeder stream, as I reported in *Piscator* No. 79, but successful breeding has taken place on only a limited scale. Artificial stocking has therefore been required to maintain the trout population.

The source of the Umgeni is in a large vlei, which it is to be hoped will not be dammed, since vleis in their natural state are now rare in Natal. After emerging from Lake Lyndhurst, which was built in 1969, the river flows to the edge of the plateau

Tempting a brown trout: Umgeni River, Natal.

and plunges down through a wooded gorge to the farms New Forest and Umgeni Poort where, for the first time, pools of adequate size for trout make their appearance.

The river flows south-east to its confluence with the Furth stream that rises on a high plateau to the south. The valley now opens out, with a gradient of less than 3 m per kilometre, and the Umgeni winds between high, overgrown banks, with long pools interspersed with shallow riffles.

Breeding places for the brown trout that have lived in the river for 96 years are not abundant. Overstocking is therefore not a problem; indeed numbers have had to be boosted from time to time by introduction of hatchery stock. Nevertheless, the descendants of the trout introduced by John Parker in May 1890 probably continue to form the bulk of the fish.

The Natal Fly Fishers' Club has rights to some of the best water, but the Umgeni is not an easy river to fish. Canon G.E. Pennington, who published a book on trout fishing in 1911, considered that the Umgeni proved profitable only late in the day.

At the eastern boundary of the farm Beverley, the river passes under the bridge on the Impendle-Lions River road and then drops over a fall into a narrow, rocky valley. The water swirls attractively past dolerite boulders and this was at one time well-known trout water, including the section in State Forest land at Dargle. Recent years of drought have resulted in the virtual disappearance of trout from the river below the falls. Perhaps a cycle of more favourable seasons will see a reversion to the position of former years. In 1911 the *Descriptive Guide and Official Handbook* for Natal mentioned the "splendid trout fishing" available here.

Turning again to the dams that have been built on tributaries of the Umgeni, one of the most productive group of man-made lakes in South Africa is situated in the catchment of the Furth stream. Hastings Farm has a dam on which visitors pay to catch trout, while the two Rainbow Lakes form the basis for a commercial enterprise in which ova are collected from the fish inhabiting the lakes. These eggs are then incubated and sold to trout farmers in other parts of South Africa and overseas. Other dams belong to syndicates who use them for recreational angling. Loch Furth, as one of the dams is called, is particularly interesting because its stock is almost entirely self-maintaining. The Furth stream that feeds the dam provides good spawning facilities, in seasons of normal rainfall, and natural breeding produces as many young rainbow trout as the dam can provide food for.

Well below recognised trout water is Midmar Dam, the main reservoir for Pietermaritzburg. Prior to 1970 two large brown trout, the bigger one 3,6 kg, were caught in the lake, proving that trout do move downstream beyond their normal habitat.

Not far from Midmar Dam, the Lions River joins the Umgeni from the north. The source of the Lions is near Fort Nottingham and, like the upper Umgeni, the Lions River catchment is liberally dotted with dams, many of which have been stocked with trout. The stream itself can offer interesting fly fishing at times. Although there are few places where trout can breed, the brown trout that were first introduced in 1899 have been able to maintain a rather sparse population. The most notable fish was a brown trout of 4,5 kg that was found stranded below a weir on the farm Sarsden. More recently, Chris Hadley Grave, of the Natal Fly Fishers' Club, landed a fine 2,3 kg brown trout below the Mill Falls at Caversham in 1979.

Within the Umgeni River catchment area are the sites of John Parker's historic hatcheries. The first, used for hatching the original trout that became acclimatised in South Africa in 1890, is on a small forest stream between Lidgetton and Balgowan. The second, which was in operation between 1899 and 1907, is on Parker's farm Tetworth, through which flows the Jackson's Spruit, at one time well known as a minor trout stream. It joins the Karkloof River that flows into the Umgeni near the head of Albert Falls Dam.

The Karkloof is not a trout water but its northern tributary, the Yarrow, or Mrolweni, is a charming example of one of the lesser rivers that provide sport for the enterprising angler. The two main feeder streams of the Yarrow rise on top of the Karkloof range at about 1 700 m above sea-level. The stronger south fork has pools large enough to hold trout of over a pound in weight. Several of the pools lie at the foot of steep chutes, where the water flows over rock slabs. One autumn day in 1948 my father was intrigued to see a 14 inch brown trout ascending the sloping surface, which was covered with only a trickle of water, by turning on its side and flapping its tail energetically, the sound of which had drawn attention to the fish. With considerable effort the trout reached the next pool on its arduous journey to satisfy the urge to seek a gravel bed in which to lay its eggs.

From the plateau, the two streams plunge over a series of spectacular waterfalls to join at the foot of the mountain, along the slopes of which is one of the largest areas of indigenous forest in Natal. For the next 4 km the Yarrow dances over a stony bed, with pools here and there, to reach the bridge on the Howick-Rietvlei road. At this point it is already below the 1 200 m contour, commonly regarded as the lower limit of trout water in Natal.

The stream remains cool enough for trout, however, for at least another 8 km, down to about 1 050 m above sea-level. This is due to the rapid descent of the river through a well-shaded course.

The Yarrow has a remarkably prolific stock of brown trout, some of which are probably the descendants of the original 1899 stocking. Rainbows have been introduced several times since 1904, but have disappeared again after a few years. But the brown trout breed, even in years of drought, and the upper part of the Gala water has provided hundreds of yearlings taken out by Hugh Huntley's electric shocker to stock dams belonging to the Natal Fly Fishers' Club.

The best fishing is on Yarrow farm, where the stream meanders quietly between banks overgrown with long grass and nettles make the wearing of shorts inadvisable. R.B. Fyfe, who owned the farm, retained the section near his house for himself. He was especially keen on using a dry fly on the long stretch above a weir in October, when hatches of big mayflies would make the trout go wild at sunset.

Generally, a fish of a pound is a good one on the Yarrow, but anyone who doubts that big fish lurk in some of the pools should read Jolyon Nuttall's appendix, "The Goose Pool", at the end of Neville Nuttall's *Trout Streams of Natal.*

Flowing northwards from its source close to that of the Yarrow, on top of the Karkloof range, is the Inyamvubu. It winds across a broad, marshy plain, where its narrow channel used to produce brown trout of two pounds and more, but agricultural development and tree planting seem to have put an end to the fishing. Farther downstream the Inyamvubu has been impounded by the Craigie Burn Dam, in which trout are occasionally caught.

In the same area, the upper Umvoti River is within the trout zone. On one of its tributaries is Merthley Lake, the reservoir that supplies Greytown. This was one of the first still waters to be stocked successfully in Natal. In 1935 it yielded Cyril Browning's 10-pound trout that stood as a Natal record for many years. This trout was caught as a yearling in the upper Mooi River and transferred to Merthley Lake.

The Mooi River is the best-known brown trout stream in South Africa. Although it rises away from the main Drakensberg escarpment, on a spur projecting eastwards from Giant's Castle, it maintains a more constant flow than many other Natal streams. Its relative constancy, as well as the presence of good breeding grounds, has enabled the Mooi River to support a population of brown trout, without restocking, ever since the introduction of 400 brown trout fry in 1899.

Paradoxically, the favourable environment provided by the river has caused a problem: the production of too many fish. Ever since the initial breeding stock built up, the average size has been reduced by competition for food. For this reason, the best sport has been in years that have followed droughty seasons in which the numbers of trout were reduced. Deliberate extermination of trout over considerable stretches, by the use of rotenone fish toxin in 1963 and 1968, produced a temporary boost in growth rate.

The Mooi rises at an altitude of 2 500 m and flows down a narrow valley on State Forest land, before dropping over a waterfall on the farm Game Pass. At 1 800 m above sea-level a strong tributary joins the main stream and from that point, for more than 60 km, trout inhabit the river. For several kilometres the gradient remains steep, with frequent cascades among massive sandstone boulders. Near the lower boundary of Game Pass is a tributary which was the site of the 1899 stocking. In 1890 Parker put 500 fry into the Mooi River, but much farther downstream near Rosetta, where conditions were unsuitable for their survival.

On Gladstone's Nose, a farm that forms part of Kamberg Nature Reserve, the gradient of the river flattens to less than 10 m per kilometre, its winding course lined with indigenous nchichi and other shrubs. Close to the upper boundary is a weir which diverts river water into the Natal Parks Board's hatchery where rainbow and brown trout are reared for stocking dams and rivers.

Water flowing out of the hatchery is channelled into a series of large ponds in which public fishing is available. Most of the fish put into these ponds are rainbows, but there are also some browns. Camp Dam is the largest pond, with an area of 1,4 hectares.

The clear water and attractive combination of pools and running water make the Gladstone's stretch of the river appealing to fly fishermen. The wary brown trout are not easy to catch, and the better-sized ones generally live in the more inaccessible places, where skilful casting is required to place the fly within sight of their discriminating eyes. High banks add to the novice's problems and many of the visitors who stay in the huts at the camp prefer to spend their time on the dams. This suits those who enjoy testing their skill on the river.

Below Gladstone's Nose (named after the Victorian British Prime Minister, whose jutting nose was thought to be of similar shape to that of a conspicuous rock formation overlooking the valley) the river flows through farmlands where the Natal Fly Fishers' Club has rights on a particularly attractive stretch of water, above and below the bridge on the road to Rosetta. The river banks are more open than farther upstream, and an almost ideal balance between pools and riffles makes the stream particularly tempting for a fisherman. Although the average size may be no more than 150 g, considerably larger trout are not uncommon.

On Stillerust, the more easterly portion of Kamberg Nature Reserve, the river loops to and fro across an open plain with a comparatively flat gradient of 5 m per kilometre. The trout are less numerous than farther upstream, but the average size may be better.

After being joined by the Reekie Lynn tributary, the Mooi plunges over a 10 m fall into a gorge, whose fine pools and deep runs have yielded many brown trout of a pound or so, although not many bigger ones. Large brown seem to prefer more quietly flowing water. Four kilometres below the falls, the valley opens out as the gradient becomes less steep. Runs alternate with pools that average some 15 m in width and trout have all they need for breeding and survival (except in years of severe drought).

These are the waters of the Trout Bungalow, a name going back to 1902, when Harry Singleton, proprietor of the Nottingham Road Hotel, erected accommodation for anglers. The wood-and-iron buildings stand to this day on a bluff overlooking the stream, carefully maintained by their present owner, who also keeps up to date a record book of the trout caught over the past 60 years.

The material used for the bungalow originally formed the officers' mess at the British cantonments in Harrismith during the South African War. In 1910, Singleton charged visitors 15 shillings a day, including fishing. Those who arrived by train were transported by horse and trap for 15 shillings each way, or 10 and sixpence each for two or more passengers. The 18-mile journey took two and a half hours. Most of Singleton's clients apparently came from Johannesburg. Thus trout were instrumental in bringing profit to Natal from the City of Gold.

Singleton advertised a plentiful supply of trout running three to the pound. Fish up to two and a half pounds were not uncommon and one of 6 lb 12 oz. was caught on a No. 12 Butcher on 27 September 1910.

Below the Trout Bungalow the river offers excellent fishing through half a dozen privately owned farms to the falls on Inchbrakie, where a vertical drop of about 7 m prevents any upstream movement of fish. Below the falls, scalies are plentiful and smallmouth bass may also be found. Above the falls brown trout are the only fish in the Mooi, apart from some rainbows. The latter have been introduced several times, either deliberately or through fish escaping from dams in the catchment. Rainbows bred in the river in the early 1970s but in recent years the only ones reported have been a few that had apparently escaped from the hatchery in Kamberg Nature Reserve.

From Inchbrakie, the river winds along a course that is heavily overgrown with osier willows as well as indigenous vegetation. Although siltation of the river-bed gives little opportunity for breeding, some big trout occur in the area down to the bridge on the Rosetta-Kamberg road, and even past Rosetta. Fly fishing in winter and early spring sometimes gives good results as far down as the confluence of the Little Mooi a few kilometres above Mooi River township.

The Little Mooi River is noteworthy, not only for the large brown trout it has produced, but because its valley has numerous dam sites, many of which have been developed into productive angling waters.

Near the source of the Little Mooi on Highmoor State Forest, two dams are widely known to fly fishermen. One is about 10 hectares, the other three hectares. So popular have they become that the Directorate of Forestry has had to limit access to prevent an undesirable concentration of anglers. Although dams normally have no close season, visitors are not permitted when a pair of Wattled Cranes, which are resident in the area, are engaged in nesting activities. These rare birds nest in vleis with shallow standing water, and it is a matter of concern to conservationists that dam-building may destroy a natural breeding site. Experience at Highmoor proves that the creation of a man-made lake is not necessarily inconsistent with the needs of the cranes.

Below the dams, the sources of the Little Mooi plunge down steep gorges cut into the sandstone plateau and emerge far below, at the top end of Fairview farm, which has been subdivided into a number of smallholdings. The main stream flows on the northern side of Cleopatra mountain, while a large tributary flows on the southern side, to the confluence at Fairview boundary.

Five kilometres down the valley is Sans Souci farm, where I caught my first trout at the age of five, using a wattle stick to which was attached a length of string, some gut and a fly. The trout was scarcely big enough for my supper but its capture remains a vivid memory.

On Sans Souci the Little Mooi is still a small stream, perhaps 8 m in average width, but it has pools of sufficient depth to hold substantial brown trout. Wattle trees, brambles and long grass make the angler work for his fish, while the next farm, Kilmore, is shaded by numerous weeping willow trees. Although unwelcome to someone unskilled in the art of switch casting, the willows give shade to the stream which is mostly shallow. Without the shelter provided by the trees, it is doubtful if the stream would have produced as many good trout as it has.

Kilmore was the site of the original stocking of 200 brown trout fry in 1900. Other introductions were made later, using fish caught on fly in the Mooi River, and rainbow trout have also been put into the Little Mooi, but the descendants of the first planting are probably there to this day. Brown trout remain the dominant species and, indeed, no rainbows have been reported in recent years from the Little Mooi.

Below Kilmore, the river consists of long pools, with shallow stickles in between. In years of drought the pools become almost stagnant, but normally a fair number of well-grown trout await the fisherman.

Breeding can take place only here and there, so overstocking is not a problem in this part of the Little Mooi.

The valley is broad and flat, stretching to the slopes of Kamberg mountain, which gives the district its name. A succession of streams flow northwards off the mountain

The overgrown banks of the Little Mooi River, Natal, pose a challenge to the fly fisher.

to join the Little Mooi, each in a shallow valley of flat gradient. It looks as if the landscape had been specially planned to encourage dam building. If one flies over the area, at least a score of water bodies will be visible within an area of a few square kilometres. The size of each impoundment varies from less than one hectare up to more than 15 hectares. Here is a remarkable collection of trout waters. Some are not fully utilised, but six dams are managed by the Natal Fly Fishers' Club, and others belong to landowners who take an interest in angling. Luckily, bass have not found their way into these dams, in which rainbow trout, as well as some browns, find conditions to their liking.

After meandering across the Kamberg valley, the Little Mooi tumbles over the lip of a dolerite sill that forms a 12 m waterfall. This was a natural barrier to the scalies, indigenous to the last few kilometres above the confluence with the Mooi River. As happened on the Polela, an early settler transferred scalies above the falls, where they multiplied. In the 1920s and '30s scalies were numerous as far upstream as Sans Souci. My father used to fish for them with bait when the river was discoloured after rain. Although he used mealie paste, which trout are not supposed to relish, he was horrified to find he had hooked a three-pound brown trout on one occasion. Luckily it was liberated unharmed. More embarrassing, was the arrival of a neighbouring farmer on the scene of the Doctor's fishing activities. To the explanation that scalies were the only quarry, our neighbour replied politely that of course that was all he ever fished for himself!

Large numbers of fungus-infected scalies were seen dying in the river in 1938 and there have been no reports of scalies in the Little Mooi above the falls for many years. Chubby-head minnows (*Barbus anoplus*) on the other hand, which were also introduced by human agency, are common in the river and its tributaries.

The Hlatikulu River joins the Little Mooi a short distance above its confluence with the Mooi. It is of minor importance as a trout stream, partly because of its small size but also because it has very little in the way of gravel beds in which trout could breed. In addition, in the lower part of its course where the best pools occur, sheets of flat bedrock force the stream to spread into broad shallows that raise the water temperature.

The road from Kamberg to Giant's Castle crosses the Hlatikulu as it meanders eastwards across a broad valley in which several small streams provide sites for dams that are suitable for trout.

North of the Hlatikulu valley lies the Bushman's River, which some might rate above even the Mooi as the premier brown trout stream of southern Africa. The Bushman's originates on the main Drakensberg, its headwaters draining a segment of the escarpment from Giant's Castle northwards for 15 km. This upper catchment provides a breathtaking view from the rest camp in Giant's Castle Game Reserve. Over millions of years, since the uplifting of the Lesotho plateau, the power of running water has carved deep chasms through the sandstone foothills, leaving the dark volcanic cliffs of the main range towering above a terrain of immensely high relief.

Headstreams hurtle down the mountainsides in a precipitous descent of 1 000 m or more. At about 1 800 m above sea-level the main stream of the Bushman's has gained sufficient volume to provide pools that may harbour trout, although it is not for another kilometre or so that the gradient eases sufficiently to give trout a permanent home.

About a kilometre upstream from the camp, a large tributary joins the main Bushman's and from that point down is a popular fishing stretch, where the watercourse, averaging 6 m in width, has pools at intervals along its stony bed, with small brown trout sheltering behind rocks and under banks.

The gradient is steep (about 27 m per kilometre) but gravel is available for spawning and, in favourable seasons, a lot of young fish survive; in fact too many for the available food supply. In consequence, yearlings may be only about 100 mm in length, compared with those from less crowded situations where the fish are often more than 150 mm at the end of their first summer.

Farther down, the floor of the valley becomes narrower and steeper, with a gradient of more than 50 m per kilometre. In this section the trout cannot breed freely, but some of half a pound or more may be found wherever there is shelter from the torrent. The gradient flattens to 18 m per kilometre below the confluence of a sizeable tributary, but the river remains too swift-flowing to support many trout until it leaves the Game Reserve at 1 450 m above sea-level. The trout-rearing ponds of a commercial enterprise are to be seen close to the river and some rainbow trout have escaped from time to time to form an unintentional supplement to the brown trout that inhabit the Bushman's River.

Through the farms Snowflake and Elands Park, the stream flows parallel with the road in a series of inviting pools and runs, with a favourable gradient of 8 m per kilometre. Below Elands Park, in the KwaZulu area, the gradient becomes only half as steep, with pools taking up a greater proportion of the waterway.

With the road running close to the river, all the way to the confluence of the Ncibidwane, the Bushman's is easily accessible. Moreover the banks are open, with few trees to hinder the angler. Although weather cycles cause great fluctuations in the trout population, over the years the section from the Ncibidwane up to the Game Reserve has provided splendid sport for a great many fishermen. Records submitted by successful anglers over the period 1950-70 indicated that 250 to 300 fishing trips were made to this area each season with an average bag of six trout per trip, and a total weight of 1 kg.

An average of slightly over 150 g may not seem very impressive, but considerably larger fish were often taken and a kilogram of trout per day, from a well-fished river, is a very satisfactory catch-rate. Interestingly enough, we have accurate information about the size of the trout in that same section of the Bushman's River between 1914 and 1930. Hugh Beavan, who lived at Elands Park, kept a meticulous diary of his fishing results. Surprisingly, perhaps, his trout were similar in size to those taken 40 years later. The only apparent difference was that he could catch half a dozen fish in an hour or two instead of the three or four hours needed in later years. Obviously, trout were easier to catch when fewer anglers were on the water.

Further downstream, the Bushman's has never attracted a great many fishermen, mainly because of its inaccessibility. There is a stretch 8 km in length between the

Ncibidwane, which joins the river from the south, and the Mtshezana, which joins the river from the north. This is prime fishing water, with a succession of pools averaging 20 m in width, but without any road access. Again, below the Mtshezana confluence, the river zigzags through a deep valley for 27 km to Dalton Bridge. Not only is this long stretch far from a road, but for most of the distance its heavily overgrown banks make fishing difficult.

One of those who used to fish this part of the river regularly was Q.E. Carter of Ennersdale. He took many notable brown trout but, as he put it, wore his legs "short as a duck's" with the effort. Another man who made outstanding catches was Roy Drummond of Estcourt. The biggest trout taken since 1950 weighed 3,1 kg, but many of between 1 and 2 kg were landed.

A turbulent run on the Bushman's River. Dark dolerite boulders are characteristic of many Natal trout streams.

The gradient near Dalton Bridge is somewhat steeper than farther upstream — between 5 and 6 m per kilometre. This ensures well-oxygenated pools as the river flows over dolerite sills and down boulder-strewn runs. Below Dalton Bridge is a steep cataract, below which the river flows through Moor Park Nature Reserve to the top end of Wagendrift Dam. The cataract is not a barrier to the upstream movement of scalies, which regularly ascend the chute during their annual spawning migration in early summer.

The presence of Wagendrift Dam, a major impoundment a few kilometres above Estcourt, has radically changed the environment of that part of the Bushman's. The man-made lake has provided a habitat for scalies, which has boosted their population and led to the appearance of greater numbers in the river upstream. Before the construction of the dam, trout were able to live in the river as far down as Estcourt township. Although no breeding took place in that area, anglers used to catch a few large brown trout each winter and rainbows, which were introduced on several occasions, grew well. The dam has therefore curtailed trout habitat.

Even without the dam, the lower Bushman's would have ceased to hold trout. Siltation due to soil erosion in the catchment has severely affected the river as far up as the Ncibidwane confluence, reducing its capacity to breed trout. Although some of the glory of this beautiful river has faded, the descendants of the original 500 brown trout fry that Parker introduced in May 1890 will continue to provide sport for future generations. Whether the rainbows that have found their way into the Bushman's from the hatchery near the boundary of Giant's Castle Game Reserve will become established is doubtful. Previous introductions have all vanished, leaving the river to the brown trout.

Travelling north on the national road to the Transvaal, the best of Natal's trout country is left behind as one crosses the Bushman's River, below the spectacular arches of Wagendrift Dam. The ramparts of the Drakensberg still gather rainclouds on the western horizon and clear streams still cascade off their high tops, but the plains that run up to the foot of the escarpment are too low and hot for trout.

The Little Tugela or Injasuti ("well-fed dog") rises high up, at the north end of Giant's Castle Game Reserve among spectacular peaks including the Injasuti Triplets. After passing through deep gorges, the river emerges onto Compensation, a farm now included in the reserve, where the swiftly flowing stream offers attractive fishing when the water is in good order. In the adjoining KwaZulu area larger pools are to be found, but with a gradient of 20 m per kilometre the stream soon reaches too low an altitude for trout. Both brown and rainbow have been introduced on several occasions, the first brown trout being stocked in 1905, but of recent years only rainbows have been reported.

A tributary of the Little Tugela is the Sterkspruit, which rises on the slopes of Cathkin Peak and tumbles down a steep valley to the foot of the escarpment where it flows between high, grass-clad banks. It was stocked and restocked on a number of occasions and some of the fish, both brown and rainbow, grew well, but breeding was never successful enough to maintain the population.

At Cathedral Peak, the magnificently sculptured terrain of the high Drakensberg gives birth to the Mlambonjwa, which flows past Cathedral Peak Hotel, close to which a successful trout farm has been established. The river flows clear and sparkling over a bed of sandstone boulders, with holding places for trout here and there in the course of its rapid descent.

After it leaves State Forest land, the Mlambonjwa has a series of pools that have produced well-grown brown and rainbow trout. Better conditions for trout are, however, provided by its southern tributary, the Mhlwazeni. For several kilometres above the road that approaches the hotel the river drops from one rocky pool to another. In years of good rainfall some excellent autumn fishing has been enjoyed by energetic anglers.

Between Cathedral Peak and Mont-aux-Sources, the Mnweni valley drains a segment of the escarpment. For a short distance, the Mnweni River was known at one time as a producer of rainbow trout, but severe soil erosion has taken place and of recent years no one seems to have made the journey to see if any trout survive.

At Royal Natal National Park, the Tugela River and its tributary, the Mahai, both offer a limited amount of trout fishing. The Tugela, after dropping more than 1 000 m off the Amphitheatre, is in a great hurry to continue its long journey to the sea. Below the Gorge, well known to hikers from the Royal Natal National Park Hotel, the river flows across a highly unstable flood plain, covered with waterworn fragments of white-speckled basalt from the main range and pale sandstone from the cliffs of the Little Berg. Wherever a small pool occurs, fat little rainbow yearlings will be prepared to rush at one's fly. There always seem to be enough adult fish to produce a crop of young ones, although the adults are few and far between. Below the bridge on the road up to the Park more extensive holding places for trout occur, before the river becomes suitable only for the indigenous scalies and mudfish.

In the trout zone numerous rock catlets (*Amphilius natalensis*) shelter under the rocks. Scalies also work their way well upstream and give a good account of themselves if they deign to take an artificial fly.

The Mahai comes off the Little Berg to the north of the Tugela and its clear waters, cascading over sandstone terraces, supply not only the hotel but also the Natal Parks Board's trout hatchery. In times of drought there may not be enough for both. The normal flow is, however, adequate to satisfy all domestic requirements and also to keep the pools well filled. Some of these pools are deepened by the construction of weirs and, thanks to the hatchery as well as a certain amount of wild breeding, sizeable trout may be caught by anglers who can avoid entangling their flies on the overhanging trees and shrubs.

Two dams are available for the trout-fishing visitor at Royal Natal National Park. One is on the banks of the Mahai, in front of the hotel. This is a popular venue for casting clinics, with the additional attraction of offering the chance of hooking one of the trout transferred from the hatchery. The other dam is on a stream a couple of kilometres away and is also kept well stocked.

From Royal Natal National Park, one might head off to the northern corner of Natal, where the Incandu and Ingogo are well known to the residents of Newcastle as producers of surprisingly large trout in the wet years of each rainfall cycle. One might travel north of Utrecht, to the highlands close to the Transvaal border, where the Slang River flows west and then south to join the Buffalo, while the Pivaan goes off eastwards to join the Pongola. Both the Slang and the upper Pivaan have given sport to justify the effort involved in stocking them, but they are insignificant in comparison with the major trout waters of Natal.

If one wants to go north, an exciting prospect awaits the trout angler in the Orange Free State, over the top of Oliviershoek Pass.

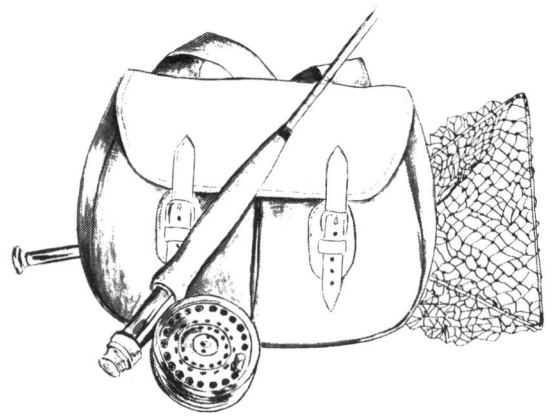

8. Orange Free State and Transvaal

Sterkfontein Dam has made the Orange Free State a province that is visited by trout fishermen from far and wide. Hitherto, trout were found only in a few minor dams.

The road over Oliviershoek Pass, between Bergville in Natal and Harrismith in the OFS, takes one onto a high plateau at 1 700 m above sea-level. On the western side of the road are the sources of the Nuwejaarspruit, an insignificant tributary of the Vaal River. Its valley forms an elongate irregular basin extending northwards. In this valley a dam has been built, the Driekloof, which holds back a considerable volume of rather dirty-looking water.

Nearly 15 km down the valley a second, larger wall has created a lake that is beautifully clear. When full, the surface area of this splendid body of water is about 6 900 hectares with a maximum capacity of 2 600 million cubic metres (according to Hughes, *Tight Lines,* August 1985). It has an endless series of bays and promontories, with a backdrop of flat-topped hills, typical of the eastern Free State. The austere, treeless landscape contrasts with the vast expanse of water that is there as if by magic.

The magicians who placed this superb habitat for trout on the stark Highveld were engineers in the Department of Water Affairs. They had no thought of trout. Their concern was to supplement the water supply to Reef cities and industries. They approached their colleagues in the Electricity Supply Commission and asked how much it would cost to pump water over the escarpment from the upper Tugela River in Natal. The expense looked daunting, until someone had the brilliant idea of designing a pump-storage scheme that would meet the needs of the suppliers of both water and electricity.

Water can be stored, whereas electricity cannot. Two reservoirs were therefore constructed, one at the bottom of the mountain, on the Natal side, and one at the top, the Driekloof Dam. Pumping to Driekloof takes place at off-peak periods, when spare electrical capacity is available, and some of the stored water is allowed to run back through a 5 m-diameter pipeline to generate the electricity needed at periods of peak demand. The rest of the water from Driekloof flows on into Sterkfontein Dam, where it is held until required to supplement Vaal Dam.

Most of the sediment that is present in the water pumped from Natal settles out in Driekloof. At times there is still considerable turbidity in the upper part of Sterkfontein, but the middle and lower parts are extremely clear. This is an important

Top end of Sterkfontein Dam, O.F.S., where Tugela water is pumped into the Vaal River catchment.

point in the lake's favour as a habitat for trout. In addition, the high altitude and large volume of water keep the temperature below 20 °C for most of the year.

Since 1981, the Nature Conservation Branch of the OFS Provincial Administration has been stocking the lake with 35 000 to 40 000 rainbow trout annually. The fish have grown rapidly and some of well over 2 kg have been reported. A biologist, W.G. Dörgeloh, recorded an increase from 78,5 g mean weight for stocked fish, to a mean of 479 g six months later. At a fishing competition in June 1985, trout of less than two years were weighing up to 1 kg. Garrett Evans (*Piscator* No. 115) mentions catching as many as 20 trout in a day, averaging 800 g, in the autumn of 1985 (many of these he returned). Dörgeloh has found that daphnia, mayfly and other insect nymphs, midge larvae and snails are the main food items for rainbow trout in the lake.

Small fish might be eaten, especially by the bigger trout, as there are two species of minnows, as well as yellowfish, mudfish (two species) and catfish (or barbel). Sterkfontein is probably unique in having both catfish and trout. The catfish are potential predators on trout and large ones have been seen pursuing hooked fish. Cormorants are probably more significant predators, and Garrett Evans mentions that trout with beak wounds on the side are not at all unusual.

Tilapia are said to have been introduced to the dam, but the winter temperature of 8 °C will almost certainly prove lethal to these warm-water fish. The Vaal River yellowfish are doing well in Sterkfontein; one of nearly 3 kg was taken on a spinner by Mark Wilson.

Any type of artificial lure may be used, but natural bait is prohibited. When the trout are feeding in the shallows, where beds of submerged aquatic weed are to be found, small artificial flies, including dry flies, are said to give good results.

The lake shore, except a limited area near the wall, is privately owned. A boat is therefore needed, even when the trout are feeding along the grassy margins. The boat must be seaworthy and equipped with an outboard motor, since dangerously large waves develop if a storm blows up.

The size of Sterkfontein Dam, together with its abundant food supply and good physical conditions, makes it the premier stillwater trout fishery in South Africa. There is every likelihood it will produce a record rainbow.

Not far from Sterkfontein, the Qua Qua Homeland offers good fly fishing in a dam, while the mountains of Lesotho have beautiful, high-altitude trout streams of legendary quality. Regrettably, the modern reality does not live up to the legend: much of the black volcanic soil of the upland valleys has been washed into the rivers, leaving them choked with sediment. The headwaters of the Malibamatso River are among the most favourable for trout. If ever the Oxbow scheme to dam the Malibamatso is put into effect splendid fishing might be provided.

To the north, the vast tableland of the Transvaal Highveld is intersected by rivers. But they offer nothing of interest to the fly fisherman, unless he is prepared to seek quarry other than trout. A large area is drained by the Vaal River and its tributaries that eventually join the Orange River on its westward course to the Atlantic. Indeed if the length of the watercourse were to be used as a criterion, the Vaal would be considered the main river, as it rises much farther from the sea than its bigger sister. But, whereas the upper Orange originates in high, mountainous country, the Vaal is a plateau stream. Although the river remains for a long distance at a height above sea-level that one commonly associates with trout in South Africa, it is a murky and uninspiring watercourse. A hopeful trout lover might seek encouragement by following the Vaal River eastwards towards its source. But disappointment awaits him. The Highveld rises gradually, with never a hill in sight, to form a featureless plateau from which sluggish watercourses meander languidly, some going west to form the Vaal, others east to the Incomati. The continental divide in the Carolina district is unspectacular.

As one travels along the watershed northwards towards Belfast and Machadodorp, quite suddenly a change becomes evident. Hills and valleys appear as the Highveld plateau is tilted up to form a ridge of increasing altitude, reaching 2 330 m (7 650 ft) north of Dullstroom. Tributaries of the Crocodile River, fed by the high rainfall of this elevated terrain, have the unmistakeable appearance of trout streams. So does the Steelpoort that flows northwards to join the Olifants River, together with the Blyde and the eastward-flowing Sabie. The trout country of the Eastern Transvaal is about 4 000 square kilometres in extent, roughly crescent-shaped, with its base in the region of Belfast and Machadodorp. It includes the Dullstroom district, Lydenburg, Sabie and Pilgrim's Rest. Apart from some spring-fed streams to the west of Johannesburg, the only other Transvaal area in which trout occur is near Magoebaskloof, west of Tzaneen, where the Drakensberg escarpment makes its final appearance at the sources of the Letaba River.

The Elands is the most southerly of the trout streams of the Crocodile River system. It rises on the high plateau north-east of Belfast and flows south for about 15 km before swinging eastwards towards Machadodorp, where it is joined by two tributaries large enough to carry trout. The Taute River comes in from the north and Leeuspruit from the south. This section of the Elands is in close proximity to the cheerful little town of Machadodorp, founded in 1894 and named in honour of Machado, Governor of Mozambique at the time the Pretoria-Maputo railway line was under construction.

Twenty-six kilometres of the Elands, Taute and Leeuspruit are available to members of the Machadodorp Trout Club, which makes provision for visitors on a daily basis. Originally, the upper Elands and its tributaries must have had grassy banks with no trees, but exotic species are now established, especially silver wattles which make casting difficult in places. Although narrow, with a width rarely exceeding 10 m, the Elands has pools with ample holding space for large trout. The gradient is fairly flat, about 7 m per kilometre, with stony runs between the pools and enough gravel

Eastern Transvaal trout areas.

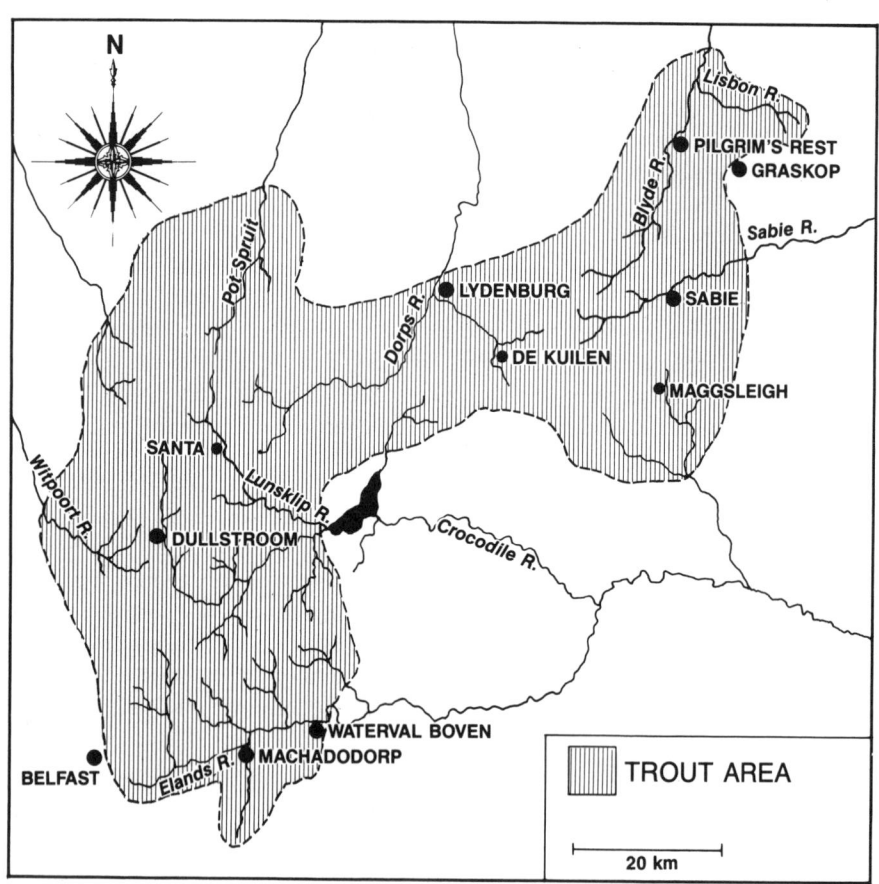

— at least in the area above the town — to enable natural breeding to occur, although the stock of trout is augmented by regular introductions of hatchery-reared fish. Some of these are probably unintentional donations on the part of the owners of three trout farms, two on the Elands and one on the Taute River. As well as escaped trout, the fish farms contribute feed to the stream, increasing the natural productivity, which was always considered to be good. The water is slightly alkaline, with chemical nutrients derived from the volcanic dolerite rock of the catchment. Deposits of clay give the Elands a slightly milky colour, even in the dry season.

Below Machadodorp, the river winds across an open valley past Waterval Boven before entering a spectacular gorge, with a vertical drop of 90 m over the ZASM Falls, to reach Waterval Onder, whence it hurries away towards the Lowveld and its confluence with the Crocodile, far from trout country.

Trout have been in the Elands since 1900, when a consignment of rainbow fingerlings reached Waterval Boven by rail, consigned from the Cape to a local farmer. Some of the fish had already died and the remainder were in distress when they reached Waterval Boven, so the local station master dumped the whole lot in the Elands River, where the survivors established themselves.

West of Machadodorp is the Belfast district where Michael Salomon (author of *Freshwater Fishing in South Africa*) took his best rainbow, weighing 3,6 kg. In the same area Ernest Farnworth caught one of 4,8 kg on 20 September 1970.

The road north from Belfast towards Dullstroom runs through the heart of Transvaal trout country: the plateau of the Steenkampsberg, with 1 500 square kilometres of land at an altitude of 1 800 to 2 300 m above sea-level.

The Nature Conservation Division of the Transvaal Provincial Administration devoted a whole issue (No. 41) of its journal *Fauna and Flora* to the Steenkampsberg. Articles, with colour illustrations, describe the attributes and problems of this unique and beautiful area. Problems include the familiar ones of overutilisation and denudation of the grassveld, as well as large-scale planting of exotic trees, some of which have spread aggressively, especially along watercourses. The construction of dams for trout fishing is a cause for concern where this has involved destruction of natural vleis, but, as Dr S.S. du Plessis points out, the use of large areas as holiday farms has served to give the land a rest from annual burning and heavy grazing, thus contributing to its conservation. The main objective of those who own or manage these holiday farms is to provide trout fishing; more than 200 trout dams of various sizes have been built on the plateau.

That those whose prime interest is trout fishing may be better conservationists than officials of the Department of Agriculture was made apparent to me on a property near Dullstroom. This property is excellently conserved, but one of its trout dams is subject to discolouration from a furrow on a neighbouring farm. The furrow is part of an officially approved project to drain an extensive vlei. While some types of modification of natural habitats may be economically justified, in this case the drainage operations appeared to have caused gratuitous destruction without any benefit to the farmer.

Trout farming and the provision of angling have in recent years become of increasing significance in the Eastern Transvaal. In 1985, 11 of the 15 members of the Trout Farmers' Association of South Africa were situated in the Machadodorp-Dullstroom-Lydenburg-Sabie area. The Provincial Fisheries Institute at Lydenburg was built in 1948 primarily for trout production, while the De Kuilen site was developed more recently, south-east of Lydenburg, to give the Nature Conservation Division the largest trout hatchery and rearing station in Africa.

Private trout farmers dispose of their fish in three ways: many trout are marketed for the table, either fresh or smoked; some are sold for stocking angling waters; and others are put into the farmers' own ponds to be caught by members of the public, who pay according to the weight of fish they take. The main purchasers of live trout for stocking are syndicates of townsmen who own or lease angling waters.

These syndicated waters include rivers such as the upper Crocodile, which rises north of Dullstroom, together with its tributaries to the north and south of the main stream. The relatively small size of these plateau streams favours their modification by weir building to create pools of a size and depth adequate for large trout. At the same time they are not subject to severe flooding, so hatchery fish remain in the stream long enough to satisfy those who pay for the privilege of catching them. Food supplies are limited and the stock of trout is usually maintained at a level far beyond the natural carrying capacity. This is achieved by artificial feeding with commercial trout pellets.

Such intensive stream management, plus the use of small dams on tributaries, gives excellent results in terms of fish production. A well-known syndicate on the Crocodile caters for a total of 16 members and their guests. Over the 40 weekends of each season, anglers are permitted to take 100 trout per weekend. Since this limit is often achieved, the potential yield could exceed 3 500 fish averaging 700 g, or approximately two and a half tons per annum. The total area of water is no more than five hectares, so the yield might be as much as 500 kg per hectare, compared with a yield of 15 to 20 kg per hectare from the natural productivity of the water. The costs of intensive management are, of course, high, but members of well-run syndicates are satisfied with the return on their outlay. There is keen competition for any vacancies that may occur.

To obtain fishing in the Eastern Transvaal one does not need to belong to an exclusive syndicate. At Dullstroom the municipal dam is open to the public and many rainbows have been taken by visitors, although the standard of sport is dependent on the amount of stocking that has been carried out the previous year. With a surface area of 11,25 hectares, the dam is set in attractively natural surroundings.

Less natural are some of the privately owned commercial angling waters, although others provide an attractive setting (see, for instance, the photographs in *Tight Lines*, July 1985). Several establishments in the Belfast-Dullstroom area offer both accommodation and fly fishing. At Lydenburg, the large, deep P. T. C. du Plessis Dam may be fished on permit from the Town Council, while no permit is required to try the Dorps River within the municipal area. This somewhat murky stream with high banks and numerous wattle trees has deep, narrow pools that yield rainbow trout, introduced from the provincial hatchery. On the banks of the river is the F.C. Braun

Park, dedicated to the memory of the man who played a major part in stocking the streams of the Lydenburg and adjoining districts.

Lydenburg is situated in a broad basin at about 1 300 m above sea-level, with the lofty Steenkampsberg to the south-west and another high massif to the east, culminating in Mount Anderson, 2 282 m above sea-level.

These mountain ranges are composed of hard quartzite, which is resistant to erosion. Little sediment accumulates, with the result that the headwater's streams remain remarkably clear. Another effect is that stream-beds are rocky and steep, with waterfalls much in evidence. These precipitous streams have deep pools, but few gravel beds in which trout can spawn. Regular restocking is probably needed to maintain the population, but with the disappearance of such energetic trout lovers as F.C. Braun there seems to be little interest in the more inaccessible, untamed waters. Those that are accessible are developed for intensive angling.

A splendid scenic drive from Lydenburg to Sabie takes one over the high plateau with spectacular gorges that carry tumbling streams down to the Lowveld. On the eastern side of the escarpment, which gathers rainclouds moving in from the sea, an annual rainfall of as much as 2 000 mm is ideal for the growth of trees. What is perhaps the world's largest man-made forest now covers what must have been a superbly varied natural scene.

One of the features that has remained little affected by man is the multitude of rivulets that unite to form such well-known rivers as the Sabie and Blyde. Many of these rivulets originate as dolomitic springs, with a constant flow and a temperature that remains between 15 and 17 °C all year round. Spring-fed streams are less affected by drought than those that rely more directly on rainfall. Deep springs may reduce the influence of the pine plantations, which are known to cut down available ground water during dry periods. A noticeably adverse effect of forestry is siltation of streams from the roads used to extract timber.

The township of Sabie is situated at an altitude of 1 100 m on a gently sloping hillside above the Sabie River, of which 9 km are controlled by the Sabie Trout Angling Club. The stream near the town has a moderate gradient of about 8 m per kilometre, but is much steeper near the foot of the mountain, with a waterfall above which brown trout have continued to survive since their first introduction in 1904. (The Auxloop stream also has brown trout, but otherwise rainbows predominate throughout the area.)

Since the club makes fishing available to visitors, who may purchase temporary permits, its section of the river is regarded as public water and has therefore been stocked regularly by the Nature Conservation Division. There is no close season. The river is less than 10 m wide, but it flows invitingly through a series of pools, connected by deep runs and shallow stickles with gravel beds offering spawning places, although silt has accumulated in what used to be a stony bed.

Parts of the river are quite heavily bushed, placing a premium on skilful casting to reach some of the likely places, where the larger trout take refuge. The river is easily accessible by road, amid pleasant parklike surroundings. A variety of wildlife is to be seen, especially early in the morning. On one occasion a keen fisherman,

Father Wakeling by name, set off for a favourite pool before sunrise on a summer morning. As he approached the river he was surprised to hear splashing sounds. He was even more surprised when he looked over the bank to be confronted by a full-grown hippo! Although hippos occur in the lower river, in the Kruger National Park, it was remarkable that the animal had managed to work its way so far upstream, past the falls at the lower end of the town lands.

Above the club water, the Sabie River flows through land owned by the Directorate of Forestry and by the Mondi Timber Company. The latter operates an up-to-date trout farm that produces some 35 tons of trout annually, some of which are purchased by angling syndicates and clubs, including the Sabie Angling Club.

Twenty kilometres north of Sabie is the historic settlement of Pilgrim's Rest, redolent of the romance of the gold mining days a hundred years ago. Scars left by the men who tore open the hillsides in search of the yellow metal remain visible, but only as well-healed irregularities in the natural contours. The Blyde River and its tributaries run clear and sparkling, with the promise of rewards for the fly fisherman.

The road north out of Pilgrim's Rest crosses the river and then follows its course down the valley. The gradient of the stream is steep, more than 20 m per kilometre, but good trout-holding pools are frequent, with rocky rapids in between. The banks are stable, with a luxuriant cover of grass, reeds and shrubs preventing erosion of the sandy soil. Pools are seldom more than 6 m in width.

This part of the Blyde River is open throughout the year for fishing by any licensed angler who buys a daily ticket. Farther downstream, on the property of Transvaal Gold Mining Exploration, trout continue to find conditions to their liking, while large shoals of indigenous yellowfish occur as well. The water remains cool enough for trout well below 1 200 m above sea-level, due to the rapid descent from a higher altitude and the perennial flow of dolomitic springs. One of these springs provides

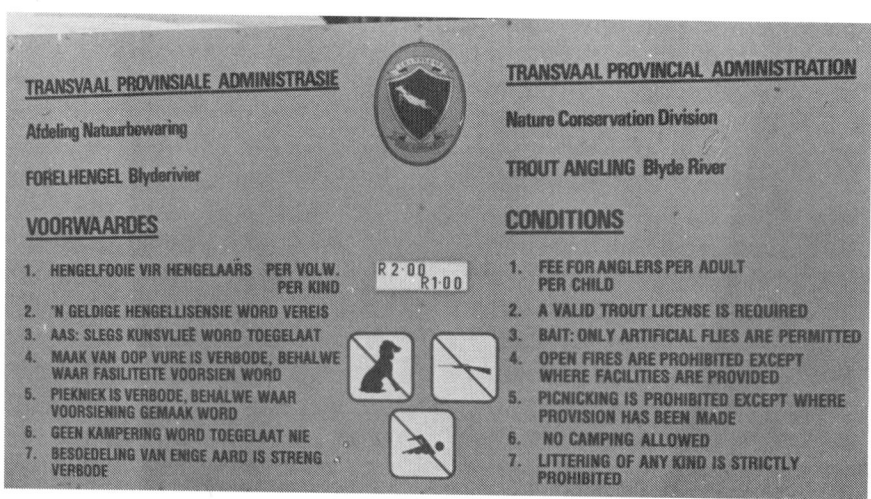

Notice board on the banks of the Blyde River, near Pilgrim's Rest.

50 litres a second to four trout-rearing ponds in which rainbows are grown out to a size of 800 to 1 000 g to stock the main river as well as the Lisbon, a tributary with a series of large pools that joins the Blyde from the east. Some of these pools have been deepened by building boulder weirs.

Large trout, released from the rearing ponds, lose condition in the river, but wild-bred fish grow up to a pound or so on the natural food supply. No artificial feeding is carried out, as is commonly done in other intensively managed rivers in the Transvaal.

Below trout water, the Blyde River passes through the well-known Blyde River Canyon on its way to join the Olifants River.

The main tributary of the Olifants is the Letaba River, which rises on the northernmost outpost of the Drakensberg where the Wolkberg plateau reaches an altitude of 2 050 m above sea-level, south-west of Tzaneen. Here, according to Horst Dombrock of the Magoebaskloof Hotel, is a "magic land of the Silver Mists". Stephen Jupp (*Piscator* No. 110) gives a graphic account of "rainbows in the swirling mist". Paul Smit, to whom I am indebted for information about trout in the Magoebaskloof area, remarks that fishing is generally poor during the very hot summer months, but improves from April onwards.

The Broederstroom was first stocked in 1904 and the Haenertsburg Trout Association was formed in 1906, making it one of the oldest associations in the country. At present it controls fishing in part of the Broederstroom, including the 12-hectare Dap Naudé Dam which was built in 1958, as well as the four-hectare Lakeside Dam and one kilometre of the Helpmekaar River below the dam.

Dap Naudé is well stocked by natural breeding in the Forestry area above the dam and numerous rainbows of 28 to 30 cm are to be caught, as well as an occasional larger one. Below the dam the stream is narrow and overgrown, but Stephen Jupp caught a two pounder, as well as smaller ones. Lakeside Dam is regularly stocked with 500 g rainbows.

Some distance downstream of Dap Naudé Dam is Ebenezer Dam on the Broederstroom. This large body of water has bass and other fish, but trout of up to 2 kg are caught there, and regular stocking is carried out with rainbows raised in cages.

Brown trout breed in favourable parts of the streams in the Magoebaskloof area, where visitors are assured of fly fishing in this far corner of the Republic, a thousand miles from Cape Town.

III THE ART OF FLY FISHING

9. Tackle

The sort of tackle a man uses may give a measure of his opulence. More significantly, it shows his attitude to the sport of fly fishing. If he regards expensive equipment as a prerequisite to the enjoyment of catching trout, he will always find an excuse to lavish his resources on what the tackle dealer has to offer. On the other hand, some people like to keep their equipment simple to a degree that might be regarded as parsimonious. There are keen and successful fishermen who use the same rod and reel for years on end and buy a new line only when the old one becomes unpleasantly rough. This type of angler probably restricts himself to a few favourite flies and the minimum of accessories. The older generation was perhaps less inclined to extravagance than are modern fishermen, many of whom take pride in equipping themselves for every possible eventuality. Tackle manufacturers are constantly developing their gear, thereby placing temptation in the way of addicts who are as easily seduced as a fashion-conscious woman in a dress shop. Not long ago an auction sale of the personal collection of fishing tackle and books that belonged to a well-known angler yielded more than R4 000.

An outlay of this magnitude bears no relationship to the needs of a beginner. To the uninitiated the task of selecting suitable gear from the vast array on offer in a well-equipped tackle shop may seem daunting, but good advice is easy to come by — usually from the salesman himself. At least one knowledgeable member of staff is to be found in each of the shops, of my acquaintance, which specialise in fishing goods in South Africa.

The essential items are comparatively few in number. First the rod, which must be critically examined before purchase. A rod's performance is not necessarily related to its price; on comparing the action of several rods of varying cost one may find the cheapest is the best. The product of even such famous firms as Hardy or Orvis should not be accepted without trial. Doubtless the quality will be superb, but the purpose for which the rod was designed may not coincide with your particular needs. To be effective, a rod must be able to deliver the fly accurately to the point where you wish it to go. Accuracy is generally more important than an ability to reach out to a great distance, a point well made by Frank Sawyer in his book *Nymphs and the Trout*. Above all, if one is going to fish South African rivers with their high banks, long grass and other obstructions, one needs the "high speed/high line" action advocated by Charles Ritz in *A Fly Fisher's Life*. Charles Ritz was a millionaire and a perfectionist, with friends who were not merely devoted to the art of fly fishing, but who also possessed the technical know-how and resources to develop rods with almost ideal characteristics. Few of us can hope to own a rod of the standard laid down by Ritz, but we can look for a rod that will do what we require. And we may find what we are seeking in a batch of mass-produced and inexpensive rods.

Individual rods of the same make vary, especially the cheaper models, so patience may be needed to find the right one, and obviously we have to know what we are looking for. To begin with, we must decide what material we want. For many years split bamboo or cane was the material of choice, replacing the greenheart and lancewood of an earlier era. Cane rods are still manufactured, but anyone who buys one does so for sentimental rather than practical reasons. The elegance of an expensive split-cane rod is undeniable, but for efficiency the modern synthetic materials are supreme. For some years fibreglass has been firmly established as the most popular material, but carbon or graphite rods are claiming an increasing share of the market. Carbon rods are lighter than fibreglass, which seemed featherweight compared with cane, and the performance of the more expensive models is superb. Because of the strength of the material, carbon rods are extremely thin, which reduces air resistance when casting. The same applies to the newest material, boron, which is also the most expensive of all.

For cheapness and versatility, however, fibreglass is hard to beat and the beginner cannot go wrong by restricting himself to this material. Final choice of a rod should be based on length and action. A general-purpose fly rod should not be too short, and in my opinion the trend towards shortness has been taken too far. H.D. Turing, in his book *Trout Fishing*, advocated a 10-foot rod, which is longer than most anglers use today. Anything less than eight feet creates problems on overgrown river banks and nine feet is probably better. Incidentally, metrication, accepted unwillingly in all fields related to angling, seems to have bypassed rod measurements entirely.

Action is less easy to define than length or weight, but a rod's action is its most important feature. It is the resilience and bend of a rod that transmits power to the line, leader and fly. Charles Ritz, early in his fishing life, became convinced that most trout rods were inefficient owing to too much bend near the tip. To this day it is a common fault for which one should watch. Simply thread a line through the rod rings and note how the rod bends when the line is pulled. Under load the rod should curve throughout its length, right down to the butt. If only the top part bends, the so-called tip action which Ritz condemned, hand the rod back to the salesman. Above all, a rod must give a feeling of steely springiness, neither wobbly nor unresponsively stiff.

Rods are, of course, designed for various weights of line. In order to assist the fisherman in matching these two essential parts of his equipment, the Association of Fishing Tackle Manufacturers (AFTM) has a system of numbers. A rod of medium power is labelled 6, a light rod 4 and a rod suitable for heavier work 8. Lines have corresponding labels. One should never try to cast a No. 8 line with a No. 6 rod, which will become overloaded except for very short distances. Conversely, too light a line will fail to flex the rod adequately to bring out its resilience.

Whereas one need not necessarily buy an expensive rod, it pays to obtain a really good line. The line is not, as in bait fishing or spinning, a mere connection between the hook and the reel. Delivery of the fly to the point where the trout is lying depends on the pull of the line as it goes out from the rod tip. The weight of the line is of critical importance. In order to do its work effectively a line must be tapered, thin at the end with a section of increasing diameter to the mid-section or belly. Level lines are cheaper, but not worth buying, even for a beginner.

There are two main types of tapered line: double taper and forward taper or weight-forward. As its name implies, the double-tapered line is symmetrically tapered and either end may be attached to the leader. When one end becomes worn, the line may simply be reversed, thus extending its useful life. Apart from the obvious aspect of economy, a double-tapered line has other advantages for ordinary fishing. Its more gradual taper as compared to a weight-forward line makes for more delicate presentation; line splash may frighten fish in clear water. The weight-forward is really a specialised line for long-distance casting.

A final point about line weight is that the AFTM number for a particular line is based on the mass of the first 30 feet. A length in excess of this, and hence a greater weight of line, will be in the air when long casts are being made. If one makes a habit of casting well in excess of 30 feet it may be a good idea to use a line of lower rating than the AFTM number of one's rod. An overloaded rod cannot perform efficiently.

Having decided to purchase a double-tapered line of suitable weight, the question remains whether it is to be floating, floating with a sinking tip, neutral density (that is neither floating nor sinking), normal sinking or fast sinking. Each type has its uses, which will be discussed later, but the most generally effective for catching trout in South African rivers and still waters is a normal sinking line. If you are buying two lines, one should be a floater.

A reel is the next item to consider. It is of less importance than either rod or line, but must be mechanically sound and reasonably durable. There is no pleasure in fishing if the reel does not run freely to draw off and recover line. The check must be of correct strength to prevent an over-run and yet not provide so much resistance that a fine leader will break when a fish makes a dash for freedom. An adjustable check is a great advantage and is always provided on more expensive reels. A reel that is to be used frequently should have a line guard to prevent the line, as it is pulled off the drum, wearing the reel frame. It is surprising how a line cuts into the relatively soft aluminium alloy from which the frame is usually made. Such wear is unlikely to affect the function of the reel, but it creates a rough surface that plays havoc with the smooth finish of a fly line. In modern reels the line guard is stainless steel, replacing the agate used in former times and familiar to the owners of those beautiful old ballbearing Hardy reels.

Another obvious difference between old and new reels is their weight. Modern reels are much lighter, in keeping with the reduction in the weight of rods. Not that a heavy reel should go with a heavy rod; the lighter the reel the better, irrespective of rod mass. It is important to have a reel with sufficient drum capacity to take both the line and at least an equal length of thinner backing. A big trout may make a run of 50 m or more when hooked, so the backing supplies a margin of safety.

The business end of the line is, of course, attached to a leader, or cast, on which one ties the fly or flies. Since the design of the leader differs according to the number of flies it carries, we must decide whether to fish with one or two flies. Traditional anglers on lakes and rivers in the north of England and Scotland mounted a team of three or four flies, but in South Africa two is usually regarded as the limit and most anglers use no more than a single fly. While it is certainly inadvisable to have two hooks when fishing for large trout in either rivers or still water, my own preference for most rivers is to have both a tail fly and a dropper fly. The object of using a second fly is not to catch two fish simultaneously, although this does happen, but to offer a choice of different flies at varying depths. A purist would probably say that a single fly is more sporting, especially if the angler finds himself with two fish on at once. The second trout may have grabbed the spare fly because it was being pulled to and fro in a lifelike manner by the first trout, that had already been hooked, thus giving the angler an unfair advantage. In practice I have yet to meet a fisherman who was unwilling to accept the lucky bonus presented by two trout on the same leader. A more valid reason for avoiding a second fly is the risk of a free hook snagging an obstruction while the fish is being played. There is also the question of delicacy of presentation. In very clear or calm water a single fly causes less disturbance than two.

A great deal has been written about the length, strength and design of leaders. Ivens's *Still Water Fly-Fishing* and *Fly-Fisherman's Primer* by Fling and Puterbaugh, provide detailed instructions for those who want to make up leaders with scientific precision. As with any refinement in tackle, complex designs are necessary only if the angler thinks they are. For someone who enjoys being meticulous about his equipment, a leader offers an opportunity to indulge in a search for perfection. Less fussy anglers still catch fish.

However simple or elaborate may be the make-up of leaders, certain fisherman's knots are essential. For joining line to leader, a very neat connection may be made by using the needle knot as described by various authors, but my practice is simply to put a loop on the end of the leader and attach this to the line by means of a detachable figure-of-eight hitch.

To attach fly to leader the Turle knot is both neat and secure (see diagram). For joining two lengths of nylon the Blood knot is the recognised method. It was named after its inventor, who may seem to someone trying to tie this knot for the first time to have been unduly clever. The trick is to hold the ends that have to be joined well apart, while twisting them as shown in the diagram. Also, one has to change one's grip at the half-way stage. But it is worth practising until one is adept as there is nothing more frustrating than trying to tie an unfamiliar knot at the waterside when the trout are rising invitingly. Particularly galling is to lose a good fish due to an insecure knot coming apart under strain. Every knot should be carefully tested.

Horsehair was replaced by silkworm gut, which has now been entirely superseded by nylon as the material for leaders. Nylon is, however, far from uniform in strength,

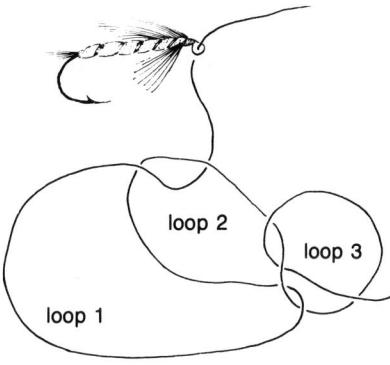

The Turtle knot. Tighten loop 3, then loop 2, and finally pass loop 1 over hook from behind to tighten around eye.

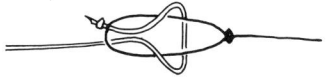

Simple method of attaching line to leader.

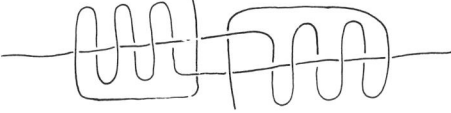

The Blood knot: to connect two lengths of nylon.

suppleness or elasticity. The manufacturer's label generally gives the diameter and breaking strain and, since one wants nylon that is as thin as possible for a given strength, one should compare the figures for different brands. It does seem, however, that some manufacturers are more optimistic than others. Actual tests with a spring balance have proved that the true breaking strain of samples of nylon may be either higher or lower than the printed figure on the label. Apart from the inherent quality of the monofilament, three factors may reduce the expected breaking strain. First, even the best-made knot reduces the strength by about one third; second, nylon that has absorbed water is weaker than dry nylon; third, and most significant, strength deteriorates with age. Allowance has to be made for the effects of knots and water, but old nylon should be discarded especially if it has been exposed to the sun. Last year's leaders are seldom safe to use.

The danger of breakage raises the question of what strength nylon to use. Some anglers make a point of fishing with the thinnest possible leader, priding themselves on their sportsmanship in landing heavy fish on ultra-light tackle. In my opinion, this practice should not be carried to extremes. There is nothing sporting about leaving a hook embedded in a trout's jaw, especially if a length of nylon remains trailing in the water. It may certainly be considered sporting to use barbless hooks or very small flies, but nylon that is liable to break when playing a fish should be avoided. Charles Ritz considered nylon of 0,008 inches (0,22 mm) diameter suitable for use with a No. 14 fly, which is small by South African standards. A diameter of 0,008 inches corresponds with a nominal breaking strain of about 6 lb. This I regard as a good standard for ordinary river fishing, whereas nothing lighter than 8 lb nylon should be used where large trout are to be expected. Nylon from a spool labelled 8 lb test will probably withstand a working load of 5 lb under fishing conditions.

Apart from breakage, another disadvantage of very fine nylon is its lightness and tendency to loop back on itself to form a tangle, especially if one is trying to cast against the wind. Thick nylon, on the other hand, may perhaps be more easily visible to the fish and it also tends to inhibit natural movement of the fly. Nylon varies in flexibility according to its method of manufacture and one should choose soft nylon in the heavier grades, but stiff nylon for fine work. It is extremely difficult to cast really thin, soft nylon. Incidentally, a tangled leader should simply be scrapped: even if one succeeds in unravelling a bird's nest, the nylon will never straighten properly afterwards.

Several different grades of nylon should be carried in your tackle bag to meet various requirements. When using a single large fly there is no need to depart from a straight length of nylon of adequate thickness. For smaller flies or long-distance casting, however, a tapered leader is a great advantage. One can buy ready-made leaders with a continuous taper from butt to tip, but most fishermen make up their own leaders by joining two or more pieces of nylon of differing thicknesses. For ease of casting, a leader with a thick butt section is best and the experts advocate starting off with nylon as heavy as 0,016 inches or about 20 lb breaking strain. To end with a 0,008-inch tippet several intermediate sections are required, since one cannot join pieces with too great a difference in diameter. My usual practice is to start with 12 lb, then 10 lb and finally the 6 lb tippet. If the leader is to take two flies, the easiest way of making a dropper is to leave a long end projecting when tying the tippet to the middle section. The dropper should not be too long — about 4 inches (10 cm) is enough. With a total length of slightly over 8 feet (2,5 m), good balance is achieved if the dropper is 3 feet from the end. For extremely clear, calm conditions a longer leader is advisable, with a thicker section added to the butt and a fine tippet.

Whereas a rod, reel, line or leader may be selected on objective criteria, the choice of a fly depends almost entirely on the personal preference of the angler. This does not imply that trout fishermen lack scientific knowledge: an immense amount of effort has been devoted to studies of the natural food of trout and to the creation of objects to simulate anything from a mayfly to a tadpole. The point is that trout usually grab whatever stimulates their predatory reflex, with very little discrimination. Angling writers often emphasise the success achieved by offering a trout an imitation of the particular insect on which it happens to be feeding at the time. While there is no doubt that a fish may concentrate its attention on one type of food to the exclusion of others, it is not correct to assume that one should attempt to catch such fish only by means of an exact imitation of the natural insect. Even if a trout is temporarily specialising in what it consumes, there is always a chance that it will take something quite different if this comes invitingly close. Perhaps more significantly, one may question whether an artificial fly can ever really look like a natural insect. Certainly, to the human eye there is a vast difference between a live mayfly and any of the dressed-up hooks that anglers put in front of trout. Clarke and Goddard in their beautifully illustrated book *The Trout and the Fly* reproduce underwater photographs comparing their new dressings with the natural insects on which they are modelled. While there is a closer resemblance than one finds in other artificial flies, the differences in form and texture remain obvious.

Some people take pleasure in doing their best to match the hatch, or to match the numerous underwater creatures on which trout feed. Books such as Ernest Schwiebert's classic, *Nymphs*, provide meticulously researched information for anyone who wants to pursue the art of exact imitation. On the other hand Frank Sawyer, in his *Nymphs and the Trout*, concludes that it is pointless to tie dozens of different dressings to represent all the different species of nymphs. He finally reduced his repertoire to two dressings. Charles Ritz, T.C. Ivens and other leading figures in the fly-fishing world dismiss the concept of exact imitation in favour of correct presentation of an artificial that offers a generalised representation of what the trout are feeding on. David Jacques (*The Development of Modern Stillwater Fishing*) regards dogged persistence and care not to frighten the fish as criteria for success, together with frequent changes of flies and tactics. For floating flies, he suggests that size and contour determine acceptability, while a sunken fly's appeal lies largely in its colour.

In South Africa, as elsewhere, the modern trend is for fishermen to tie their own flies rather than relying on the commercial product. There is no question that using the creation of one's own nimble fingers adds an extra dimension to the pleasure of catching trout. It is easy to feel more confidence in a fly that is "just so", as Kipling used to say. Not that you should be concerned if your home-made flies look less elegant than bought ones. The trout may prefer them that way. Nor is there any need to stick to a recognised dressing. You may refer to Courtney Williams, John Goddard or one of our South African writers to read up a "standard" pattern, but every fly in the book was invented by an angler, or perhaps by a professional tier, who liked that particular combination of silk, tinsel, feathers or fur. You can sit down with a fly vice, some hooks and whatever material is at hand, and put together your own Drakensberg Special. Provided you adhere to certain basic principles, your Special will catch trout as freely as the most orthodox Invicta. In Britain, especially, one encounters the cult of the local pattern. If you seek success, say the experts, stick to the tried and trusted flies used by the local fishermen. To express my scepticism of this cult I have deliberately tested the reaction of British brown and sea trout to flies tied with the feathers of game birds indigenous to South Africa. Scottish trout accepted the foreign concoctions with apparent enthusiasm.

If we agree, in the first place, that it is unnecessary to attempt exact imitation of natural insects and, secondly, that deviation from standardised artificial patterns is permissible, does this mean we should regard the choice of a fly as unimportant? In fact, the size, shape, colour, texture and sinking or floating properties of a fly may make all the difference to its acceptance by the trout. There is also the question of visibility. This is not significant in clear, relatively shallow water where any trout on the lookout for food will have no difficulty in seeing even the smallest and most inconspicuously coloured fly. But South African trout are often to be found in turbid water or in deep artificial lakes where underwater objects are not readily visible. Under such conditions, it is necessary to offer the fish something that will attract their attention. Hence Ivens's term "attractors" for flashy, brightly coloured flies that bear no close resemblance to any living creature and yet often catch trout. Size obviously affects visibility, so large flies are generally recommended for murky or turbulent water, but size also plays a part in stimulating a fish to seize the fly. If the artificial is much larger than the creatures on which a trout is feeding, a favourable response may not be forthcoming. Nevertheless it is surprising how often a trout will go for a fly that is far more bulky than the natural food items available. A very small fly may occasionally be necessary to tempt particularly selective fish, or to avoid disturbance on flat, calm water, but in most cases the reason for its use is that the angler wants to prove his skill by landing a trout on a tiny hook. For those of us who like to make things easier, rather than more difficult, reliance may generally be placed on the greed of trout. I have found when fishing with two flies, one smaller than the other, that more often than not the larger fly has been taken. This is understandable when one examines the stomach contents of fish of various sizes. An eight-inch trout may swallow a 50 mm tadpole or minnow, while a big trout can easily accommodate a frog or crab that looks enormous compared with the largest legal artificial fly.

Trout fly hooks in general use range from No. 2 (35 mm long) down to No. 14 (10 mm). The largest legally recognised hook is a 2/0 (41 mm) and the smallest size for practical use is a No. 18 (6 mm). Were I to be restricted to a single size for all my fishing I would choose a No. 8 (19 mm). Any trout, from four inches upwards, can be caught on a No. 8 hook. If one wishes to enjoy the delicacy of presentation possible with a small fly, one should include some No. 14's in one's box, but by far the majority of South African trout are caught on hooks from No. 6 to No. 12.

When asking for flies of a certain size, confusion may occur owing to the existence of short-shank and long-shank hooks, in addition to the standard shape. A further source of confusion is that two other scales exist (in addition to the generally accepted "old" or "Redditch" scale) for measuring hooks, but luckily one is unlikely to come across them in this country.

Size, then, is an important feature of any trout fly, and it is advisable to carry at least two sizes of each of one's favourite patterns. What these patterns should be is a matter on which no two anglers will agree. In 1948, Courtney Williams included 345 different dressings in *A Dictionary of Trout Flies*. Even then this was very far from being a comprehensive list and recent years have seen a vast proliferation of published descriptions of new, named flies. Unnamed and non-standard creations are to be found in every amateur fly tier's collection. Given the virtually infinite combinations of material possible it says much for man's attachment to convention and precedent that one can walk into a tackle shop north or south of the equator and find certain standard patterns that have become hallowed by tradition. An Invicta, Connemara Black, March Brown, Butcher, or Coachman is known and recognised throughout the fly-fishing world. There are dozens of others that have stood the test of time. *Flies and Fly Fishing in South Africa,* by Jack Blackman, includes an illustrated list of 124 patterns, most of which are available in local tackle shops. The shape or contour of an artificial fly is important. A badly formed fly will fail to give the trout an impression of something edible. A common fault of winged wet flies is a wing that stands out at an angle to the hook. Always choose a fly that has the wing well laid back, parallel with the body. This does not apply to dry flies, which are intended to imitate an upwinged floating insect, but in wet flies a streamlined contour is essential. This is one reason for the success of modern streamers and bucktails, and flies dressed with a row of small overlapping feathers on each side such as the Walker's Killer or Mrs Simpson. A simple, wingless hackled fly or nymph has a shape conducive to natural movement under water.

Colour is a highly controversial attribute of artificial flies. Although trout have been proved to have colour vision, the extent to which colours show up under water depends on the amount of light as well as the angle from which the fish is looking. Objects silhouetted against the sky must appear dark. Red, orange and yellow are the colours most easily seen by trout, which may account for the success of flies that incorporate these colours. Since most of the underwater creatures on which trout feed are predominantly dull green or brown, the attraction of brightly coloured artificial lures is presumably due to their visibility and not to their resemblance to any aquatic animal. Whatever the reason, there is no doubt that differently coloured flies evoke different reactions. One day, or at one time of day, a yellowish fly may be the only pattern that catches trout, while at another time something totally different may be required. That is why a successful angler is ready to change flies when necessary. I do not believe, however, that minor differences in colour are of any significance: it is a major contrast that counts. As a general guide, the old adage "bright day, dark fly; dull day, red fly" seems to work. Towards evening a yellowish fly often proves attractive, while the white wing of a Coachman or some other conspicuous material may help to bring a trout up under conditions of very low light intensity. Several types of synthetic material are on the market for fly tiers who want to increase the visibility of their lures.

A fly fisherman might resent any suggestion that he used lures, but a great many of the objects intended for the capture of trout should not really be called flies. Even an artificial nymph that is supposed to represent a larval insect is not, strictly speaking, a fly and other trout lures have no entomological connections at all. A Walker's Killer might be regarded as representing a dragonfly nymph, but a fish is probably just as likely to take it for a tadpole or minnow. If the definition of a fly was restricted to imitations of natural insects, a large proportion of the patterns in common use would fail to qualify. For convenience, therefore, and to satisfy the legal requirement that trout may be caught only on "an artificial, non-spinning fly", a wide variety of what might well be termed lures are accepted as "flies".

Whatever materials a fly is made from, the texture of the finished product is important. Anything that makes a fly look rigid and unlifelike should be avoided. A fly tier may concentrate his efforts on trying to imitate the shape of objects eaten by trout, but succeed only in creating something that looks dead. Some of the nymphs and other patterns that appear realistic when lying in a box probably seem most unappetising to a trout. You may see so-called flies made of latex or plastic, but no matter how accurately they may be modelled on a real insect, they are totally lacking in natural movement. An effective fishing fly is a work of art that presents the right visual image to a hungry trout. There is no need for superfluous detail. One may see a cranefly imitation, for instance, in which fibres of feather have been knotted to simulate the joints in the legs of a natural insect. Such anatomical minutiae may appeal to the human eye but are most unlikely to attract a trout.

In many a successful painting the artist conveys the essence of his subject in a few brushstrokes. Similarly, the most successful flies are those such as the one tied by W.J. Lunn in the spring of 1917. When asked what it represented, he replied: "Nothing particular, Sir." For nearly 70 years, Lunn's Particular has been held in high esteem by anglers as a consistent killer of trout.

Wet flies are intended to sink, whereas dry flies float. The latter are effective only if the fish are rising to surface food, whereas a wet fly may be made to sink to any required depth. Selecting the right type of fly and other equipment, as well as adjusting one's fishing technique to meet specific conditions, will be considered in the next chapter. A final word on tackle concerns the various accessories that may be considered necessary.

To carry the fish one catches, a bag is usually slung over the shoulder, or perhaps a wicker creel. The latter keeps the fish cool and free from bruising but may be considered somewhat clumsy. Standard fishing bags generally contain compartments for tackle as well as a waterproof pocket for the fish, which is alright as long as it is lined with fresh newspaper or other absorbent material. Otherwise the fish become slimy and unpleasant to handle. A plastic bag is the worst possible container in which to carry fish, especially in hot weather.

A landing net may save the trauma of losing a trout at the last minute and should be big enough to accommodate the outsize fish that everyone hopes to catch one day. There are fishermen, however, who prefer to take a chance on losing the trout they cannot secure by hand, either because they like to give their quarry a sporting chance or because they cannot be bothered to burden themselves with a net.

A spring balance is an important item for anyone who wants to know the true weight of his fish. Not only may fish be returned to the water; any destined for the frying pan should be cleaned at the riverside, so it is not good enough to leave a scale at home.

Comfortable clothing is, of course, essential and provision should be made for the sudden rainstorms and temperature changes that characterise the South African summer climate. Bright colours that make the angler conspicuous are to be avoided.

Special fishing waistcoats are fashionable, with pockets to hold fly boxes, scissors and so on. These useful garments are known as vests, reflecting their transatlantic origin, but locally made ones are available.

Wading is often desirable, both on rivers and still waters. Whether to plunge boldly in or wear waterproof waders depends on the angler's hardiness and the coldness of the water. If waders are not used, gumboots or some other protection for feet and ankles may be considered prudent, if only to make one feel more comfortable at the prospect of meeting a cobra or puffadder. Waders are clumsy and hot for walking, so one sees them in use more often for fishing dams than rivers. This applies particularly to chest-high trouser waders.

The ultimate for anyone who wants to move out into deep water without sitting in a boat is the float tube, a device that originated with the bright idea of using a tractor tube to keep afloat. The lower part of the angler's body and his legs are encased in waterproof material, while frogman flippers give efficient propulsion. Those who have taken to float tubes speak enthusiastically of their manoeuvrability and the ease with which fish can be approached without frightening them.

Boats are used on many of the larger dams, and there is a single piece of equipment that should always be provided: an anchor. A boat that is being propelled by a stiff breeze is a most unsatisfactory fishing platform, so always have a 10 m length of cord and a weight adequate to hold the boat in place when required.

10. Technique and tactics

"This is going to be a fisherman's day," my father would remark on a bright, windless morning, with the river running crystal clear. On such a day every trout landed would have to be earned by a careful approach and accurate casting. The real pleasure of fly fishing is to succeed when the odds are against you.

For a beginner, or for someone who is feeling lazy, there are two possible ways of catching a trout. On a well-stocked river, if you stand at the top end of a pool where the water is moving fairly fast and let the current carry your line downstream, there is a good chance of a fish grabbing your fly, particularly at the moment you start pulling the line in. If a river is not available, boat fishing on a dam may bring easy results. Perhaps someone will agree to row the boat, while you let your fly trail in the water. It is, however, inadvisable to boast about a trout caught in this way. To rely on the movement of a boat to pull the line through the water constitutes trolling, which is severely frowned on in sporting circles. A troller is looked on in a similar light to the person who uses a 12-bore shotgun to tumble a sitting guineafowl out of a tree. Even more reprehensible than rowing is to employ a motor to propel the boat while fishing. This is strictly forbidden on most club waters. When fishing for trout one is expected to cast and work the fly without relying on adventitious aids.

To become a reasonably competent fly caster is not difficult, provided you start correctly. The best way to learn is obviously to receive tuition from someone who knows how to teach the correct way to handle rod and line. Just as there is a right method and a wrong method of swinging a golf club or a tennis racket, so it is with a fly rod. Whereas most serious golfers and tennis players receive lessons from professionals, who have themselves been properly taught, fly casting is seldom the subject of authoritative instruction. As a result many of the anglers to be seen in action have never developed the right technique. Indifferent casters still catch fish, but real proficiency in handling a rod makes an immense difference to the pleasure of a day on the river. Even when the trout are in unresponsive mood, there is great satisfaction in watching the line go smoothly out to drop the fly exactly where you intended. Accuracy of presentation may make all the difference between success and failure. My father used to recount a lesson he learned from A.A. Hamilton, who owned a stretch of the Mooi River at Kamberg. One day, watching my father fish, Hamilton said, "There's a trout under that bush on the opposite bank", but several casts produced no results. Remarking that the fly had not gone close enough to the trout's feeding spot, he took my father's rod and placed the fly right under the bush. A moment later the trout was hooked.

Consummate skill comes only from long practice, but it is important to understand the basic principles of fly-rod operation. With these principles in mind, one can achieve the muscular co-ordination that becomes, through practice, an automatic sequence of movements. Casting depends on the laws of mechanics and is therefore subject to strictly scientific analysis, unlike so much of the art of angling. One of the first writers to recognise this was an American, Fred G. Shaw, who published *The Science of Fly Fishing for Trout* in 1925. The book dealt with many aspects of angling, so the title may seem a little presumptuous. As an exposition of casting technique, however, Shaw's work remains a classic to this day. More recent writers on fly casting include such well-known names as Eric Horsfall Turner, who was associated with Captain T.L. Edwards; Tom Ivens, a leading exponent of long-distance

The author fishing on the Polela River.

casting; and Charles Ritz, whose book *A Fly Fisher's Life* has been an inspiration to more anglers than any other. An excellent up-to-date account of casting technique is to be found in *Fly-Fisherman's Primer* by Paul Fling and Donald Puterbaugh, whose text and graphics are crystal clear. Jack Blackman provides some useful hints in his *Flies and Fly Fishing in South Africa*.

There is plenty of good advice available and personal instruction is obviously much superior to the written word. To enrol for a professionally run fly-casting course, or to attend one of the fishing clinics that are organised from time to time, will be immensely helpful. Probably the pupil who will benefit most from expert tuition is one who has already learned to catch fish, but who wants to improve his technique by learning some of the tricks of a top-class angler.

It is all a matter of energy correctly applied. The rod's function is that of a spring which stores energy as it flexes and releases the energy as it straightens. Energy is passed on to the line, which carries the leader and fly out over the water. The angler's task is to impart energy to the rod: the right amount of energy at the right time. Perhaps the most striking difference between the action of an experienced caster and that of a novice is the apparently effortless way in which the former wields his rod. Considerable muscular power is required for a long cast, but a forced, jerky movement is fatal.

For the normal overhead cast, two distinct movements are involved: an upward/backward stroke to extend the line behind the caster and a downward/forward stroke to send the line to its destination. It is a common fault to thrash the water by using the rod like a whipstick, in a single, semi-circular movement. Back-pause-forward is the correct sequence. A skilful fisherman does learn to get his fly out across the water without letting his line go behind him, by using the roll or switch cast, which is accomplished by a single continuous movement. But this should be attempted only after the normal casting technique has been mastered.

At the start of a cast the line must lie straight without any slack, to ensure immediate transfer of energy from rod to line. The rod tip must then accelerate as rapidly as possible, although not with a jerk, in order to impart maximum energy. Remember $e = mc^2$. Energy depends on mass times velocity squared, so twice the speed means four times the energy. That is why Charles Ritz's "high speed/high line" casting technique works so well. The object is to move the line as rapidly as possible off the water and keep it as high as possible as it extends behind the angler. If the rod travels too far back, the line will drop low enough to enable the fly to hook whatever vegetation may be growing on the river bank. And if that seems to imply a deliberate intention on the part of an inanimate object, I can only say that fly hooks and bushes have a mutual attraction that defies explanation. So the loop of the line must be kept well above the ground as it straightens on the back cast.

Split-second timing is required to start the forward cast at precisely the right instant. Too late, and the result is a sickening jolt as the fly catches an obstruction; too soon, and the line gives a whip crack as it comes back on itself, minus the fly. Beginners should watch the line by a turn of the head, and start the rod moving a moment before the line has straightened completely. Timing becomes automatic with practice, but it never does any harm to watch the back cast, if only to make sure there is no unexpected tree looming up.

The correct stopping position for the rod at the end of the back cast is generally slightly past the vertical, but it may be stopped either sooner or later, depending on what the fly has to clear on the bank. For a really long cast the rod has to move through as wide an arc as possible and therefore, if there are no obstructions behind the angler, the rod butt may be allowed to go back beyond the usual one o'clock position. In any case, the danger of the line dropping too low on the back cast is not eliminated by an early stoppage of the rod. If the line is moving too slowly, or if there is too long a pause before the start of the forward cast, the line will fall to the ground whatever the rod's position. Bringing the rod to a sudden stop, after a smoothly accelerating upstroke, is the key to effective casting.

As the rod is stopped, it flexes backwards under the pull of the line until the tip is almost horizontal. The line travels in the shape of a loop, which straightens progressively, re-forming on the forward cast. The dimensions of the loop vary according to the way in which the rod is handled. A narrow or tight loop travels faster than a wide one, since it meets with less air resistance. To achieve maximum distance, therefore, the loop must be kept as tight as possible. This calls for movement of the rod tip back and forwards in approximately the same path as that followed by the line. In making a long cast, the angler pushes his hand forwards, rather than swinging it down. A downward movement of the hand opens the line loop and reduces its forward impetus.

One of the difficulties in reaching out for distance is that the narrower the loop the greater is the likelihood of the fly catching in the line. The resulting tangle is something we all experience. A skilful fisherman learns to reduce this danger by avoiding an unnecessarily tight loop when using a short to medium length of line. The tightness of the loop must be varied according to circumstances.

If the rod is moved back and forward in a single plane, the line will also move in that same plane, which is what one wants if the object is to achieve a narrow loop. This plane may be either vertical or inclined towards the horizontal. What most authorities seem to stress is that the rod tip should not move back in one plane and forward in another. A wide sweep of the rod creates a wide loop in the line, which is undesirable if the intention is to cast a narrow loop. But, in practice, a narrow loop is often more nuisance than it is worth. This applies particularly when a wind is blowing from behind or from either side. To drive the line into a head wind one does need a tight loop, but if the wind is from any other direction one's main concern is to prevent the leader from being blown across the path of the line.

With a wind blowing from my left, I swing the rod well over to the right on the back cast and bring it overhead on the forward cast. A wind from my right calls for the reverse procedure, starting with a backhand stroke to get the line moving downwind. Again, my rod tip follows an elliptical course in a wind gusting from the rear. This unconventional, wide-swinging action seems to do away with the danger of hooking either my rod or my person, and minimises the risk of wind knots and tangled leaders.

Performance of rod, line and leader depends on the movement of the angler's arm — or rather, arms — since the left hand (or right hand in the case of a left-handed caster) plays a vital role in controlling the line. A beginner is often told to use his wrist. A natural response to this advice is to copy the flapping movements of a child patting a balloon to and fro. The elbow goes out at right angles to the body and the wrist wobbles ineffectively. Teachers who appreciate this danger have tried to introduce wrist control by various devices, of which the silliest was to make the pupil hold a book under the armpit. Captain T.L. Edwards suggested sitting on a chair and keeping the elbow of the rod-arm firmly on the knee while learning to put the rod to work. Eric Horsfall Turner advocated this procedure, after it became apparent that the earlier idea of strapping up the learner's wrist, to prevent excessive flexing of the joint, did not really help to teach correct control of the wrist when the device was removed.

In fact, there is no need for any artificial restriction on wrist movement. Control is automatic, provided attention is concentrated on bending the *elbow* joint. If you hold your arm out, thumb uppermost, and move the hand smartly back to touch your ear, the wrist bends hardly at all. The backward movement you have just made is the correct action for the back cast when you have a rod in your hand. But don't worry about a rod for the present: hit forward as if making a karate chop at an object level with your shoulder. Again it is elbow and not wrist that provides the action. As long as the thumb remains on top, the structure of the wrist prevents the joint bending more than a few degrees.

Now pick up a rod, with reel attached, and point it straight out in front. How are you holding the handle? There is only *one* correct way, whatever you may have seen other people doing. The thumb must be on top, pointing along the rod, while all four fingers grasp the handle. One may see anglers, who have fished for years, casting with the thumb at the side of the handle, perhaps extending the forefinger towards the rod-tip. However used they may have become to holding a rod like this, it remains a handicap, except for very short distances. Ritz's "high-speed/high line" technique is the method that is followed, whether consciously or not, by all the leading exponents of the art of fly fishing. Ritz insisted that "thumb-on-top" is the only grip to use. As long as the thumb remains on top, casting is easy provided the wrist is not allowed to twist sideways. To ensure this, the flat of the reel must be kept in the same plane as that in which the rod is moving.

When making a horizontal cast, that is moving the rod roughly parallel to the ground, the angler's arm is, of course, rotated. But the thumb must remain in the same position, relative to the reel. A horizontal cast is required to throw the line under overhanging bushes. It is also less likely to frighten fish which may be able to see the flash of a rod high in the air under very clear, calm conditions. Effective fly casting calls for an ability to vary one's technique, moving the rod in any required plane, either forehand or backhand. For short distances, the elbow is the main pivot, but for a long cast the whole arm swings freely from the shoulder. There is no harm in letting the elbow move away from the body. To hold a book under the armpit is therefore a pointless restriction. Just remember to watch out for that sideways twist of the wrist. The simplest way to avoid undesirable wrist movement is to concentrate on the thumb, which must be pressed firmly against the top of the rod handle. A firm grip automatically restricts flexure of the wrist.

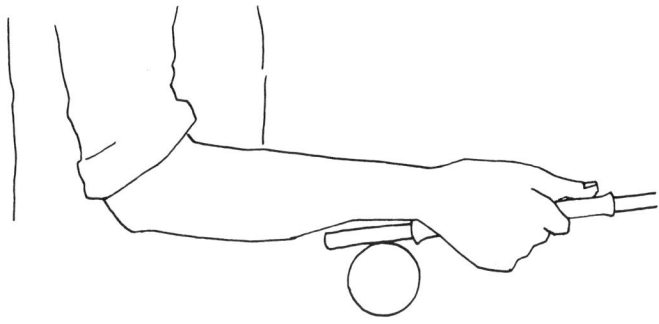

Position of arm at start of short cast. Note thumb on top of rod.

Perhaps the most neglected element of fly casting is correct use of the left hand (or right hand, in the case of a left-handed caster). A modern trout rod is easily wielded with one hand. Some people are therefore tempted to leave the left hand out of action, or perhaps to use it for holding a landing net, while they cast and draw the fly through the water. To fish like that is manifestly inefficient. Once the fly is in the water, it should be worked by pulling in line with the left hand, thus covering a considerable distance before the rod is raised for the next cast. Trout often follow a fly for several metres before taking it, so each cast should be fully fished out if one is to avoid the frustrating sight of a trout vainly chasing a prematurely airborne fly. The line is drawn in over the right index finger, which is held ready to clamp the line against the rod in preparation for a strike, should a fish take the fly.

What to do with the line as you pull it in with the left hand remains a problem. The loose coils may be held in the hand or allowed to fall to the ground. In either case there is a risk that the coils will become entangled, with disastrous results if a hooked trout makes a quick bid for freedom. A good idea, if you have the patience to put it into practice, is to use T.C. Ivens's method of figure-of-eight bunching in the palm of the left hand. Line held in this way unravels smoothly. My own practice is to form fairly large coils, controlled by thumb and forefinger. For stillwater fishing, where one is not moving about very much, a stripping basket may be attached to one's waist. As the line is retrieved, it is dropped into the basket, reducing the danger of entanglement.

However the line is handled on the retrieve, it has to be paid out again for the next cast. If several metres have been drawn in, two or three false casts may be required to get the full length airborne. A false cast involves the normal casting action, except that the line is not allowed to land, whether behind or in front. When lengthening line there is no excuse for the sloppy practice of whipping the water by allowing the fly to alight and then snatching it off again.

Each hand has a part to play in any type of fly fishing, but correct timing and co-ordination between the rod-hand and the line-hand become critically important in long-distance casting. As explained by Ivens, the task of the left hand is to keep the line taut, both at the beginning of the rod's upstroke and at the start of the forward stroke. Rather than merely holding the line, the left hand should actively haul the line to give additional acceleration at the critical moment. This is easily done on the upstroke: as the right hand raises the rod to lift the fly off the water, the left hand moves rapidly down and sideways, with finger and thumb firmly grasping the line. To achieve the tournament caster's double haul requires considerable practice. The object is to accelerate line speed, not only on the upstroke, but also at the start of the forward stroke, when the line is extended behind.

Whereas in ordinary casting the hands remain well apart until the cast has been completed, for double hauling the left hand must start to follow the right as soon as the line begins to move backwards. As the left hand moves upwards, line is fed through the rod rings. The forward punch of the right hand is then accompanied by a simultaneous downward haul of the left hand, giving the acceleration needed to send the fly out to the maximum distance. To complete the cast, the line is released to allow the loop held in the left hand to shoot through the rod rings.

Long-distance casting involves swinging both arms from the shoulder and should not be attempted until complete proficiency has been achieved in casting a short line using elbow and controlled wrist movement. Initial concentration on developing a good punch to get the line moving quickly off the water, and another good punch on the forward cast, will pay dividends. With practice the whole process involves little expenditure of energy, as timing takes the place of brute force. Reaching out for distance does become strenuous if a continuous spell of long casting is required, but in practice this is seldom called for. Even when fishing a dam from the bank, casts of varying length give better coverage of the water than constant efforts to achieve maximum distance.

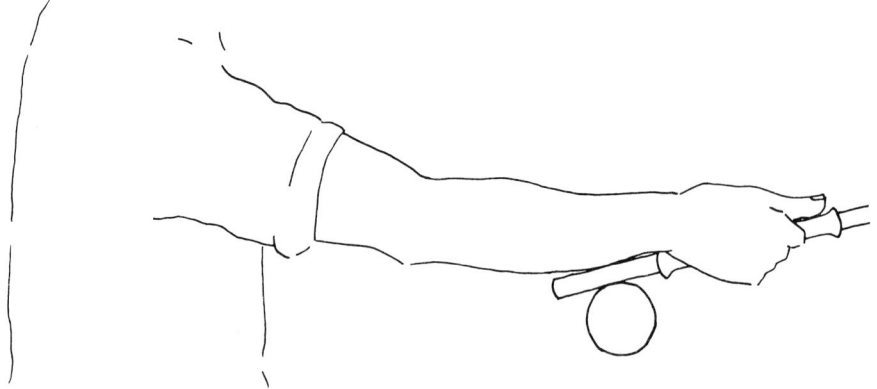

Position of arm at start of long cast. The whole arm swings freely.

author holds an 850 g rainbow from the Umzimkulu

Joan Crass plays a trout in an Underberg dam

Club room, Cape Piscatorial Society. Ross-Munroe, seated, Hugh Huntley and Jack Blackman

As well as the normal overhead or horizontal cast, in which the rod moves back and forwards, trickier methods of casting become necessary when fishing a river with heavily overgrown banks. Inaccessible places often hold the best fish, so skill in avoiding obstructions may be rewarding. By using the roll or switch cast it is possible to drop a fly 20 metres away without allowing the line to go behind where you are standing. To do so requires a radically different action from the back-pause-forward motion of the overhead cast. The line is raised from the water in a smooth semicircular movement of the rod tip, accelerating into a downward hit. In contrast to overhead casting, a roll cast requires flexible wrist action. It also requires a quick-actioned, resilient rod with sufficient power to whip the line forward. Above all, it needs a great deal of practice, as do all facets of the process of co-ordinating the angler's muscles and the capabilities of his tackle.

To practise or demonstrate casting, a lawn may be used if water is not available. The main drawback is that the friction of a grassy surface differs from that of water. A complete outfit, including line, leader and fly should always be made up although it is advisable to break off the hook point at the bend to avoid catching in grass or the ears of bystanders. Practising on water that holds trout is, of course, more interesting and sometimes results in a pleasant surprise. A few years ago my daughter gave me a copy of Charles Ritz's *A Fly Fisher's Life*, so we proceeded to the banks of the Polela River to try out the author's precepts. An open stretch of water, barely knee deep, was selected for a casting demonstration. There was no thought of catching a fish in a place where only tiddlers could be expected. We wanted to see if the "high speed/high line" technique worked. Encouraged by the initial efforts, a long cast was attempted, using a tuft of grass on the opposite bank as a convenient target. As the fly settled close to the overhanging grass, there was a swirl and a moment later a two-pound rainbow was firmly hooked.

This experience emphasises that trout are not always where we expect to find them. Nevertheless the experienced angler will generally pick out the most likely lies, even in a strange river. Fish-catching ability always involves more than mere technical excellence in the use of tackle. A man who casts his flies with superb precision may have fewer fish at the end of the day than a less polished performer. River craft is based on qualities that are hard to define, although intense concentration and unflagging perseverance certainly play a part.

A point overlooked by inexperienced fishermen is that a trout is always on the lookout for danger. Anything that appears dangerous inhibits the feeding response on which an angler's success depends. When a trout is on the alert for food it is also on the alert for anything that may pose a threat. Little notice is likely to be taken of stationary objects, whether to eat or to avoid. The angler's task, therefore, is to present the fish with something that looks good to eat (the artificial fly), while avoiding any action that may stimulate the trout's flight reflex. An obvious precaution is to keep out of sight, which may be easy or difficult, according to circumstances. If the water is murky, or turbulent owing either to streamflow or wind action, concealment is easy. Clear, flat-calm water presents a challenge. Trout feeding in the shallows are more likely to take fright than those in a deep pool. This is due not merely to the transparency of shallow water, but because fish appear to feel more secure in deep water.

The first point to remember in seeking concealment is that the higher above the water surface an object moves, the more conspicuous it becomes. We referred earlier to the investigations of Clarke and Goddard and their conclusion that anything below an angle of 10 degrees from the horizon is so indistinct and distorted as to be virtually invisible to the fish. The practical implication is to keep below the critical angle. At a distance of 10 m on a flat surface a man 1,76 m (5 ft 9 ins) tall can stand upright without intercepting the 10 degree line. At 5 m he would have to bend down to half that height. Therefore one should keep well back from the edge of the bank. Alternatively, one of the best methods of keeping a low profile is to wade. A tall man knee-deep in water can approach to within easy casting distance of a fish, provided he moves cautiously.

This brings us to the second important point — movement. A stationary object may be completely ignored, even if it is well within a fish's field of vision. A sudden movement is recognised immediately. Not only must the angler guard against waving his arms where they are visible: many a trout has been warned of danger by the flash of a rod. The line is also liable to scare fish. An angler may take care to use the thinnest possible nylon for his leader, in the hope of deceiving the fish, without realising that the line is a far more important source of trouble. Obvious disturbance is caused by the splash of a clumsy cast, but one tends to ignore the frightening effect of the line once it is in the water. Underwater photographs in Clarke and Goddard's *The Trout and the Fly* show with startling clarity how visible a line may be. This applies particularly to a floating line.

The question of visibility is one of the considerations that determine what type of line to use. Earlier I stated that a sinking line is generally preferable to a floating line, under South African conditions, and a point in favour of a submerged line is that it is less conspicuous in calm water. Nevertheless many anglers favour a floating line, which is, of course, essential for dry-fly fishing and also for using a nymph in shallow water. Even where the water is deep, a floating line combined with a long leader may be effective. The ease with which one can pick a floating line off the surface makes for pleasant casting. Personal preference plays a larger part in selecting a particular item of tackle than any objective criterion.

Two anglers fishing together on a dam or river may adopt entirely different techniques. In still water, if the fish are feeding near the bottom, one man may attach a small nymph to a long leader on a floating line, while the other may try a flashy attractor-type fly on a sinking line. The nymph fisherman will draw his line slowly, watching carefully for any tell-tale line movement that indicates a take. Patience is required, since a fast retrieve will bring the fly up close to the surface out of sight of deep-lying fish. Pulling a floating line across the surface will also create an alarmingly visible wake. A sinking line, on the other hand, lends itself to the often successful technique of giving the fly rapid movement by stripping the line in through the rings with the rod tip held close to the water. A heavy line keeps the leader well below the surface, except in turbulent water.

In a rapidly flowing river it may be necessary to weight the fly in order to keep it at a level where the fish will see it. Turbulent upwelling around underwater boulders will lift the leader and fly away from the river bed, even if the line is well sunk. It is common practice, therefore, to clip a split shot onto the leader a short distance in front of the fly. Alternatively, the fly itself may be weighted by incorporating lead or copper wire into the body. I dislike using a heavily weighted fly, as it spoils the normal rhythm of casting. A small nymph with a few turns of wire round the hook is not unpleasant to cast and yet sinks rapidly. A nymph of this sort may be cast upstream and allowed to drift down through likely trout lies in swift water.

Where the stream is flowing more quietly, the same technique of allowing the fly to drift freely in the current may be practised with an unweighted nymph or other type of fly. An artificial that is tied with feathers and silk on a light hook will, in fact, have much the same density as a natural nymph, which one is trying to simulate. In principle, therefore, I favour flies without additional weight.

Having persuaded a trout to accept your fly, a sharp pull is generally needed to set the hook. Some fish seize the fly and dash off with it, hooking themselves, while in swift water the weight of the line may embed the hook. More often than not, however, the trout will find the fly is inedible and will reject it without getting hooked, unless the angler strikes at the right moment. The strike should be merely a sideways or upward twitch of the rod point. Timing is all-important. In clear water it is easy to strike too soon. When a fish can be seen coming to the fly, one must wait until it turns away, or the hook will simply be jerked out of its open mouth. This applies particularly to a dry fly, for which a good formula is to see the rise, say "One thousand, two thousand, three thousand" and then tighten the line.

With a wet fly or nymph the fish is likely to be invisible. A floating line may give a clue and one should watch intently for any movement or unexpected stoppage of the line. A quick strike may hook a fish that has quietly sucked in the fly. Similarly, with a sinking line quick action is called for if any resistance is felt as the line is retrieved. A slight nibble, on the other hand, may indicate that the fish is merely plucking at the fly and that one should wait for a solid pull. Experience is the only guide in many cases, and even the most skilful angler misses a good proportion of the fish that come to his fly. Much seems to depend on the mood of the trout. On some days one after the other is firmly hooked. On other occasions the trout come "short" with infuriating consistency and either avoid the hook altogether or go free after being lightly hooked on the edge of the mouth.

Over the years, I have landed about one in three of the trout that I have seen or felt come to my flies. Contrary to the popular idea that larger, and therefore older, trout are more cunning than small ones, I find that I hook a higher proportion of the former. Small trout often seem to play with a fly, whereas if a big one is attracted it generally seems to mean business. Very likely the big trout is more prone to ignore an artificial fly. Older fish feed less energetically than small ones and for a shorter period each day.

Finally, comes the question of how to play a hooked trout. My suggestion is that more fish are lost through the angler being over-cautious and allowing slack line than through pulling too hard. We have, of course, all seen an excited youngster hanging on for dear life and giving the fish no line, until the hook pulled out or the leader broke, but going to the other extreme is also the mark of a novice.

11. Ethics and regulations

Trout fishermen surround their sport with a network of restrictive rules and regulations. Ever since trout were first introduced to South Africa, an interminable succession of legislative provisions has been brought into effect to protect the fish from undue exploitation, or from capture by methods considered unethical.

A provincial licence has for many years been the first requirement for anyone who wanted to catch trout. As with most fishing licences, no one has ever defined accurately why a trout licence should be required. Usually, the ostensible reason for imposing a licence is to raise revenue. Another possible justification is to exercise control over those participating in the licensed activity.

As a means of raising revenue, trout licences in South Africa have never been related to the amount spent by the provincial authorities in the Cape, Natal or the Transvaal. Initially, only small amounts of tax-payers' money were spent on trout propagation. The imposition of a £1 licence might have seemed an adequate levy on those who benefitted by the expenditure. But with the vast proliferation in funds allocated to trout production from about 1947 onwards, licence fees became of relatively little significance. For several decades provincial legislators were content to see a widening gap between the tens of thousands of rands brought in by licence fees and the hundreds of thousands spent on trout culture and law enforcement. In any event, the revenue from fishing licences has always been treated simply as an item of general provincial revenue and has not been made available to the nature conservation authorities whose responsibility it is to provide a service to anglers. This lack of any direct relationship between revenue and expenditure has been to the advantage of trout fishermen, who have received far greater benefits than they have paid for. Recently, however, a change in attitude has become apparent. Officials in charge of nature conservation no longer regard trout as a high priority for the allocation of funds and manpower. Indigenous fauna and flora and the upkeep of real estate, in the form of nature reserves, are considered more appropriate recipients of available resources than introduced species such as trout. The extent of this change in attitude differs from province to province.

In the Cape, the year 1985 saw the institution of steps by the Department of Nature and Environmental Conservation to cut down quite drastically on trout propagation, while formulating legislative changes to remove overall protection of trout. Trout fishermen are no longer required to buy a licence, other than the R1 licence needed for any type of freshwater angling. In the Orange Free State, where trout have never received much attention, there is also no separate licence. In the Transvaal a licence for public trout waters costs R8, compared with the R5 licence for other fish. On private dams, however, Transvaal anglers do not require any licence at all. This shows good sense on the part of the authorities.

In Natal the existing R3 trout licence is likely to be increased to R10, with no licence required for juveniles who have hitherto paid half price. On officially listed trout waters, any adult angler except the riparian owner and his family is obliged to have a licence. Dams, whether privately owned or not, that lie within the catchment of a scheduled trout stream are deemed to be trout waters for licensing purposes. A dam lying outside a trout area is not a trout water in terms of the law, even though it may be stocked with trout.

In view of the variation in policy and in the cost of licences in the four provinces, the purpose of maintaining the present system is unclear. As already indicated, revenue is relatively insignificant. Control over angling activities is not affected by the licensing laws, which are not aimed at limiting the number of licensees. Nor would any limitation be desirable. Overfishing may be a problem on certain easily accessible waters, but this is a matter for local regulation.

Licence statistics are of interest to show trends in the number of anglers, but there is little of practical import in such information. Attempts to use licences to obtain catch records for research purposes have met with a poor response. The argument that the users of a resource should pay for the maintenance of that resource is valid in principle, but is irrelevant to the issue of trout licences. The multiplicity of rivers and still waters scattered over South Africa constitutes a resource that is available to licensed anglers to a widely variable extent. Availability is dependent not on the possession of a licence, but on the arrangement made by each individual angler with the owner of the land on which a river or dam is situated. The owner may be a farmer, municipality or state department, but it is always necessary to obtain permission to fish. Payment is generally involved, either directly or through membership of a fishing club that has made an agreement with the landowner. Possession of a licence gives no one the right of access to fishing, nor would the granting of such a right be equitable. If each angler is to make a fair contribution to the amenity which he enjoys he must, firstly, pay in proportion to the extent to which he uses the resource. Someone who fishes only occasionally should not pay the same as a man who fishes a great deal. Secondly, the angler's money should go to the supplier of the amenity, not into the general revenue fund of a provincial organisation. Neither of these conditions can be met by making a South African angler pay a licence fee.

Objectively, then, a trout licence appears to be an unjustified imposition. But an important consideration is the attitude of the fisherman himself. Anglers in general, and trout anglers in particular, share a strong bond of fellow-feeling with others who practise their art. Members of clubs proudly display their membership badges. In a broader context the possession of a fishing licence may be regarded as a badge of membership of the brotherhood of anglers. There is little prospect therefore that licences will be abolished. Possession of that piece of official paper gives the owner a feeling of group identity.

To obtain a licence is easy in Natal, since a large number of tackle shops, hotels and other agencies are authorised to sell fishing licences, for which they are paid a commission by the provincial accountant. In other parts of South Africa one may have to find an official receiver of revenue, since the all-pervasive red tapeworm is loth to allow collection of public monies by private operators. In the Transvaal, some public-spirited individuals have persuaded the authorities to let them sell fishing licences, but they may do so only if the books of licences are bought, and paid for in advance, without any recompense for the trouble and financial outlay.

Having bought a licence, the angler finds his way beset with rules and regulations to prevent him wandering from the path of good sportsmanship. He must use a rod — no hand lines or set lines are permitted — and in Natal his reel may not be of the fixed-spool variety (the other provinces allow any sort of reel). Hooks may not be doubles or trebles and may not exceed 42 mm in length. The reasons for these limits are far from clear. Double and treble hooks are used for artificial flies in Britain, especially for salmon. As far as size is concerned, it is most unlikely that anyone would want to use anything larger than a 42 mm (2/0) hook.

Then comes the question of what is permissible to adorn the said hooks. One may use only "artificial non-spinning flies". Fortunately no legally binding definition has been attempted. It is easy to distinguish between a conventional "fly" and such things as minnows, plugs or spoons. But there are borderline cases for which it would be impossible to set a standard in terms of the law. Consensus among anglers generally serves to separate the acceptable from the unacceptable.

Whereas a natural product in the form of feathers, fur or silk is happily incorporated into the dressing of an artificial fly, bait is anathema to the trout fisherman. South African trout lovers long ago insisted that bait fishing be made illegal in the waters listed in the official gazettes of the provinces concerned. In Europe, mere moral outrage has apparently had the desired effect. Jack Olsen tells the story (published in Ritz's *A Fly Fisher's Life*) of the shock and horror of Monsieur Vernes, proprietor of a famous stretch of Normandy chalk stream, at finding a British major using, horror of horrors, a "Wuhhhhm". The story has a happy ending. The major, one may assume, had turned to a worm after having had to leave his fly-fishing equipment behind when he set off for the D-Day landings. He gratefully accepted Monsieur Vernes's generous offer of a good fly rod and some flies, which doubtless proved more effective for taking trout than the wrigglers shamefacedly dug from some farmer's manure heap.

In the days before bait fishing was made subject to the rigours of Natal law, my father accepted a challenge from two farmers to see who could catch the most trout in a day on the Mooi River. My father would stick to his flies, while his competitors might use grasshoppers, frogs and other natural fauna. The result proved that more fish were to be caught on artificial fly than on bait, although the latter accounted for the two largest trout. There are times, of course, when a succulent morsel of truly edible material does the trick under conditions that are unsuitable for fly fishing. I went, some years ago, to a stretch of the Umzimhlava River, near Kokstad, and obtained the permission of Mr Brownrigg, the owner, to try his water. On enquiry as to the likelihood of finding a trout his reply was, "Oh, yes. A couple of weeks ago, when the river was full and a bit dirty, I tried that pool at the corner. Soon had a bite, gave a good heave and there was a three pounder on the bank behind me."

Then there is the story told by Dicky Southworth, founder of Basutair, the first regular charter company in Lesotho. Dicky flew two Johannesburg visitors, father and son, from Maseru to Semonkong, for a day's fishing. However, the Maletsunyane River, which flows past the airstrip, was swollen by a thunderstorm that had swept over the catchment the previous day. The two fishermen set off for the river, but Dicky held out little hope of success. After enjoying a cup of tea with the storekeeper, he started turning over old packing cases at the back of the store, with the intention of finding a cricket. A mouse scuttled away, leaving a nest with four naked baby mice. Dicky left two for the mother and carried the other two off to the river. The first was impaled on a hook and allowed to drift into a backwater. Sure enough a fine four-pound rainbow took the bait and was duly landed. The second mouse secured a brown trout of almost identical size. When the two fishermen returned empty-handed, they were delighted to be offered a choice of either a brown or a rainbow to take home.

In support of the contention that bait fishing is not worth the trouble, or the risk of being found out, are two authentic instances of anglers who found that neither of the flies they were using was proving successful. A frog was then attached to one of the fly hooks, which had the desired result but in each case the trout left the frog and took the unadorned dropper fly. Frogs are, of course, generally attractive to trout and a lady of my acquaintance once found herself in an embarrassing situation through making use of this affinity. When she hooked a hard-fighting rainbow in the Polela River, her companion came to her assistance to net the trout, which had a half-swallowed frog in its mouth. Tact forbade mention of the fact that the hook was embedded in both frog and fish.

What might be termed unintentional bait fishing is not unknown. Large trout may have their cannibal instincts aroused by a small fish struggling on the end of a line. When fishing the Mooi River, on a section now included in Kamberg Nature Reserve, my father one day hooked a six-inch trout that was seized by what looked like a four pounder. Instead of letting go of its prey, the big trout remained attached to the leader and was eventually brought within reach of the net. At this stage the hook, which had penetrated the trout's lip, pulled out and the cannibal escaped, removing the temptation to claim it as a fair catch.

Few anglers are, in fact, likely to be faced with such a decision in the case of a fish caught by dubious means. But fair fishing will, if successful, raise the question of killing or releasing the trout we catch. On most waters there are limits, set either by provincial regulation or by a club or landowner, that control the number and size of fish that may be taken. In the past the emphasis was on returning undersized fish, while attempting to attain a limit bag. Because of this attitude, and because the limits were often excessively generous, these so-called control measures had virtually no effect in reducing the impact of fishing on the trout population.

In recent years, limits have tended to be stricter, with fewer fish of larger size permitted in the angler's bag. Another development has been a removal of restrictions on the taking of small trout in heavily stocked waters. This makes sense in many of the headwaters of Natal rivers where breeding often produces far more young fish than have any chance of growing to a size that anglers will want to catch. But the mere fact that a small fish is of no great interest to the fisherman means that removal of restrictions on taking trout of, say, less than 20 cm has scarcely any effect. A stretch of river that has a large stock of fingerlings holds little attraction, compared with a place where well-grown fish are present. Therefore fishing pressure is low on an overstocked water. In addition, the feeling that it is unethical to kill young fish makes many sportsmen loth to take them. Fear of ridicule may also be a factor. No one likes to be accused of bringing home sardines. In fact, of course, three or four six-inch trout make a delicious meal and where a bounteous supply is available there should be no qualms about taking them.

Where one should consider the ethics of killing fish is in waters with a stock that is below carrying capacity. To remove a fish that has a good chance of growing bigger is to deprive another angler, or maybe oneself, of an opportunity to make a more exciting catch later. A thoughtful angler will always behave in a way that is consistent with the welfare of his sport.

Good fly fishing depends, primarily, on the presence of an adequate stock of well-grown trout. If this is to be maintained there must be a balance between what the water can produce and what is taken out of it. Natural production will never keep up with the drain imposed by unrestricted fishing. Greedy fishermen have no place in an angling community and, however much we may admire angling skill, if a man uses his skill simply to take excessive bags admiration will turn to distaste. A well-known former member of a Natal angling club was one of the most successful fly fishers, but he showed little ability to control his killer instinct when trout were on the move. Nor could he afterwards resist the temptation to broadcast his exploits. When an indignant dam owner complained that the club member in question had taken eight fish instead of the limit of four, the committee was forced to impose a penalty for breach of club rules.

The rules imposed by fishing clubs, or by those who control waters to which the public has access, are designed to share out the available resources. As well as limiting each angler's catch, the rules generally ensure that fishermen respect one another's rights. An unwritten code of conduct also does much to enhance the pleasure of fly fishing. We all know instances when this code has been broken. Neville Nuttall, in *Trout Streams of Natal*, describes how a big trout was located one morning by a fisherman called Carruthers, who told his fellow guests at lunchtime where the trout was lying and how he hoped to catch it that afternoon. Carruthers was sitting on the riverbank waiting for the fish to rise, when one of those with whom the secret had been shared appeared on the opposite bank and unceremoniously hooked the fish. Carruthers then showed the calibre of his sportsmanship by wading in to net the three-and-a-half-pound trout for his rival, who, one hopes, had some qualm of conscience at such chivalrous behaviour.

There may be a narrow dividing line between what is acceptable and what is unacceptable. Mrs Hilliard, who fished at Underberg for many years, made a practice of using a shot to sink her fly, as did many others. My father referred to this practice as "lead slinging". One day he found himself fishing the south bank of the Umzimkulu River, with Mrs Hilliard on the north bank. When asked, on his return, whether he had been successful, the scornful reply was: "How can you expect to catch fish when there's someone throwing cannon balls into the river?"

Highmoor Dam, Natal. Their expressions say it all!

When fishing from a boat, trolling is regarded by high-minded anglers as a heinous offence. Yet many of us leave the line trailing while we row upwind. My only complaint about trolling is that, more often than not, a trout takes the fly, the reel screams and the fish is gone before one can pick up the rod. Trolling, at least while someone else is rowing, is certainly a lazy way of fishing, but it is also inefficient and that, to me, is more significant than the ethical aspect.

Angling ethics are mainly concerned with the effect one's actions may have on another angler. In rivers or dams that are heavily fished, the standard of sport enjoyed is reduced by the constant removal of sizeable trout. One way of countering this loss is to keep restocking with catchable-sized fish. An alternative is to cut down losses by returning captured fish to the water. This "no-kill" concept has fired the imagination of anglers in America and Europe, and has become widely accepted in South Africa. As with most good ideas, however, it is a concept that should not be applied uncritically. As an aid to managing trout waters, catch-and-release will come up for discussion later. From the ethical viewpoint it may seem entirely commendable not to kill trout, but there are dissentient voices.

Correspondence in *The Field* has shown that some British writers view with alarm the possibility that anti-cruelty lobbyists might use catch-and-release as an avenue for their attack on angling. Perhaps there is some substance in this fear. Few people would object to catching a fish on a hook, if the fish is going to be killed and used for food. All fish die eventually and a fish that meets its end at the hands of an angler may suffer no more than if it were killed in some other way. In any event, a fish's nervous system is not highly organised and cannot register pain to the same extent as the brain of a mammal. But are we entitled to say that a fish suffers *no* pain or trauma when hooked and played to exhaustion? The question may be asked, therefore, whether we are morally justified in catching a fish simply for the fun of deceiving it, with the intention of letting it go again. We may derive pleasure from the exercise of our skill, but is that a sufficiently substantial reason to subject the fish to what amounts to an unnecessary life and death struggle? One devotee of no-kill fly fishing has described trout as "pleasure machines".

An advocate of fish's rights might well argue that the practice of catch-and-release fishing amounts to playing a game that gives pleasure to one participant and pain to the other. Contrariwise, a thoughtful fly fisherman might say that it is surely worse to kill a fish than to let it live out the rest of its natural life, and that being hooked leaves no lasting impression on a trout's consciousness — if it has any consciousness, anyway.

My personal preference is to catch only those fish which I intend to keep. I am happy to return a trout that is below the size limit — or above the size limit, if one is trying to preserve the bigger fish. But I do not deliberately set out to hook a fish that is to be put back. Having caught my quota I would rather leave the fish to rise in peace. If trout are in need of protection, I would rather see that river or dam temporarily closed. Where only a limited kill is desirable, I would prefer to accomplish this by restricting the number of anglers and tightening up on the bag limit, as well as on the methods of fishing. Superb sport is provided by the traditional control over chalk stream fishing in the south of England. Each angler has his own beat in which he must stalk and catch individually selected trout, using either dry flies or nymphs offered to only a few fish in the course of a day. This approach is far removed from the practice of hooking as many trout as possible, even if they are to be returned.

Under the heading *Trout: Tagged or Meunière*, in *Piscator* No. 115, July 1985, appears a plea for consideration to the fisherman who wants to continue to catch his "one or two trout — and eat them". This plea is sandwiched between articles by Tom Sutcliffe and H.A. Biggs, both practitioners of catch-and-release, although not to the extent of sparing *every* trout they land. The no-kill philosophy is a virtue, but let there be moderation in all things — even in virtue.

IV DEVELOPMENT OF TROUT FISHING IN SOUTH AFRICA

12. Pioneers and personalities

Pioneers are fortunate. To them is given the opportunity to start something new; to launch a great endeavour. When we look back to well-known figures of the past perhaps we may feel that the opportunities they enjoyed are no longer open to us.

That is true enough. We no longer need to concern ourselves with making trout a part of the South African scene. Trout have become firmly established here, thanks to the pioneers. But that is not the end of the story. Each generation has new problems to face, new challenges to meet, new work to do. Most important of all is to make sure that future generations enjoy the sport of fly fishing. The mantle of the pioneers is on our shoulders.

If we want to go back to the very beginning of South African trout acclimatisation, perhaps we should start with Frank Buckland, the English naturalist, who showed that salmon eggs would retain their vitality after being kept frozen for 100 days. As a result of his experiments and his personal supervision of the packing, a consignment of salmon and brown trout eggs that left the United Kingdom in January 1864 was transported successfully across the equator, leading to the establishment of brown trout in Australia, Tasmania and New Zealand.

News of this success reached the Cape Colony and encouraged a group led by Charles Fairbridge, a member of the Legislative Assembly, to pursue the idea of bringing trout to South Africa. It was not until 1875, however, that any action was taken. In that year, A.R. Campbell Johnston brought a consignment of ova with him on the mailship. Part of this consignment was offloaded at Cape Town and the rest taken on to Durban. All the eggs were dead on arrival.

From 1882 onwards, John Clarke Parker, of Natal, became involved in attempts to acclimatise trout. He finally succeeded in March 1890, thus giving Natal the honour of having the first rivers stocked with trout in sub-Saharan Africa. I shall take up the story of the Natal pioneers later.

In the meantime, Lachlan MacLean, in charge of the Donald Currie steamship office in Cape Town, had arranged for a shipment of 20 000 brown trout ova in 1884. This was done on his own initiative and at his own expense. The eggs arrived in good condition and 17 000 hatched in troughs fed by a furrow from the upper Breede River, near Ceres. All but 60 of the alevins died, possibly of zinc poisoning from the metal lining of the troughs used for hatching the eggs. An unseasonal flood carried away 57 of the survivors, leaving three, which lived for six years and grew to about three pounds in a small pond. No breeding took place, so this initially promising enterprise came to nothing.

In 1890, the Cape government, possibly encouraged by Parker's success in Natal, agreed to provide funds for trout importation and acclimatisation. It was furthermore resolved to employ a professional fish culturist. This led to the arrival of South Africa's first full-time hatchery supervisor, Ernest Latour, who brought with him 60 000 ova from Guildford, Surrey. Latour seems to have been a somewhat pig-headed man. The local Fisheries Committee, consisting of L. MacLean, R. Trimen, W.G. Fairbridge and Anders Ohlsson, had made preparations for hatching the ova in the old building at Mr Ohlsson's brewery at Newlands. Things were not to the Frenchman's liking, however, so he took the eggs and dumped them in the Eerste River near Stellenbosch, where it seems certain they all perished in the heat of the Cape summer.

A few weeks later, another consignment arrived from England and these eggs were hatched with fair success. Fry were later transferred to the Eerste, Lourens, Berg and Breede Rivers. Further batches were successfully reared in 1893.

Owing to space limitations at the Newlands site, the government leased part of the farm "Jonkers Hoek" in the valley of the Eerste River 8 km from Stellenbosch, towards the end of 1893. The object was to develop a hatchery, but Latour did not take kindly to the proposal that he should live there. He supervised the construction of some ponds, but continued to base himself at Newlands, where he hatched imported ova early in 1894, before taking a post with the Frontier Acclimatisation Society and leaving the Western Province.

The Cape government was now committed to trout acclimatisation and spent about £7 000 over the next five or six years. It employed John L. Scott from the Solway Fisheries, Dumfries, to carry on Latour's work. Scott built the first permanent building at Jonkershoek Hatchery in 1894, a substantial masonry structure that stands to this day. In June 1895, he stripped the first South African brown trout ova from imported fish held in ponds at the hatchery.

The first success with rainbow trout followed an importation in 1897. The eggs came from Britain, where this American species had been bred in hatcheries for some years. Two years later, on 1 July 1899, Scott stripped the first rainbow ova. The previous season he had initiated a system of sending trout eggs by post to distant destinations in the subcontinent, thus making possible the early establishment of both brown and rainbow in all the main trout areas of South Africa and adjoining territories.

In the meantime, Latour (working for the Frontier Acclimatisation Society that had been formed in 1894) imported, hatched and distributed the first brown trout near King William's Town in 1895. The following year he departed for his native Europe and was succeeded by A.N. Stenning from England, another professional fish culturist. The amateur efforts of J.D. Ellis, of King William's Town, had nearly succeeded in February 1884. A consignment of 20 000 ova arrived in good condition and began hatching, only to perish for want of sufficient ice to keep the temperature down.

136

Jonkershoek Hatchery. Mike Scott stands in front of the hatching house built by his namesake in 1894.

Stenning remained in the service of the Frontier Acclimatisation Society until 1903 and succeeded in establishing breeding stock from which he produced ova for stocking rivers over a wide area. His place was taken by the man who became one of South Africa's best-known propagators of trout — F.G. Chaplin.

Chaplin took over the Pirie Hatchery in 1903 and stayed there until 1907. He then moved to the Jonkershoek Hatchery, where he remained as Curator until 1942, when Dr Douglas Hey was appointed Superintendent of Inland Fisheries, to head the newly created Department of Inland Fisheries. Chaplin went on living at the hatchery for the next 10 years, lending a hand when required. His dedication to the cause of fish culture made him known and respected throughout South Africa and beyond its borders. S.A. Hey, in his third report on a Fishery Survey of Inland Waters (1928), remarked that, at Jonkershoek, Chaplin had "put practically a life's work of ingenuity and skill into the establishment and it would be a difficult matter to compute the value of this work".

137

One of the most widely used of the devices he designed was the Chaplin hatching box. It was a wooden structure with a hinged lid, gauze ends and bottom, and floats along the sides. In use, the box was anchored near the bank of a stream that was to be stocked with trout. Eyed ova were then placed on the gauze bottom until they hatched. Whoever was in charge of the operation would remove dead ova each day to prevent infection spreading to healthy eggs.

Innumerable batches of eyed ova were sent by post to trout streams in remote areas, where a local farmer would set up his Chaplin box. Sometimes the young fish would be fed in the box after they had passed the alevin stage, but usually they were released as unfed fry. For stocking virgin waters, where conditions were favourable, results were often good. He also invented a portable hatching container made from a paraffin tin with holes punched in it.

When Chaplin left Pirie in 1907, his place was taken by W.S. Richardson, then Hon. Secretary of the Frontier Acclimatisation Society. An engineer by profession, Richardson became widely known for his work as Curator of the Pirie Hatchery, from which he retired at the end of September 1946, when the station was taken over from the Acclimatisation Society by the Cape Provincial Administration. His wife, who was considerably younger than her husband, joined wholeheartedly in the practical work and became Assistant Curator from 1946 to 1948.

The first provincially appointed Curator of the Pirie Hatchery was Lt.-Col. J. Geddes-Page, who faced an immense task in bringing the station up to an effective standard after a long period of inadequate funding by the Frontier Acclimatisation Society, which received a subsidy of only £500 per annum from the Administration.

In Natal, the early establishment of trout was due to John Parker's determination to enjoy fly fishing, the sport of his youth in the north of England. After the abortive importation in 1875 by Campbell Johnston, Parker began corresponding with authorities in the United Kingdom and, as a result, 10 000 brown trout eggs were sent to him from Howietown in Scotland in 1882. The ova travelled by rail from Durban to Pietermaritzburg and from there for 30 miles by horse omnibus to Shafton, in the Karkloof. Only 18 alevins showed signs of life on arrival and these were too weak to survive. A year later another 10 000 ova were imported but the whole lot died.

In 1889, Cecil Yonge, a member of the Legislative Council, was inspired by Parker's enthusiasm to seek government support for a further trial. A sum of £500 was voted and a committee appointed to carry out the work, consisting of J.C. Parker, C.A.S. Yonge and Lt.-Col. Henry Vaughan.

A site for hatching the eggs that were to arrive in March 1890 was selected in a south-facing, wooded gulley through which flowed a cool, spring-fed stream on the farm Boschfontein (appropriately named!), owned by Graham Hutchinson. To this day the brick piers on which Parker rested his hatching troughs stand in the shade of the indigenous trees that were growing there nearly a hundred years ago.

Boschfontein is on the main railway line between Lidgetton and Balgowan. The proximity of the railway was important, since not only was the ova-box to be delivered by train, but Parker needed ice to keep the eggs cool enough to prevent their death. The Natal Government Railways arranged a temporary platform at which the train stopped on 8 March 1890, to offload the eggs as well as 500 pounds of ice. Further consignments of ice were delivered each day until after the alevins had hatched.

The first baby trout appeared on 10 March, thanks to the cooling action of the ice which Parker packed into a box containing a coil of 50 feet of half-inch diameter pipe through which water was fed to the hatching troughs. Within two weeks, more than 2 000 fry were beginning to feed. Thus Parker's dream came true, six years after Ellis had so nearly succeeded at King William's Town and MacLean had come even closer to success in the Western Cape.

Boschfontein was more than 12 km from Parker's home, and therefore inconvenient for his supervision of the hatchery, but the site had been well chosen.

Within less than two months, the young trout were judged ready to go to their new homes. On 2 May the Mooi River was stocked with 500 fry, on 7 May the Bushman's River received 498 and on 10 May the final batch of 444 went into the Umgeni River. John Parker and Henry Vaughan travelled together to make the historic plantings. On the Mooi, the fry were introduced near Rosetta, below the good trout water, and they failed to become established. In both the Bushman's and the Umgeni the fish bred and populated the rivers.

In 1891 and 1892 further supplies of ova were imported amounting to a total of 200 000 brown trout, besides salmon and American brook trout eggs. A few hundred young salmon were released in a tributary of the Umkomaas but were never seen again. Only 29 of the brook trout lived to the fry stage and these disappeared after release. Of the brown trout some 4 500 were distributed in 14 different rivers and streams. Government subsidies were provided during these two years, amounting to over £1 000, out of £1 334 spent by the committee, but in 1893 no more funds were made available. However, private subscriptions were raised and 50 000 ova imported from which nearly 1 500 young fish were reared and planted in various streams, the most successful result being near Harding in what is now the Weza Forest Reserve on the slopes of the Ingeli mountain.

No further trout stocking was attempted until 1899, when a new phase began and hatching equipment was removed to Tetworth, Parker's own farm near Curry's Post.

It was some years after the original stocking of Natal streams before it became certain that trout were really acclimatised. In April 1892, Graham Hutchinson caught a trout in the Boschfontein stream 12 inches long and weighing 11 oz. Three months later John Parker took a brown trout of 2 lb 2 oz., 17 inches long, from the Umgeni. This fish was caught on a March Brown fly and was one of the original introduction, being two years and four months old. These were undoubtedly the first trout caught in Natal streams, and the next record is of two from the Bushman's in 1895 and early 1896, caught on mealie meal while fishing for scalies.

By 1899 there was no doubt about the survival of trout in Natal and the Minister of Agriculture, D.H. Winter, approached John Parker to renew stocking of rivers. The government of the Cape Colony had offered 10 000 trout ova free of charge from the Jonkershoek Hatchery. Parker offered his services free, provided actual out-of-pocket expenses were paid, and it was decided to build rearing facilities at Tetworth. Everything connected with the hatchery at Boschfontein was therefore transported to Parker's farm a few miles away. The 10 000 Cape ova were hatched out and 2 500 fry distributed. Of these, 400 were placed in the Mooi River at Game Pass and did very well, populating the whole of the upper and middle trout waters.

The following year, 1900, despite the war then in progress, stocking activities continued on a modest scale, using fry hatched from Cape ova. The most successful planting was 200 trout in the Little Mooi River at Kamberg.

In 1901 rainbow trout were tried for the first time, when 10 000 Cape ova were brought to Tetworth. Rainbow had been imported to Jonkershoek four years before and were being bred successfully there. Of the 1 700 fry reared, some were used to stock the Polela and the upper waters of Jackson's Stream on which the hatchery was situated. For years afterwards Jackson's gave good rainbow trout fishing, but these fish disappeared from the Polela after doing well for two years.

From 1902 to 1905 Parker hatched and distributed ova received from the Cape, and made unsuccessful attempts to produce his own eggs from breeders held at the hatchery. In 1906 and 1907 brown trout ova were imported from Scotland, but high water temperature caused total mortality. Moderate success attended Parker's activities in stripping and fertilising eggs from his own fish, but at the end of the 1907 season he ceased work at the hatchery, having reached the age of 60.

Mortalities in warm weather, as well as losses due to flooding of the ponds, caused Parker considerable frustration. He was particularly upset by the loss of the final consignment of imported brown trout ova. Nevertheless, the only major Natal rivers in which trout were not established by 1907 were the Ngwangwana and Umzimkulu.

In his final report Parker expressed the view that rainbow trout were "a snare and a delusion" although he admitted that they fought harder than brown trout. He also indicated that the Tetworth hatchery site on Jackson's Stream, at less than 1 300 m above sea-level, was not really suitable for trout propagation and that sites should be found at a higher altitude in the Drakensberg foothills.

Parker's contemporaries seem to have held him in high esteem. On 10 February 1904, he was presented with a silver dinner service and gold watch by the Hon. G.M. Sutton, Prime Minister of Natal, whose son, Cherrington, was to become Natal's second Inland Fisheries Officer 32 years later. After his death a memorial sundial was erected at the Trout Bungalow, overlooking the Mooi River.

The real reward for all Parker's hard work came from fishing the rivers he had stocked. A particular favourite of his was the swift, clear Loteni, where he took many a good trout on Willie Root's farm Oorpoort (now part of Loteni Nature Reserve). Finally, there came a day in March 1925, one of those beautiful autumn days on which the valley is at its finest, when age and infirmity were weighing heavily upon him. Although he still cast beautifully, he could no longer see what he was doing. After repeatedly hooking the tall tambookie grass on the river bank, he gave up, saying he would come back in the spring, when the grass was short. But a few weeks later, on 29 April 1925, John Clarke Parker was dead.

In view of the work he put in over a period of 30 years in the interests of trout acclimatisation, one might assume that Parker was a man of considerable private means. He received only enough to cover some of his actual out-of-pocket expenses, without any salary from the government. Yet the total value of his moveable assets, when realised after his death, was £602-7-6, including a canteen of silver (presumably the one presented to him in recognition of his services) valued at £20.

Hatcheries in Natal received no serious attention for more than 40 years after Parker ceased operations. Lionel Day, who became the first Inland Fisheries Officer in April 1926, rightly concentrated on other aspects of trout management.

Local enthusiasts persuaded municipal authorities to set up small hatcheries at Henley, near Pietermaritzburg, and at Estcourt, but in view of Parker's experiences it was only to be expected that results would be disappointing. A small station was started at Royal Natal National Park, but it was soon abandoned.

Sundial erected in memory of John Clarke Parker, Trout Pioneer, at the Trout Bungalow.

Operations were, for a time, resumed at Parker's old hatchery on Tetworth, now owned by Felix Deane, who undertook to look after the rearing of trout on behalf of the Lions River District River Conservancy. In 1929, both brown and rainbow ova from the Cape were successfully hatched, but a row developed in May 1930 when it was discovered that no trout remained in the ponds. In response to a query from the Fisheries Board, which had made a grant from provincial funds, Deane submitted a highly illuminating report on what had taken place. First, explained Deane, a flood had brought down rubbish which had clogged the outlet screens; "consequently the screens had to bear the weight of water in the ponds, which they could not withstand, so they broke". Many of the young fish had escaped through the unscreened outlets. The screens had holes that "were too small and the material quite unsuitable for the purpose". Deane had not bought the screens; "they were sent to me to put in".

Having restored the situation as best he could, Deane then had to face a further disaster. A storm washed away the sod and earth wall from the top of the dam and cut off the water from the stock ponds. He decided that some of the fish must be released immediately, so, "as members of the conservancy seemed to favour rainbow trout, I decided to release the brown to save them and concentrate on keeping the rainbow intact. After letting the brown go, storms were a continuous source of trouble and I had a very difficult week indeed in keeping the rainbow trout continually supplied with water. Eventually on March 14th I had no alternative but to let them go or they would have died.

"I would point out that had I got the empty bags promised me the dam would not have given any trouble. I used every grain bag, fertilizer bag, sugar and flour pocket I had, but all these were only half enough."

The objective tone of a man who must have felt intense frustration continued to the end: "I hope I have covered all the particulars you need. I shall be pleased to give any further details. Signed Felix Deane."

Poor results from hatcheries that were badly sited, ill-equipped and staffed by part-time supervisors, vindicated Lionel Day's decision to concentrate on other methods of trout management. He wrote in 1933 that he regarded artificial breeding as unnecessary where trout were already established (he was referring to rivers: Merthley Lake at Greytown was at that time the only stillwater fishery for trout in Natal).

At the end of 1935, Day submitted a report on the inland waters of the Natal province, in which he described transportation of wild-bred trout from overstocked rivers as "cheaper, quicker, more economical, and certainly more satisfactory . . . than stocking streams by planting trout fry hatched from ova obtained from the Cape". He attached a schedule listing the numbers of trout transported from overstocked rivers to other waters (including Merthley Lake) between 1926 and 1935. The total was 2 430 brown trout and 18 025 rainbows. These fish were caught by parties of fly fishermen on overstocked sections of river.

In order to carry the trout that had been caught, Day designed special metal tanks, each with an inner liner of perforated zinc. This inner liner could be removed and placed in running water. As trout were caught by the fly-fishing party they would be put into the liner, until the time came to leave, when the whole thing, fish and all, would be inserted into a tank without any handling.

Day actively organised the stocking of Natal waters with both trout and bass through the various river conservancies and Honorary Fisheries Officers. Membership of conservancies was confined to riparian owners, while the great majority of Honorary Officers also resided in the country. A few townsmen bought licences and enjoyed their visits to the trout rivers, but it was the landowners who did the work. As long as he had the farmer's permission, all a townsman needed was a licence. Incidentally, the willingness of South Africans to put up with red tape seems to extend back for more than half a century. To obtain a licence in 1930, Natal anglers were required to complete an application, duly signed in triplicate, before the document could be issued.

Lionel Day was an ex-schoolmaster who seems to have become accepted by the farming community despite his somewhat pompous and dogmatic manner, which irritated some of those with whom he came in contact. To his credit, he was prepared to learn from people with practical experience.

His successor as Inland Fisheries Officer was Cherrington Sutton, who took over the post in September 1936. Sutton was a farmer in the Howick district of the Natal midlands, a keen and competent angler, despite the disability resulting from the loss of his right hand early in life. His wife, Helen, shared his interest in fishing as well as his public-spiritedness. Cherrington's father was Sir George Sutton, one-time Prime Minister of the Colony, and his son, Bill, has also made a career in politics. Cherrington, or Cherry as he was widely known, made the development of inland fisheries the objective to which he devoted 10 years of his life. The time and energy which he spent in the interests of angling were totally unrelated to the £300, plus the use of an official vehicle, which he received each year from the Provincial Administration. His wife received no recompense whatsoever for all the typing, clerical work and general assistance that she tackled with unfailing good humour.

Sutton, being a farmer himself, developed an excellent liaison with the farming community. He realised that farmers, to use his own words, "hate like poison" anything to do with writing. He relied more on direct contact with Honorary Officers and river conservancy members than on written reports.

A question which had been discussed over the years was how to ensure a reasonable degree of public access to the trout streams of Natal. At the insistence of two members of the Natal Fisheries Board, A.E. Carlisle and H.L. Crockett, a formal meeting took place on 16 November 1932 to consider the following suggestions: "(a) To declare all perennial streams or rivers to be public rivers for the purpose of fishing; (b) To give the Government the right to expropriate rivers or sections thereof that have been stocked from public moneys." Similar suggestions have been made since that time, always with the same result: uproar on the part of landowners.

Sutton realised that any attempt to remove the right of an owner to control access to his land was doomed to failure. Instead, he set out to persuade farmers to lease their "fishing rights" to the Provincial Administration, which would then offer angling to members of the public, on payment of a fee. "Fishing rights" meant, in practice, permission to enter a property for the purpose of angling. In contrast to the United Kingdom, where fishing and shooting rights are a legal entity distinct from ownership of the land, South African law makes no provision for such rights. Our law merely makes it an offence to fish without the owner's permission.

Sutton concentrated attention on the Underberg-Himeville district, where he negotiated agreements with riparian owners on the Ngwangwana, Umzimkulu, Polela and Umkomaas rivers. He persuaded the Provincial Executive Committee to appoint the first full-time Fisheries Inspector, Leslie Acutt, part of whose duties would be to control the use of the leased waters.

Thus, when Cherrington Sutton handed over the post of Inland Fisheries Officer (now to become a full-time position) in 1946, he had provided a sound basis for a co-operative system whereby anglers would enjoy the privilege of fishing waters in private ownership, while farmers would receive not only a small amount of cash but active assistance with management. The system has changed over the years, with privately run clubs taking over the role originally assumed by Cherry Sutton. Had he not acted as he did, using a small amount of taxpayers' money, there seems little doubt that the good relationship that exists today between landowners and fishermen might not have become established. His good work paved the way for mutual trust to develop between all concerned.

Sutton was the last of the three Natal pioneers to whom modern fly fishers look back in gratitude. Parker, Day and Sutton each received subsidisation from government sources, but they remained amateurs, in the best sense, doing a job for the love of it.

In the Cape, Arthur Cecil Harrison stands out as South Africa's most remarkable personality in the field of freshwater fishing. He, too, was an amateur, without any university training. Yet he made a greater contribution to our knowledge of fisheries biology and management, in relation to angling, than any professional scientist. His studies of indigenous fish and stream insects provided a base for future workers.

Harrison held the posts of Provincial Inland Fisheries Officer, Secretary to the Provincial Advisory Committee for Nature Conservation and Secretary to the Cape Piscatorial Society, while continuing to run the typewriter servicing business that was his main source of livelihood. He was a founder member and the main driving force in the Cape Piscatorial Society from its inception in 1931 until shortly before his death in 1980. Under his editorship, the society's journal *Piscator* rose to a standard unique in South Africa. To refer to him as Editor is, in fact, a travesty of the truth: a large proportion of the most authoritative articles were written by A.C.H., as he was known to the wide circle of his admirers. Innumerable reports, memoranda and correspondence with fishery scientists all over the world stand to his credit. His knowledge of the rivers and reservoirs of the Western and Eastern Cape, their history and management, was encyclopaedic.

In 1960, when the Underberg-Himeville Conservancy and Fishing Club sought the services of a leader in the field of trout management to join the staff of the Natal Parks Board in a survey of the rivers in that district, the choice fell naturally on A.C.H.. Tributes to him have appeared in Nos. 106 and 107 of *Piscator*, as well as elsewhere, but his own publications stand as the memorial which best indicates

Top, left to right: Claude Ledward, Leslie Acutt, Harry Towner Coston.

Above: A.C. Harrison.

Left: Frank Braun in the days when hunting still ranked higher than fishing.

145

the contribution he made. He richly deserved the degree of Master of Science, conferred on him by the University of Cape Town.

As well as immense knowledge and untiring industry, A.C.H. possessed the ability to project the powerful force of his personality in a manner that made him not merely respected, but cherished as a friend by all who knew him. His sense of humour never failed, whether he was gently deflating some ill-informed theorist or employing a down-to-earth metaphor. John Geddes-Page, Director of the Natal Parks Board and formerly Curator of the Jonkershoek Hatchery, tells how A.C.H. roused him early one morning in 1949. They were on a fishery survey trip and had agreed to be up at daybreak. John was still asleep when a deep voice rang out: "Come on, the dawn bird has farted!"

It was impossible to shake A.C.H.'s composure, although he reacted decisively to anything foolish or slipshod — but always with a twinkle in his straight blue-grey eyes. Inessentials concerned him not at all. He never learned to drive a car, taking the train to work each morning and letting others transport him when a journey by road was required.

A.C.H. was actively involved with inland fisheries for more than half a century, from the early 1920s to the late 1970s. The fact that a man of his calibre was happy to devote so much of his life to the interests of anglers should be enough to convince one that fishing is important, after all. And so it is, if one views it, as did A.C.H., in the broad context of environmental conservation — the wise use of our natural resources.

In the Transvaal, among those who established trout in the streams of the eastern Highveld the best-known pioneer was Frank Charles Braun, a German immigrant from the Black Forest who was apprenticed to a watchmaker in Dublin, where he took to trout fishing, and finally settled in Lydenburg in 1908 at the age of 32. There he opened a jeweller's shop and made hunting his main recreation until H.J. Gurr, the Postmaster at Lydenburg, began stocking the local streams with trout in 1915.

Braun, together with Morgan and J.F. Huggard (the local Inspector of Roads), had excellent fishing in the Potspruit in 1923. This inspired him to start introducing trout into unstocked rivers himself. For £2 he bought 1 000 eggs from the Jonkershoek Hatchery and proudly liberated 680 trout fry a few weeks later. The following year Braun became Hon. Secretary of the newly constituted Lydenburg Trout Protection and Angling Society. Annual subscriptions and donations enabled him to purchase 600 000 ova during the next 24 years. For the care of the ova, he made himself personally responsible. In his third report on the Fisheries Survey of Inland Waters (1928), S.A. Hey mentions that he urged the Town Council of Lydenburg to provide a small shelter in which to house a large hatching trough to obviate the need for the floating Chaplin hatching boxes that Braun looked after.

Hey wrote: "This year the secretary of your society has, I notice, handled 22 000 eggs in four boxes. The sites chosen . . . are anything but convenient for attending to the contents of the boxes. Lying on one's stomach on the damp banks of a water-furrow for a couple of hours each day, attending to trout ova, can hardly be described as a healthy pastime."

Not only was Braun unconcerned about the inconvenience of looking after ova, he was prepared to tramp far and wide over the roughest country to take young fish to the more remote streams. Trout acclimatisation and fishing replaced hunting as his spare-time occupation. He was, indeed, ready to close his shop at any time if his beloved trout required attention or if some visitor sought guidance to the angling waters he knew so well.

Hey remarked in 1928 that the Cape Provincial Administration was spending over £1 000 per annum on freshwater fish culture and Natal approximately £500, and he hoped that the Transvaal Administration would also contribute towards the stocking of the streams under its control. Twenty years later the Transvaal Nature Conservation Division was established and the Provincial Fisheries Institute developed under the able guidance of S.S. du Plessis.

In the meantime, however, Braun carried on indefatigably. He spent £125 of his own money on materials for a small hatchery in 1936 and took the keenest interest in all matters affecting conservation. Worried about denudation of catchments, he bought seeds of trees which he encouraged school children to plant. He campaigned against bad farming practices, such as autumn burning and overgrazing.

F. C. Braun's philosophy is summed up in his words to Lt.-Col. Henry Birch-Reynardson in 1933: "Yes, up here they think I am mad — a *dumkopf*. But I say to them, well you have your tennis and your billiards — they are your hobbies. But my sport is to make things grow — my hobby is Life."

13. Official organisations

Before Union, in 1910, trout acclimatisation had proved successful in both the Cape and Natal, as well as in some parts of the Transvaal. Financial support was made available, on a small scale, for trout propagation in Natal, but only to cover costs incurred by private individuals. The Cape colonial government employed a professional fish culturist from 1892 onwards and developed the hatchery at Jonkershoek, while subsidising the Frontier Acclimatisation Society's Pirie Hatchery. In the Transvaal, private enterprise was solely responsible for trout stocking.

After Union, inland fisheries remained a regional responsibility under the control of the respective provincial councils. It is somewhat curious, therefore, that a debate took place in the House of Assembly in 1925 on the question of the possibility of fish production in the inland waters of the Union. Clearly, the provinces had not yet developed the jealousy apparent in later years at any infringement of their statutory rights.

Following the debate in Parliament, a Fisheries Survey Committee was set up under H. Warington Smyth, Secretary for Mines and Industries. It was decided to carry out a general survey of all the inland waters of the Union and the man chosen for the job was S.A. Hey, a civil servant in the Department of Posts and Telegraphs, who was seconded for the duration of the survey to the Department of Mines and Industries. Hey tackled the job with great energy and enthusiasm, although he found that his subsistence allowance was so niggardly as to leave him heavily out of pocket. However, as only Parliament could increase the laid-down rate, and Parliament was otherwise engaged, nothing could be done to improve matters. With great conscientiousness Hey went ahead and completed his assignment, writing a lengthy three-part report on the results of his field-work. He included many useful comments, although his terms of reference seem to have been extremely vague.

In submitting the third part of Hey's report to the Minister of Mines and Industries, in 1928, the Chairman of the Fisheries Survey Committee commended the author and mentioned that "Mr Hey has been and still is inundated with correspondence from interested persons requesting expert advice and information." The Chairman went on to suggest that the survey should be followed up by practical steps towards further development of inland fisheries on a national scale. He continued: "It is here that one is faced with the delicate question of possible overlapping with the Provincial Government functions, for fish preservation is one of the subjects in regard to which, by the South Africa Act, the Provincial Councils may make Ordinances."

The whole concept of a Fisheries Survey Committee reporting to a central government department on matters of regional concern was dubious. It seems to have been one of those hares chased up by politicians wanting to impress their constituents. The committee could never have become more than a body with some responsibility but no authority.

Fortunately, the Hey report was written by a practical angler and a man of common sense, so something useful resulted, at virtually no cost to the taxpayer. Involvement by politicians in setting up investigative committees does not always leave the public exchequer unscathed, as anyone in public life could confirm.

Natal was the first province to have any identifiable official body dealing with fisheries matters. In 1912 the Natal Fisheries Board was functioning for the control of coastal fishing, which had been reserved by Natal as a provincial responsibility in contrast to the position in the Cape. Trout regulations had been promulgated before Union in terms of Law 21 of 1884.

By 1914, W. Dick, Secretary to the board, was co-ordinating the activities of the Natal Fisheries Department, concerned with both coastal and, to some extent, inland fishing. Dick was given the title of Honorary Principal Fisheries Officer. In 1916, Inland Fisheries became an accepted part of the responsibilities of the Principal Fisheries Officer. That year saw the first comprehensive Provincial Fisheries Ordinance. In 1919 new regulations appeared restricting methods for the capture of trout to artificial fly only, while the limit permitted to a licensed angler was 20 trout per day.

H.W. Bell-Marley was now Principal Fisheries Officer, with 37 Honorary Fisheries Officers under him — 31 on the coast and six inland (on trout waters). The most active Honorary Officer appeared to be L.A. Day, who submitted a lengthy report in his capacity as Hon. Secretary of the Estcourt Trout Acclimatisation Society.

The year 1926 saw the creation of the post of Inland Fisheries Officer, with L.A. Day as its first incumbent. He received an honorarium of £240 per annum, while the salary of the Principal Fisheries Officer was £500 per annum. Other items of expenditure budgeted for the Inland Fisheries Department were £36 for the Curator of the Estcourt trout hatchery and £50 for expenses.

The post of Inland Fisheries Officer was made a full-time salaried position in 1946, when H.E. Towner Coston took over from Cherrington Sutton. By this time Inland Fisheries had been separated from Coastal Fisheries, each with an advisory board.

In December 1947, the newly formed Natal Parks, Game and Fish Preservation Board assumed responsibility for the fields covered by the Inland Fisheries Board, the Coastal Fisheries Board, the Zululand Reserves Board and the Drakensberg Reserves Board. Whereas these four bodies had been merely advisory, and their staffs had been provincial servants, the new board was an autonomous statutory body controlled by independent men of standing, appointed by the Provincial Executive Committee.

The Natal Parks Board, as it is commonly designated, started off as an essentially field-based organisation, each section having grown to meet the practical needs of a particular aspect of nature conservation. This reality of being rooted in the traditional way of life of Natal has resulted in a balance and public acceptance that have done much for the success of the organisation. There has been no distortion of values or departure from close liaison with those amateurs who have always played such an important role in looking after our natural resources.

The Cape Inland Fisheries Department dates back to 1938, when A.C. Harrison was appointed Inland Fisheries Advisory Officer. He continued in part-time service with the Provincial Administration for the next 20 years. In 1942 Dr Douglas Hey was appointed to succeed Chaplin as Curator of Jonkershoek Hatchery. Having graduated with a B.Sc. degree from Rhodes University, Hey had been appointed Assistant Curator in 1937. He embarked on scientific studies of the fertility of trout ova and was awarded M.Sc. and D.Sc. degrees by the University of Stellenbosch. His drive, ambition and organising ability resulted in a rapid expansion of the activities at Jonkershoek. Two M.Sc. graduates were employed to tackle research problems. One of these was S.S. du Plessis, a shy but extremely talented young man who, in 1947, moved to the Transvaal where he became Senior Professional Officer, responsible for the development of the Provincial Fisheries Institute at Lydenburg.

When the Pirie Hatchery at King William's Town became a provincial responsibility, under the curatorship of Lt.-Col. John Geddes-Page, Hey's designation became Superintendent of Inland Fisheries and, in 1947, he was made Director. In 1948, Geddes-Page's son, John Trevor Geddes-Page, was appointed Curator at Jonkershoek, where he remained until 1954, when he was offered the post of Inland Fisheries Officer with the Natal Parks Board.

As he developed his Department, Douglas Hey became widely recognised as an expert in the field of inland fisheries. He was particularly keen on the concept of fish for food from reservoirs and farm dams. The Inland Fisheries Department Report No. 7 for 1950 includes a policy statement setting out the following admirable principles: "The primary object is to develop all inland waters to their maximum productive capacity, selecting the most suitable species of fish from the viewpoints of table and sporting qualities. In so doing, there should be a nice balance between the interests of economic fisheries, sport fishing and the natural fauna . . . The Department is well aware of its obligations to provide well-stocked waters for resident anglers and the attraction of visitors. Care should be taken to preserve the indigenous fish fauna in certain areas for scientific and educational purposes."

In 1953, Douglas Hey became Director of Nature Conservation, as additional responsibilities were added to his Department, which is now known as the Department of Nature and Environmental Conservation. The present staff of the Department includes scientific specialists with a strong interest in the indigenous fish fauna of the Cape. Propagation of exotic species has been scaled down at Jonkershoek Hatchery, while the Pirie Hatchery has become the responsibility of the government of Ciskei.

With a very much reduced involvement in trout fishing, the Cape Department of Nature and Environmental Conservation has, in 1986, moved far from the position — formerly held by the original Inland Fisheries Department — of leadership in matters of interest to anglers in South Africa. There are good reasons for this change in attitude. Fishermen cannot expect taxpayers' money to be spent unproductively. Operations at the Jonkershoek Hatchery were, for years, grossly uneconomic and there is little doubt that, in most of the Cape waters where regular restocking with trout has been undertaken, the cost of each fish caught has been unreasonably high.

On the other hand, any policy change that is thought to be contrary to their interests is resented by anglers. A storm of protest arose in 1985 when the Department of Nature and Environmental Conservation drew up amendments to the laws governing inland fisheries. An important innovation was the removal of the traditional protection for trout. This went further than anglers had expected and seemed to upset the balance between the interests of sportsmen and those of conservation of the natural fauna, as envisaged in Dr Hey's statement in 1950.

A sensible compromise was indicated by the following statement, made by C.M. Gaigher in 1973 (*Piscator* No. 88): "Nature Conservation, as applied to inland waters, has traditionally aimed at the protection, management and encouragement of sport fishing . . . which has been based on exotic species. In recent times, however, on the grounds of ethics, the concept of Nature Conservation has been extended to include the less obvious species which are endangered. Trout and bass, and the excellent angling they have produced, have given very many people an added interest and involvement with their environment. If, however, one claims to be dedicated to Nature Conservation, one is committed to the conservation, where possible, of even those lesser species." A total suspension of all further stockings of trout in certain areas therefore seemed called for, together with the creation of sanctuaries for isolated populations of indigenous fish.

With the necessity to reduce inessential expenditure, it probably seemed logical to decide, in 1985, to cut down on trout propagation. Any reasonable angler would, as a taxpayer, appreciate the need for economy. Removal of statutory protection for trout, on the other hand, while symbolising the feeling among academic ecologists that exotic fish deserved no preference over those that were indigenous, gave anglers the impression that their sport was being threatened. There are times when a rigidly scientific approach might be tempered by an appreciation of public attitudes. In 1986, an unfortunate rift — perhaps largely due to misunderstanding — was apparent between anglers and conservation officials in the Cape.

This does not apply to Natal or to the Transvaal, despite the imposition of economies in hatchery operations, as well as in other aspects of the work of the bodies concerned. Some reassessment of priorities was inevitable in view of the hyperexponential rate at which the budgets of provincial nature conservation authorities increased for three decades after 1950. Expenditure on hatchery services, including trout production, went up at a rate that could not be sustained.

Involvement in trout stocking began comparatively late in the Transvaal. In 1947, S.S. du Plessis (who received a D.Sc. from the University of Pretoria in 1969) was engaged by the Transvaal Provincial Administration to develop an Inland Fisheries service. He found himself in the happy position of being able to plan and construct the largest station for trout propagation in Africa.

For years, fly fishermen had relied on the efforts of amateurs, such as F.C. Braun, to look after their interests. When the Administration finally decided to provide funds for the development of trout angling, it was done on a lavish scale. Applying himself with extreme diligence, Dup, as he is known to his friends, worked long hours, personally supervising every aspect of the construction, to create the Provincial Fisheries Institute at Lydenburg. When the trout fingerlings for which he had cared grew into active young fish, Dup took pride in loading them into tanks and personally transporting them to waters where anglers would enjoy catching them. The love he developed for the verdant Eastern Transvaal, so different from his native Oudtshoorn, shines in the words he wrote years later on the conservation needs of the Steenkampsberg.

After moving to Pretoria to take over as Assistant Director and then Director of the Transvaal Nature Conservation Division, Du Plessis retained his interest in matters piscatorial. When the Lydenburg Hatchery was converted largely to the culture of fish other than trout, he obtained authorisation for a new production unit at De Kuilen, a large and meticulously planned station a few kilometres from Lydenburg. Determined to see that everything was correctly done, Du Plessis was outraged when a badly built weir collapsed. To avoid the aspersion which ruined masonry might cast on the efficiency of his Division, he arranged to have the ruins blown to smithereens with dynamite!

The sparkling waters of the Blyde River, near Pilgrim's Rest.

700 g rainbow from the Umzimkulu

brown trout and a rainbow from a Natal dam; largest 1,4 kg

ch Leven, Scotland; a typical brown trout

Peter and Almarie Ferraz: left city life for this scene in the country

Underberg Hatchery, Natal: Jake Alletson feeds trout in a pond. Note floating shelters.

Official trout management reached a peak of activity at the enthusiastic hands of Richard Pott, who held the post of Senior Professional Officer at Lydenburg. On 5 May 1972, he wrote a letter (published in *Piscator* No. 84) explaining the Division's policy of stocking public angling waters, on the grounds that "we have to obtain new recruits in the art of fly fishing, and furthermore consider it our duty to try and reconcile man with his environment and give him a share in it. What industrialist, however hardened, would be prepared to see even 1 km of trout stream polluted, if he himself had felt the tug of a trout?"

Pott established an excellent liaison with anglers, especially those in organised angling clubs. At Dullstroom Dam, and on the Sabie and Blyde Rivers, rearing ponds were built to grow fingerlings out to catchable size before release. Young trout were made available free of charge to waters where the public had access. Privately owned fisheries had to pay for their fish.

Later on, with the development of commercial trout farms, pressure was put by the South African Trout Farmers Association on the Transvaal provincial authorities to cease the practice of selling hatchery-reared trout in competition with private producers. Of recent years, the Nature Conservation Division has confined its sales to ova, of which the De Kuilen Hatchery is capable of producing several million annually. One of the trout farms that is supplying trout to angling waters is owned by Mondi Forests, to whose employ Richard Pott transferred from Nature Conservation. Owing to the need to cut down on running costs, angling clubs have been receiving less liberal supplies of trout from the provincial authorities, but the policy of stocking public waters remains in force.

The Natal Parks Board has, from its inception, remained sympathetic to the needs of fly fishers. Its first Inland Fisheries Officer, H.E. Towner Coston, whom the board took over from the Provincial Administration, had arranged for the setting up of three small trout-rearing stations. Only one, however, produced any worthwhile results. This was at a site made available by Michael McDougall, who owned the farm Tretower on the Umzimkulu River 10 km from Underberg.

Leslie Acutt, who had been appointed Fisheries Inspector of Underberg in 1946, was given the task of building a small hatching house and two circular rearing ponds, which he used to good effect to produce trout for stocking dams. The first landowner to build a sizeable dam was R.I.P. Vaughan, in 1938. For the first few years he stocked this by catching small trout in the river. Development of the Underberg Hatchery enabled adequate numbers of fish to be introduced to the man-made lakes that began to proliferate from 1948 onwards. At first, the Natal Parks Board allocated young trout free of charge to anyone who had a water which was considered likely to provide good fishing. A market-related charge has now been made for fish for private dams, with a reduction of 25 per cent for recognised clubs.

As well as running the hatchery and patrolling the rivers (in those days great store was set on catching poachers), Acutt occupied an office each morning for the allocation of beats on the rivers that were available for public fishing through the lease agreements instituted by Cherrington Sutton. The office was a rondavel, in the grounds of the Underberg Hotel, now used for the same purpose by the Underberg-Himeville Trout Fishing Club, which was formed in 1954.

From the date of my appointment as the Natal Parks Board's Fisheries Research Officer on 1 February 1950, I was involved in trout management and hatchery development, as well as research on trout, bass and indigenous fish. W.L. Chiazzari took over as Inland Fisheries Officer from Towner Coston, to be followed, in May 1954, by John T. Geddes-Page, whose reputation for hard work and organising ability commended him to Colonel Jack Vincent, who had been the board's Chief Executive Officer from December 1948. In 1963, Geddes-Page became Director.

One of the first decisive actions which Geddes-Page took was to sort out the relationship between the board and the Underberg-Himeville Trout Fishing Club. With the formation of the club, the need fell away for a board officer to be involved in arranging fishing for visiting anglers. For a time, both the board and the club were leasing fishing from riparian owners. By mutual agreement the club took over this responsibility.

A second trout hatchery was established at Royal Natal National Park, and later a third station was built at Kamberg Nature Reserve, where the Mooi River provides an assured supply of at least 250 litres per second, in contrast to the unreliable supplies at Underberg and Royal Natal National Park. Both Jonkershoek and Pirie Hatcheries suffer from insufficient water in times of drought.

Natal Parks Board policy towards inland fisheries has remained consistent over the years, with the emphasis on encouraging recreational angling, while collaborating with the commercial trout farmers who have become established in recent years.

Unlike the Cape Department of Nature and Environmental Conservation, which has been careful to allow no accommodation for the public in the reserves it controls, the Natal Parks Board has made provision for recreational facilities in many areas. Trout fishing is an attraction in Giant's Castle Game Reserve, Royal Natal National Park, Kamberg Nature Reserve, Loteni Nature Reserve, Vergelegen Nature Reserve and Coleford Nature Reserve, while Himeville Nature Reserve was acquired for the purpose of building two dams especially for public fishing. The Transvaal has no trout in its provincial nature reserves, but public waters are available under the control of other authorities.

Although economies in expenditure on hatchery operations have become essential, the importance of supplying trout for angling, to supplement those available from private sources, continues to be recognised by the Natal Parks Board. On 1 January 1986, a new administrative arrangement was instituted whereby Charles Wright, who has had long experience of fisheries management, would undertake overall direction with Rob Karssing as Hatchery Supervisor at Kamberg Hatchery. D.J. Alletson, known as Jake to his many angling acquaintances, will continue to provide technical guidance and liaison with trout fishermen.

Until the creation of Sterkfontein Dam, the Orange Free State had negligible potential for trout fishing. Fortunately the Director of Nature Conservation in that province, Pieter le Roux, began his career as a fisheries biologist, so the development of this fine water is in good hands.

It is interesting that, until the retirement of Douglas Hey, all four directors of Nature Conservation in South Africa were involved in inland fisheries in the early years of their careers.

With the creation of the KwaZulu administration, its Bureau of Natural Resources became responsible for considerable stretches of Natal trout streams. The KwaZulu government service makes permits available for anglers to fish, but otherwise no control is exercised.

Many headwater streams in the Cape, Natal and the Transvaal are on land controlled by the Directorate of Forestry, Department of Environment Affairs. This Department may well assume greater prominence in the field of nature conservation with the abolition of the Provincial Councils.

For the trout fisherman it is discouraging if those responsible for Departmental policy regard any exotic organism as out of place in an area set aside for nature conservation. Certain plants or animals are, indeed, a danger to the natural flora and fauna, but trout are as much a part of South Africa as the oak trees of Stellenbosch — not to be planted in wilderness areas where they do not already occur, but to be valued where they are established.

14. Clubs and associations

Fishing clubs generally include in their constitution some sort of commitment to conservation, but the extent to which action has been taken to make that commitment a reality varies enormously.

Most members of clubs outside trout areas are interested mainly in social outings or competitive events. There is little incentive for them to become involved in activities that are not directly related to the business of catching fish. In trout areas, however, fishery management receives more attention. The various societies, conservancies, clubs and associations connected with fly fishing have played a vital part in trout acclimatisation and management, as well as in conservation of the habitat.

The largest and best known of these organisations is the Cape Piscatorial Society, whose inaugural meeting was held on 20 November 1931. At that meeting, A.C. Harrison was asked to serve as Secretary. The annual general meeting in 1979 confirmed that he should continue as Secretary although he was then in his ninetieth year. A 48-year tenure of the secretaryship of any society is remarkable.

The lineage of the Cape Piscatorial Society (CPS) goes back to 1902, when the Western Districts Game and Trout Protection Association was constituted. This body was absorbed by the CPS in 1937.

Some of the objectives accepted by the inaugural meeting were:
"• To assist members in obtaining freshwater fishing.
• To encourage and extend the culture and protection of trout and other desirable freshwater fish in the Cape.
• To encourage the study of freshwater biology in its application to fish culture and protection.
• To foster a public demand for the purity of rivers and inland waters, and enquiry into cases of pollution and the means for their suppression."

Progress in all these fields was due to the unflagging energy of A.C. Harrison, whose secretarial duties were for many years entirely honorary, although he did eventually receive a modest stipend. Not only did he work for the society; he also provided for the transaction of the society's business from his own premises in St George's House, Cape Town. These premises consisted of the room from which he ran his typewriter agency and it is amusing to note his statement in 1947 that the room "though central, is too small and congested for the convenience of all concerned."

In fact it was an incredible junkhouse, from which A.C.H. would rescue errant typewriter nuts by means of a magnetised, three-foot steel ruler.

The society's first objective, to obtain fishing for its members, was circumscribed by the fact that few private landowners controlled waters of angling importance within reach of Cape Town. In the early years of the existence of the CPS, the Eerste River gave excellent sport and arrangements were concluded for access to a number of farms. A few other privately owned sections of river became available, but the main fishing areas were, and still are, owned by the municipalities of Cape Town and Ceres or by the Department of Forestry. Nevertheless, members of the CPS have enjoyed access to some productive waters, as the fishing returns in their magazine *Piscator* clearly show. Their best stretch of river is the Molenaars fishery in Du Toit's Kloof, while the Oostenberg section of the upper Witte River, Bain's Kloof, offers brown trout fishing. This is now a "no-kill" fishery where anglers are expected to return all the trout they catch.

The Dwars River at Ceres has given excellent fishing at times, while a number of Forestry areas, with river fishing, are available on permit (at a reduced rate for CPS members).

Still waters that are available through the society include the Steenbras and Wemmershoek reservoirs, the two Paarl Mountain reservoirs and Lakenvlei Dam in the Ceres district.

The second objective of the society, to extend the culture of trout and other desirable fish, was pursued actively over a long period.

The third and fourth objectives, to encourage scientific studies and to stimulate action against river pollution, led to the gathering of much information, although practical results have not been easy to achieve.

An important function of the Cape Piscatorial Society is to provide an information centre and focus for its members, of which there are more than a thousand, as well as for visitors. Non-members are welcome to visit the spacious club rooms in Westminster House, 122 Longmarket Street, Cape Town, where tickets are issued for available waters. The extensive library and archives form a unique store-house of South African angling records. *Piscator*, under the competent editorship of C. Ross-Munro, retains its high standard.

In the Eastern Province of the Cape, the Frontier Acclimatisation Society was established in June 1894. It is the oldest association still operating in South Africa and has played an important part in stocking the trout waters of the King William's Town and adjoining areas. The Pirie Hatchery, developed and operated at the expense of the society with the assistance of a provincial subsidy, remained under its control until 1946, when it passed to the Inland Fisheries Department. In 1983, the hatchery was taken over by the government of Ciskei.

Recently, the Frontier Acclimatisation Society has operated as a fishing club, with facilities for its members on the Maden and Rooikrantz Dams on the upper Buffalo River, below Pirie Hatchery. The 10-hectare Maden Dam has been in existence for many years, while the larger, 85-hectare Rooikrantz Dam is well known for the large rainbows — up to 3,2 kg — which it produces.

The Stutterheim Angling Club offers its members fishing on the most productive trout lake in the Eastern Province, Gubu Dam, built by the Department of Water Affairs, and first stocked in 1968. This fine 120-hectare lake became very low in the 1984-85 drought, but by the beginning of 1986 it was full and was providing good sport, with most of the trout running about 700 g. The angling club has a club-house with accommodation for members. Social functions are arranged, including an annual fly-fishing competition. The club's headquarters are in the picturesque little town of Stutterheim and visiting anglers may obtain tickets to fish on a daily basis.

The Hogsback Trout Angling Club's activities centre on the Klipplaat River, by arrangement with the riparian owners concerned, and the Klipplaat Dam (also known as the Waterdown Dam). These facilities are open to visitors who become temporary members, while reciprocity is offered to anglers who belong to clubs elsewhere. A number of private dams are available to full members of the Hogsback Trout Angling Club. Since there is little natural breeding in the Klipplaat, regular restocking is required.

At Port Elizabeth, the Eastern Province Freshwater Fish Conservancy has an interest in the Moffat Dam, which belongs to the Port Elizabeth municipality. Although only about two hectares in extent, it is a cool, clear body of water situated in the Longmore Forest Reserve 50 km from the city. Lower down the same catchment is the Sand River Dam, which contains bass as well as trout.

A Federation of East Cape Trout Angling Clubs was formed on 4 September 1982, under the chairmanship of Fred Croney, with the object of co-ordinating the activities of all the above-mentioned clubs, with special reference to stocking trout waters in the region. The main preoccupation of the federation has been to ensure adequate supplies of trout. In December 1984 a major effort was made to transport rainbow fingerlings from Jonkershoek, where the Department of Nature and Environmental Conservation had made the fish available free of charge, to stock waters in the Eastern Province.

A more ambitious organisation, the Federation of South African Flyfishers, was formed at a meeting in Stutterheim of representatives of clubs from as far afield as Cape Town, Natal and the Transvaal, on 1 February 1986. The meeting elected Fred Croney as the first President, with Dr Tom Sutcliffe of Natal as Chairman and the Secretariat based in Cape Town at the offices of the Cape Piscatorial Society.

The potential value of such a national body, to represent the interests of fly fishermen throughout South Africa, is unquestionable. There are, however, two important provisos. First, adequate support must be forthcoming from the angling fraternity, not only in terms of hard cash but also hard work. Secondly, fruitful liaison must be established between the federation and the official bodies responsible for freshwater fisheries.

It is regrettable that the immediate concern of those who called the inaugural meeting was to gain allies in opposing the policy of the Department of Nature and Environmental Conservation in Cape Town. Perhaps it would be more accurate to say that anglers found themselves in opposition to what they *believed* was Depart-mental policy.

Draft legislation removing statutory protection for trout, the setting aside of certain areas for indigenous fish only and an expressed intention of reducing hatchery operations combined to persuade trout anglers that their sport was under threat. The attitude of the Department appeared to the anglers not to have been conciliatory. Perhaps there was inadequate communication, since the proposed changes in legislation and hatchery operation, as set out by Stephen McVeigh (*Tight Lines,* August 1985) seemed eminently reasonable. Removing unnecessary controls is a praiseworthy action.

If a better understanding between all concerned with freshwater angling can be brought about, the Federation of South African Flyfishers will have accomplished an important part of its function.

In Natal, a harmonious relationship exists between trout fishermen and the Natal Parks Board. This good feeling between the provincial authorities and anglers goes back far beyond the creation of the Natal Parks Board. As early as 1916, Lionel Day was contributing to the Fisheries Department's annual report in his capacity as Chairman of the Estcourt Flyfishers' and Trout Acclimatisation Society.

The Natal Trout Fisheries Association was formed in 1919. Based in Pietermaritzburg, the association recommended various measures for implementation by the Fisheries Board.

The South African Fly Fishers' Club was formed in 1912 in Johannesburg, but the water its members used was that of the Trout Bungalow on the Mooi River. The club had rules applicable to that stretch of river and its control measures were noted with approval by the Fisheries Board.

River conservancies were established throughout the trout areas of Natal in the 1920s. These were groups of riparian owners interested in the well-being of trout. Under each conservancy were Honorary Fisheries Officers, appointed by the Administrator. In 1930, 40 of these Honorary Officers were active in 10 conservancy districts. Over the years, interest has gradually waned among landowners and, although several conservancies are still nominally in existence in 1986, only one has remained functional. This is the Underberg-Himeville Trout Fishery Conservancy, an amalgamation of two separate groups, each of which played an important part in building up the standard of fishing in the district. For more than 30 years the Chairman was Ralph Hardingham and the Hon. Secretary John Campbell.

Durban fly fishers held an inaugural meeting to create the Durban and District Freshwater Angling Club on 3 June 1947. This later became the Durban Flyfishers' Club, which grew to have a membership of 180, with interests in trout fishing at Underberg as well as bass fishing near the coast.

After the formation of the Underberg-Himeville Trout Fishing Club in 1954, however, the Durban Flyfishers' Club gradually became inactive. It was formally wound up at a meeting held on 24 January 1972 and its funds shared between a Durban charity, the Natal Fly Fishers' Club and the Underberg-Himeville Trout Fishing Club.

The Underberg-Himeville club resulted from the initiative of Ralph Hardingham and his colleagues on the committee of the Underberg-Himeville Trout Fishery

Conservancy. Their intention was to ensure that flyfishers would have access to the rivers and dams of this, the premier trout area of South Africa. Among the objects laid down in the constitution were:

" (a) To further the propagation and protection of trout.

(b) To preserve trout waters and control fishing therein.

(c) To popularise trout fishing by securing for its members the right to fish the rivers and dams situated in the Club area."

In order to ensure that control remained in the hands of the riparian owners, it was laid down that not more than three committee members could be non-riparian owners.

After an inaugural meeting in July 1954, the success of the Underberg-Himeville Trout Fishing Club was immediate. In its first season there were 310 full members and a further 400 day tickets were issued for temporary members. In 1986 the total membership, including family groups, exceeds 500.

Ralph Hardingham was the club's first Chairman. William Hughes, a local farmer (like Hardingham), acted as Hon. Secretary until 1976, but has been best known for his work as Fishing Officer since 1960. This is the key position in the functioning of the club. Innumerable visiting anglers, whether club members or people seeking a day on the river, have been grateful to the man who has sat behind the desk in the Fishing Club's rondavel at the Underberg Hotel from half past eight till ten each morning of the fishing season. Since 1976, Bill Hempson has been Secretary and has administered the club's affairs with efficiency.

In October each year, the annual general meeting is an occasion for a social evening with a buffet supper, at which trout features on the menu, provided by members of the local Women's Institute. The club forms a link between town and country.

Fishing results vary from year to year, according to the weather. Normally the Umzimkulu River, of which most of the best stretches are available to members, attracts more attention that the Ngwangwana or Polela. The total length of river included in club water is more than 100 km. In years of good rainfall, the Ngwangwana is the most reliable producer of trout, often giving returns of more than four fish per rod, compared with about two for the Umzimkulu. These are average figures; as may be expected in any fishery, 10 per cent of the anglers catch at least 80 per cent of the fish.

More than 120 hectares of stillwater fishing on a dozen dams are available to club members and an increasing percentage of the total angling effort is spent on dams rather than rivers.

Each season a trophy is offered for the best dam fish and the best river fish. The winning trout from rivers has varied in size from 1 kg to 2,8 kg, while the heaviest dam trout has usually been over 3 kg. The largest ever was a rainbow of 4,5 kg, caught by Michael Blackman in 1971.

Under the leadership of the present Chairman, Teddy Morris, and with the assistance of Jake Alletson of the Natal Parks Board, the Underberg-Himeville Trout Fishing Club has embarked on a programme of management to make the best use possible of the waters so generously provided by the owners. An effective innovation has been the use of rearing cages in one of the dams. Rentals that the club pays

Left: William Hughes of the Underberg-Himeville Trout Fishing Club.

Below: Peter Arderne (centre) with two fellow-members of the Transvaal Fly Fishers' Club.

Judge's Walk, Umzimkulu River, Natal.

remain far below the commercial value of the fishing. Thus the far-sighted and public-spirited action of the original group that formed this unique co-operative association of riparian owners and anglers has been fully vindicated.

With enough water to cope with about 80 anglers per day, there is usually little difficulty in allocating ample space to satisfy visitors, although naturally some beats are more popular than others. In Journal No. 5 of the Underberg-Himeville Trout Fishing Club, John Kirkman tells the story of an American visitor who asked for "a couple of yards of fishing". When told he could have more than a thousand yards to himself he replied: "Back home we get three yards."

Another Natal trout angling club, formed in 1965, is the Midlands Fly Fishing Club. Based in Estcourt, the club has about 60 members who fish five dams situated on farms between Mooi River and Giant's Castle. The present Chairman is Dr Romyn Every, well known as a talented fly fisherman. An ex-Chairman is Bill Barnes, an outstanding angler and now the owner of a trout farm on the Bushman's River, below Giant's Castle Game Reserve.

The Natal Fly Fishers' Club (NFFC) owed its inception to that remarkable angler and writer, John Beams, who transferred his business activities from Cape Town to Pietermaritzburg largely, so he led us to believe, because he enjoyed catching the big trout to be found in Natal dams.

An inaugural meeting was held at the Royal Hotel, Pietermaritzburg, on 1 March 1972. Beams was elected Chairman, with Mr Justice John Milne President. Mrs Edith Combes took over the secretarial duties, which she carries out to this day (after a break of a few years). The 1986 executive team consists of Eddie Combes, Chairman, and Edith, Secretary; no more dedicated or efficient team could be found in South Africa.

The task facing the Natal Fly Fishers' Club appeared daunting. Whereas both the Underberg-Himeville and Midlands Clubs operate in a circumscribed area, the NFFC had to find suitable waters wherever they might become available within reasonable travelling distance of Pietermaritzburg. Some system then had to be worked out whereby members could book whatever beat they wished to fish. A telephone booking agency had to be found. After a period of operating through the reception staff at an hotel, an excellent solution was found. Members of the medical profession subscribe to an after-hours telephone answering and paging agency which has proved ideal for the fishing club's purpose. NFFC members are able to book water by telephone whenever they wish.

The club has 500 full members, with a substantial waiting list. Temporary membership is catered for and full members may take guests on payment of a fee. A clubroom housing a library is available, but members make little use of this facility. More important for the cohesion of the club are the regular informative newsletters issued by the Chairman. A printed journal, *The Creel*, is issued at irregular intervals and has contained many instructive articles.

The number of fishing waters available to members of the NFFC has increased steadily over the years, thanks to the efforts of its respective chairmen and committee members, especially Eddie Combes. In the 1985-86 season 23 dams of various sizes had become available, as well as 13 stretches of river, of which several are prime brown trout water on the Mooi and Little Mooi. Each water has been mapped and details recorded as to the conditions under which the owner has agreed to allow club members the privilege of using his property.

Dam stocking is undertaken by the club, using trout purchased from the Natal Parks Board or private trout farmers. Brown trout have been transferred from overstocked sections of stream to some of the dams. All stocking has been organised by Hugh Huntley, assisted by other members of the Natal Fly Fishers' Club, as well as Jake Alletson of the Natal Parks Board. Fishing results vary from place to place and according to the weather. The erratic rainfall experienced from 1982 to the spring of 1985 led to poor fishing in rivers and those dams that became low. Nevertheless, returns for the first half of 1985 have included rainbow trout from dams of up to 2,85 kg and brown trout from the Mooi River of up to 2,1 kg. Most of the dams on which the Natal Fly Fishers' Club has rights are open throughout the year.

The Fly Fishers' Association (FFA) was formed by a group of anglers in the Durban area on 15 March 1980. The constitution includes for the provision of fly-fishing facilities for its members, subject to the condition that the association shall not compete with the Natal Fly Fishers' Club or the Underberg-Himeville Trout Fishing Club.

The availability of underutilised trout water in the ownership of private individuals and companies in Natal is indicated by the fact that the FFA has been able to acquire rights on 10 dams as well as some river fishing. An active stocking programme has been carried out and some good sport has been enjoyed by members. A booking service has been organised and circulars prepared to provide information on the available waters. A regular newsletter is issued and monthly social meetings arranged. The Chairman, to whom a great deal of the credit must go for the rapid expansion of this club, is Clarrie Blumrick. Membership has been limited to 110 and a waiting list is now established. Facilities are available for temporary membership.

Two active clubs, based on dams in the Swartberg area of Natal, are the Hopewell Angling Club and Tswilika Angling Club. The former was formed in 1977 when Frank Marshall Smith built a 60-hectare dam on his farm Hopewell, impounding the Krom River. Although bass are present in the dam, the use of cages to rear hatchery trout fingerlings has enabled the club, with a membership of about 60 anglers, to provide excellent sport. The part played by the Hon. Secretary, Jimmy Little, has been vital to the development of this club.

Moving to the Transvaal, interest in the establishment of trout led to the formation of the Transvaal Trout Acclimatisation Society in March 1903. The President was Lord Milner and the committee included such well-known names as Julius Jeppe and Sir Percy Fitzpatrick. The society engaged the services of A.N. Stenning, who was in charge of the Pirie Hatchery at King William's Town, to create a hatchery at Potchefstroom. A 10-hectare site was made available by the municipality, £1 000 was collected from subscribers and a small government grant obtained. Although the society's report for 1904 was (according to the notes published by A.C. Harrison in *Piscator* No. 101) mainly a catalogue of the difficulties Stenning encountered, he did succeed in distributing fry to various places on the Witwatersrand. In the ensuing few years, more trout were distributed, including 1 000 that were introduced to the Dorps River at Lydenburg. One of these was caught as a five pounder by H.J. Gurr and led to his trout-stocking activities and those of F. C. Braun. The latter became Hon. Secretary of the Lydenburg Trout Protection and Angling Society on its formation in 1924. This club continued to function until 1957, when it was officially disbanded and its funds placed in trust for the development of a recreation area in memory of Frank Braun.

The Haenertsburg Trout Association was formed in 1906. As mentioned by Paul Smit, its present Hon. Secretary, it is therefore one of the oldest associations in the country. Only the Frontier Acclimatisation Society can, in fact, claim a longer period of activity. The association controls fishing in the 12-hectare Dap Naudé Dam, owned by the Pietersburg municipality. Here the rainbow trout population is maintained by natural breeding. Included in the precincts of the dam is a stretch of 2 to 3 km of the Broederstroom River in the Forestry area, where brown trout are to be caught.

Lakeside (also known as Stanford Lake) is a four-hectare dam that is kept well stocked with 500 g rainbows grown out in cages in the large Ebenezer Dam farther downstream. A club house is provided for the association's 150 members on the shore of Ebenezer lake. Although the Haenertsburg Trout Association now has a waiting list, visitors are catered for on a daily basis.

Farther south, in the main trout area of the Eastern Transvaal, two fishing clubs which cater for visiting anglers are those at Machadodorp and Sabie. The Machadodorp Trout Club controls 26 km of river fishing near the town, on the Elands River and its two tributaries, the Taute and the Leeuspruit. According to A. Joseph, the Hon. Secretary, about 600 days' fishing is done by full club members and visitors each season. Many of the fish caught are wild-bred, but stocked trout form an unknown percentage of the total.

In the 1984-85 season 654 rainbow trout, weighing 204 kg, were recorded by anglers. Mr Joseph considered that twice as many fish were probably caught. Of the fish recorded, 72 per cent were less than 300 g and 22 per cent were between 300 and 500 g; the remaining six per cent weighed up to 1,72 kg each.

The Sabie Trout Angling Club controls 9 km of the Sabie River where it flows through land owned by Mondi Forests and through the town commonage. Geoff Gidish is the Hon. Secretary who runs the affairs of the club, makes tickets available to visitors and acts as instructor to those not well versed in the art of fly fishing.

Club members resident in Sabie number about 25, including juniors, while another 75 country members subscribe on an annual basis. Geoff Gidish estimates the number of day tickets issued to visitors at nearly 2 000 a year. Fishing pressure is therefore heavy. Only conventional trout tackle may be used: no fixed-spool reels or bait are allowed. The daily limit is four fish of a minimum length of 225 mm. To maintain numbers, although natural breeding does occur in the stream, annual stocking has been carried out. For some years, when Richard Pott was Senior Fisheries Officer at Lydenburg, catchable-sized rainbows were introduced, marked by removal of part of a fin. As many as 72 per cent of the marked fish were caught by anglers. To grow trout out to an adequate size, a rearing pond was built, but results were not very satisfactory and recently the pond has been used merely to hold fish brought from the hatchery at Lydenburg. This facilitates distribution over the whole length of the club water. On one occasion, 200 trout were inadvertently liberated into one pool, which then became unduly popular with anglers at the nearby campsites!

More sophisticated anglers have been heard to complain about the fighting quality of hatchery-reared — as opposed to wild-bred — trout. As an experiment, therefore, a batch of unmarked fish was put into the stream. Word soon spread that there was a run of wild trout and those who caught them extolled their superiority, little knowing that Pott was merely testing the objectivity of anglers.

To make up for a recent reduction in the size of the trout supplied by the provincial hatchery at Lydenburg, the Sabie Trout Angling Club has been purchasing catchable-sized fish from the trout farm owned by Mondi Forests, upstream from the club water.

A few years ago, club members devoted a considerable amount of time and energy to building weirs to deepen some of the pools. As usual with such structures, results were not generally satisfactory, owing to collapse of the weir or erosion of the banks. The most ambitious dam with a wall about 2 m high had not only failed in the engineering sense: while it was in position, it had caused heavy silt accumulation on which bullrushes had become established. A more recent experiment was an attempt to create deep holes by means of an excavator. Piles of material on the stream bank bear witness to the work of the mechanical monster, but how long it will take the river to fill in the holes remains to be seen.

A previous chairman of the Sabie Trout Angling Club, Dr Roy Wood, was against artificial modification of the stream and the introduction of catchable-sized trout, for aesthetic reasons. In fact, most of the stream retains its natural charm and large trout of well over 1 kg, presumably wild-bred, are to be found by the angler who fishes in the more inaccessible places.

On the Witwatersrand, trout fishermen are numerous, but have to look far afield for their sport. Although trout were stocked in many waters around Johannesburg, no worthwhile results were achieved. A few were caught in Emmarentia and Westdene Dams and a 3,4 kg rainbow was taken in the Klip River west of Johannesburg. Near Muldersdrift a commercial enterprise offers put-and-take angling for trout.

Many of the more affluent members of society belong to syndicates, of which the members reside on the Reef, while relying on rivers and dams in the Eastern Transvaal. Membership of syndicates is generally restricted to a select few, who pay a four-figure subscription for the privilege of fishing intensively managed waters.

Two clubs that offer their members sport at a reasonable price are the South African Fly Fishers' Association (SAFFA) and the Transvaal Fly Fishers' Club (TFFC). SAFFA originally experimented with fly fishing at Muldersdrift, but this proved unsatisfactory. Now it has more than 300 members, with several dams and a 7 km stretch of the Lunsklip River east of Dullstroom. The dams are heavily stocked with catchable-sized rainbows, while the river has a breeding population of brown trout, as well as rainbows stocked by neighbouring syndicates. Weekend accommodation is provided for members and their guests on the farm where the dams and river are situated. All facilities are leased, without long-term security of tenure.

The Transvaal Fly Fishers' Club has about 110 members, with the addition of wives and children. Originally it was the Trout Section of the Rand Piscatorial Association, a long-established society with interests in all types of freshwater angling. In 1973 the TFFC became a separate club, with fishing on dams near Dullstroom. As with other lessees of dams, the club's security of tenure was in jeopardy, until some of the members formed a private company, Dullstroom Trout Farm, which bought the farm Middelpunt. The TFFC members have provided the funds to develop and maintain the property, on which there are now seven dams, with a total area of more than 18 hectares.

Thanks to the hard work and intelligent management of a small group, notably Peter Arderne, the members of TFFC have some of the most consistent fly fishing in South Africa, as well as pleasant accommodation in the old farmhouse and additional buildings. Malcolm Meintjes (*Piscator* Nos. 105 and 112, and his book *Trout on the Veld*) has published interesting information on the progress of fishing there, while Peter Arderne's regular club newsletter details what has been going on.

As one approaches Middelpunt, the landscape is open grassland with a feeling of spaciousness. On the farm the veld is well conserved and the glistening lakes lie in two shallow valleys, with the farmhouse in between. The sandy soil, with quartzite outcrops, produces little discolouration of the water, even after rain. Cool nights at more than 1 800 m (6 000 ft) above sea-level ensure that water temperatures never rise unduly high. Soil fertility is low, but a great deal of life has developed in each dam and trout do extremely well.

In the four years from 1974 to 1978 catches increased from 545 trout to 1 270, and since then the annual catches have remained well over 1 000, with a total mass of at least 600 kg. This high catch-rate has only been achieved by regular restocking with fish of about 400 g each. Most of those introduced to the dams are raised to the required size in cages, of which 20 are in constant use. Some sizeable trout are bought from a fish farm. Although this management policy might be thought to create a somewhat artificial situation, there is no doubt that the fishing is interesting and by no means too easy. The clear dams, with their fringing vegetation, give the impression of natural lakes, while the trout often elude the angler long enough to grow to a substantial size. In 1983, three rainbows of 3,20, 3,25 and 3,45 kg were caught and many others have been landed in excess of a kilogram.

Each angler is allowed three trout per dam per day. In order to be able to release fish unharmed, club members are encouraged to use barbless hooks. Boats are allowed only on the largest dam, which is seven hectares in extent. Two problems have had to be tackled in recent years: excessive weed growth and invasion of largemouth bass. The weeds are being tackled by introducing Chinese grass carp; the bass by rotational emptying of the dams and selective poisoning.

Thanks to the large input of voluntary work, the management costs are kept remarkably low. By their own efforts the members of the Transvaal Fly Fishers' Club have built up an amenity equal to that enjoyed by some of the most expensive syndicates with professional managers.

Fishing clubs working in collaboration with landowners hold the key to the provision of good trout fishing in the future.

V CONSERVATION AND MANAGEMENT

15. Control and responsibility

Trout are found in three types of environment: first, streams that offer all that is required for breeding and survival; second, streams that lack adequate breeding places, or that become uninhabitable under unfavourable climatic conditions; and third, man-made lakes and ponds.

Waters of the first type, which may be termed prime trout streams, support trout populations that seldom , if ever, need restocking. In this type of environment, trout may be considered an integral part of the ecological system, even though they owe their presence to man's intervention. Streams of the second type may be termed marginal trout waters, in which artificial replenishment of the stock is required, either regularly or at longer intervals. Marginal waters may give good sport when conditions are favourable, but results are inconsistent.

There is no hard-and-fast dividing line between prime and marginal trout waters, nor between those that are marginal (but worth managing for trout fishing) and those that are so unfavourable as not to justify the trouble and expense of trying to maintain them as trout waters.

The third category, still waters, also includes a range of different conditions, from ideal to barely suitable. The common feature of still waters is that trout do not breed in them. A few are fed by streams where trout can spawn, but the great majority of still waters have to be restocked regularly if they are to provide fishing. As long as a dam has the right features for trout to live and grow, it is worthy of management.

It must be admitted that a great deal of effort has been wasted on both rivers and dams that are unsuitable. In the early days of trout acclimatisation there was no clear understanding of the requirements of the salmonid family, but today there is much more knowledge about where trout will do well and where they will not. Yet people, actuated more by wishful thinking than by realism, continue to put fish into places where they have no hope of success.

Whether an attempt is made to manage a water for trout fishing depends largely on the local demand, as well as on the ownership of the water. Near big centres, where demand for fly fishing exceeds the supply, every available piece of water will attract attention. In remote areas, good trout dams may remain unstocked. Wherever private ownership is involved, and this includes most of South Africa's trout waters, the attitude of the proprietor is a key issue. The same may apply to waters controlled by municipalities or State departments. Uncooperative officials may prevent public utilisation of rivers or dams.

Fishing clubs as well as exclusive syndicates are coming more and more into prominence in the management of trout fishing. The question must arise therefore as to what extent Nature Conservation authorities are going to remain involved. The answer must surely be that private enterprise has to play an increasingly important role. Attention has become focused on moves by the Cape Department of Nature and Environmental Conservation to divest itself of some of its responsibilities for trout management. These moves have been made to redeploy existing resources to meet new priorities. With regard to legislative changes, simplification of existing provincial laws seems to be a wise step. In the past, preoccupation with the welfare of trout has led to unnecessary legal restrictions.

As long as the strong arm of the law is ready to descend on those who pollute or destroy the environment, detailed rules and regulations for the taking of trout are better formulated and put into effect by local angling clubs and landowners than by a regional authority. The purpose of such restrictions is to deter the selfish few from taking more than their fair share of available fish, or from interfering with others in the enjoyment of their sport. Fishing regulations are designed for people, not for the conservation of the species *Salmo trutta* or *Salmo gairdneri*. The contention one hears bandied about that trout should be exploited with care if the stock is to survive and remain healthy, is based on sentiment, not sense. If the environment is favourable, angling will never prevent trout from surviving. Certainly I know of no examples where fly fishing has exterminated the fish in a stream in which suitable breeding places are available.

Another statement sometimes made is that the practice of returning small fish to the river while keeping the larger ones imposes an undesirable selection in favour of the slower-growing individuals. If this were true it would imply that anglers who killed only the larger fish might, in time, be responsible for a stunted population. There is no evidence that this has ever happened and to use such an argument merely invites scepticism. The truth is that where numerous small fish are present there is no harm in removing those you catch. If, at the same time, the larger fish are returned to the water, there is obviously a better chance for other anglers to catch some sizeable fish. It is not a matter of the health of the stock, but of sharing out what is available among as many anglers as possible.

In a heavily fished water, where anglers are removing a significant proportion of the trout, the "window-limit" is a sensible management tool. Under this system one can take small fish up to a certain size; above that size the fish must be returned, except for trophy-sized individuals which may be kept. Jake Alletson of the Natal Parks Board is a strong protagonist of the window-limit and he persuaded the committee of the Underberg-Himeville Trout Fishing Club to try it out on the Umzimkulu River. Unfortunately, the limit was put into effect at a time when there were so few fish in the river, owing to severe drought conditions, that an angler might work all day for a single trout. If it fell within the window-limit, as it probably would, the fisherman had to find a supermarket on his way home to buy some frozen hake fillets for his supper. Since few people took the trouble to fish the river under such unfavourable conditions, the number of trout that were saved to fight another day was negligible. Which goes to show that good ideas work only if they are applied with a sharp eye to practical implications. In a water carrying a good stock of trout of assorted sizes and well patronised by anglers, the window-limit is well worth putting into operation. But on the Umzimkulu all it did in 1983 was to cause Jake unnecessary embarrassment, especially when Dr George Hughes, the Natal Parks Board's Assistant Director of Conservation (and a highly skilled angler), caught a delicious-looking pounder that had to go back into the river. There was, I believe, no supermarket open on the Assistant Director's return journey.

Any type of limit, whether based on size or on the number of fish that an angler may take, is effective only if it serves the purpose of sharing out the crop among all the anglers concerned. On a water fished by only a few people in the course of a season there is no point in having any limits at all. Conversely, on a water that is fished by an excessively large number of anglers, whatever limit may be imposed has no practical effect. If there are 100 sizeable trout to be caught and 10 anglers are on the water, a limit of 10 fish will share them out fairly. Indeed, a lot of fish will be left, as only a minority of the anglers will achieve their limit. If, however, 200 anglers are each allowed to take even a single fish, no one will have worthwhile sport. A possible solution in such a situation would be to have a "no-kill" rule. Otherwise, constant restocking on a put-and-take basis would have to be practised.

Another point about limits that is often lost sight of is that they are commonly set in terms of permissible catch per day. This means that an angler who is frequently on the water takes far more than his colleague who has an outing, perhaps, only once a season. The difficulty was overcome some years ago by the Driffield Angling Society in Yorkshire. Each member was limited to a kill of 10 trout per season. Once he had taken his limit, he had to put back every trout he caught. Undoubtedly, such a rule implies adherence to a strict code of ethics, but then any angling regulation is effective only if it is freely accepted by the people concerned.

An intensively managed fishery, where anglers are under close scrutiny by someone in authority, may rely on policing to control wrong-doers, but this sort of situation is exceptional. Certainly the days are long gone when the taxpayer was expected to pay for fisheries inspectors to wander around trout rivers in search of anglers using illegal methods, or fishing without a licence. In 1931, there was official correspondence between the Inland Fisheries Officer and the Principal Fisheries Officer of Natal to determine whether the magistrate at Bulwer had been within his rights in ordering a man, who had been convicted and fined £2 for using a worm in the Polela River, to buy a licence within two days. Imagine the waste of everyone's time!

The truth is that the control of angling waters, and of the anglers themselves, should be in the hands of those directly responsible. Landowners are naturally involved, but it is entirely commendable that many landowners are willing to allow fishing clubs to use and manage the waters on their properties. In Natal the activities of the four major trout fishing clubs have not only provided fly-fishing opportunities for a large segment of the public, through full or temporary membership of their clubs, but have made an immensely important input into management of privately owned rivers and dams.

In the Transvaal, private enterprise has, to a large extent, taken over both the provision of angling and commercial trout production. It is regrettable, for the man in the street, that many of the waters have been taken over by exclusive syndicates or large industrial undertakings, but the fact remains that good conservation practices are a priority for most of these groups. One could not fail to be impressed by the care of the natural environment in, for instance, the Maggsleigh Conservation Area owned by Mondi Forests, even though the prime object was to provide trout fishing on a series of dams down the course of a small valley. Again, the Transvaal Gold Mining Exploration estate on the Blyde River is a model of a well-conserved habitat.

Cape fly fishers have less opportunity to manage their angling waters, which are mainly owned by State departments or municipalities. Nevertheless, official policy is towards devolving responsibility onto the recognised angling bodies.

It is to be hoped that, in passing responsibility into the hands of private enterprise, officials will recognise the need to grant full authority, without which effective control is impossible.

16. River management

Trout streams form a resource which cannot be increased. On the contrary, there is considerably less river fishing available today than there was 50 years ago. Some well-known stretches of river have been destroyed by dam construction, while others have been degraded by erosion in the catchment, with consequent sedimentation. Irrigation is a threat in periods of inadequate rainfall, when farmers pump large quantities of water onto their crops. There is regrettably little we can do to change the situation, except to bring abuses to the attention of those who can take action.

The natural characteristics of a river catchment have a critical influence on the flow pattern of the stream and on the amount of soil erosion that takes place. R.E. Schulze (*Hydrology and Water Resources of the Drakensberg*, 1979) has shown that different river systems vary greatly in the volume and reliability of their flow. The Umzimkulu River, for instance , has comparatively high flows and a low coefficient of variation, whereas the Umzimvubu system has a poor and unreliable water yield. This difference in hydrology can be related to my assessment of the relative importance of the two systems for trout fishing. I have indicated in Chapters 6 and 7 that the Umzimvubu is of limited significance for trout, whereas the upper Umzimkulu basin is the premier trout area in South Africa.

Schulze has also shown that soil loss from a catchment is determined largely by the natural erodibility of the soil and the relief of the landscape. He lists five control variables: rainfall energy, vegetal cover/management, soil erodibility, slope gradient and slope length. Using a model based on these variables he found that rainfall energy and soil erodibility are particularly important. He estimated that mean soil losses range from less than one tonne per hectare per year to over 70 tonnes per hectare per year. The more soil that comes off the catchment, of course, the worse it is for the river. Vegetal cover/management is the only variable over which there is any possible control. With the object of managing the veld in the best interests of the country's water resources, the government has acquired the most important mountain catchment areas, which are administered by the Directorate of Forestry, Department of Environment Affairs. In Natal, the Natal Parks Board controls several parts of the Drakensberg, the largest area being Giant's Castle Game Reserve.

Tree planting is not encouraged in catchments where water production is the priority. It has been proved that although trees reduce flood peaks, they remove water during dry periods, thus reducing the all-important minimum flow of a river. The best cover to prevent soil erosion and give optimum water yields is a well-conserved grass sward. As we all know, grass suffers if it is overgrazed. It also deteriorates if it is left unburned for long periods. That is why plumes of smoke are to be seen along the face of the Drakensberg in spring. Controlled burning is good conservation. Veld burning as a prelude to heavy grazing by cattle, sheep and goats is, however, highly destructive. The more affluent and progressive farmers are fully aware of this and manage their land accordingly. Indeed, they may manage it better than an understaffed government agency. Regrettably, however, some of the most vulnerable catchments, with high relief and erodible soil, are occupied by people without the economic resources to practise conservation. The ecological condition of rivers in such areas, as shown by their capacity to provide a habitat for trout, is dismal.

Variations in volume, and hence in the depth of a stream, are a limiting factor in South African rivers. Building walls across the bed is a possible means of increasing the fish-holding capacity of a stream. The headwaters of the Crocodile River and its tributaries in the Eastern Transvaal have been modified successfully by the construction of concrete weirs. Boulder weirs look less unnatural and examples of those that were built 30 years ago may still be seen in some Natal streams. In many instances, however, attempts at "stream improvement" have simply been washed away or, if they remain in position, are aesthetically undesirable. Dams that create deep pools are likely to be poor in natural stream organisms and therefore unattractive to trout. A river that carries much sediment will rapidly fill in an artificially created pool.

Modification of natural waterways has so many potential hazards that it is little practised today except on small streams with a limited catchment area and stable banks. Improvement of open, shallow stretches might be effected by increasing the amount of cover for fish. *Oregon Wildlife* (December 1985) has an illustrated article on the work of a chapter (local branch) of Trout Unlimited, using heavy mechanical equipment to place boulders and tree trunks in a spring creek that lacked resting places for rainbow trout. Selected sites on South African streams might benefit from similar treatment, but our high flood peaks severely restrict any in-stream modification.

Dams on sidestreams are the most effective method of increasing the habitat for trout and other fish. Most of these dams are built to conserve water for purposes other than fish culture, but without the innumerable farm dams scattered over South Africa anglers would be hard pressed to find places to enjoy their sport. Dams are of immense commercial and recreational value. Like all good things, however, they do have their disadvantages.

Dams are often said to be useful for stabilising the flow of a river as well as being of indirect benefit by providing a farmer with irrigation water and thereby obviating the need for him to pump from the river itself. The latter is undoubtedly true, but the contention that a dam may help to keep a river flowing in time of drought is subject to an important proviso: the farmer should open the valve on his outlet pipe and allow water to flow into the river when the natural flow is at its lowest.

The reason is that a substantial amount of water is lost by evaporation from a free

A boulder weir built to deepen a shallow pool; Umzimkulu River, above Underberg.

water surface. If, therefore, no water is drawn off and allowed to run into the stream course below the dam, the flow of water going down the valley will be less than it would have been in the absence of a dam. Should the dam rely on runoff from a catchment that has no permanent stream, the effects of evaporation will be obvious, as the water level shrinks in dry weather. A strong stream will continue to produce an outflow over the dam's spillway, but the outflow will be less than the inflow into the dam. The amount of water lost will depend on the rate of evaporation and on the surface area of the impoundment. If we assume an evaporation rate of 3 mm per day, which might easily be exceeded in hot, windy weather, that means about 60 000 litres of water are disappearing from each hectare every 24 hours. A 10-hectare dam would, at that rate, lose 3,5 litres per second, or enough to fill a 200-litre drum in less than one minute.

To make matters worse, a stream shows a diurnal fluctuation in rate of flow, with the lowest flow in the afternoon. This is due to evaporation losses from the surface of its pools as well as water drawn off by plants, especially trees, growing on its banks. A river such as the Polela, which has more than 200 hectares of dams in its catchment, might suffer evaporation losses of nearly one-tenth of a cubic metre per second on a hot afternoon. This loss, together with the effects of irrigation from the river, could well bring its flow to a complete halt during a drought.

Thus dams that are not managed with a river's needs in mind may be a liability not an asset, as far as the river is concerned. Anyone building a dam across the course

177

of river is normally obliged to provide what is called "compensation" water to maintain an acceptable flow downstream, but owners of dams on sidestreams are subject to no such legal obligation.

Research at the Department of Water Affairs' Hydrological Research Institute has shown that numerous small dams in a catchment may be a liability in planning water resource management.

Another important consideration in dam-building is the siting. If a vlei is flooded, a unique biological habitat may be destroyed. In addition, Schulze and others have shown that a vlei left in its natural state has a stabilising effect on the runoff from small catchments.

Man has had important effects on some of our rivers, but others have remained in a condition very close to their pristine state, at least down to the upper part of the trout zone, which begins as soon as the river has gained adequate volume and its gradient is no longer excessively steep. Small, torrential mountain streams have been stocked on many occasions, and in some cases the trout have remained long enough to provide sport for anglers. After a variable period the trout, whether brown or rainbow, leave for more roomy quarters. This applies particularly to rainbows. The headwaters of the Mooi River in Natal, for instance, were stocked with rainbows in October 1958. Over the following two seasons odd individuals, which must have come from this stocking, were caught between 5 and 20 km below the point of introduction. None could be located in the stocked area.

Peter Ferraz has a deep pool on a small stream that feeds his trout hatchery in the Umzimouti valley near Underberg. He introduced some rainbow fingerlings to this pool, and they remained there for over a year, growing to nearly a kilogram. Each day they came to be fed, until one morning they had vanished. Over the following few months several unusually large trout were caught in the Umzimouti.

In a similar case hatchery rainbow fingerlings were put into pools near the source of the Incandu River, above Newcastle. They remained until the following autumn and some of about 400 g were caught, but during the winter they disappeared.

The most important single factor — apart from an adequate minimum flow — that characterises a productive trout stream is the gradient of the bed. If it is more than 20 m per kilometre, that is two per cent, the stream is unlikely to hold more than a few trout. Unless there are rock outcrops or large boulders, the bed will be highly unstable. Rock-bound pools may offer shelter but in general the river's course will be too torrential. A gradient of less than 4 m per kilometre, on the other hand, will lead to accumulation of sediment, which not only chokes gravel beds where trout spawn, but has a smothering effect on the habitat of stream insects on which the fish feed. The actual extent of silt accumulation depends, of course, on the state of the catchment. A river with a flat gradient may show little evidence of silt if it drains a well-conserved landscape.

The days when a river might be surveyed to determine its suitability for trout are long gone. Every stream that looks at all hopeful for stocking will have received trout at some time in the past. Where trout have since disappeared, the water may be regarded as worth restocking if satisfactory catches are known to have been made.

Mike Coke uses a back-pack electric fish shocker to collect trout on the Incandu River.

A severely degraded stream may have to be written off, but marginal waters deserve attention if only for a gamble that a favourable weather cycle will restore reasonable productivity. The difficulty may be to decide who pays for hatchery fish that are quite likely never to be seen again.

A type of river management that has fallen into disuse is the transfer of wild-bred trout from overstocked waters to those that need more fish. During the 1930s and 1940s a popular activity for river conservancy members was to make up fishing parties on the Mooi, Bushman's or one of the Underberg rivers and catch a few hundred yearling trout for transfer to the lower stretches where breeding was relatively unsuccessful. One might reasonably assume that the survival rate of trout that had been reared naturally in a stream would be higher than that of hatchery-reared fish. Wild-caught fish have proved themselves in dams, as well as in rivers.

The use of easily portable electric fish shockers, which I introduced to Natal waters in the 1950s, made the capture of large numbers of young trout in shallow streams relatively simple, although requiring a considerable labour input. Private landowners as well as fishing club committee members have been authorised to make use of this equipment, which will regain its effectiveness when the recent cycle of drought (and consequently few trout) returns to normal. Incidentally, the rapid growth of small yearlings when moved from their overcrowded environment to dams has belied any suggestion that their poor growth is due to genetic degeneration.

The electric shocker units which I designed, consisting of electrodes mounted on glass-fibre shafts, attached to a handle of the same material, are excellent for small or shallow streams, but cannot stun fish in water more than about 1 m deep. Larger electrode assemblies, powered by generators of several kVA capacity, have been developed overseas, but even the largest units produce a limited electrical field. Early expectations that electric fishing equipment would be effective in large lakes or even in the sea have proved false. An attempt to construct an electrified cable to keep sharks off bathing beaches has been pursued with commendable persistence by a research team on the Natal coast for some 20 years, despite my scepticism as to the project's feasibility. Technology has its inherent limitations. In trout management, the best way of catching fish for transport to other waters is still a fly rod in capable hands if the river being fished is a moderate-sized or large trout stream.

If hatchery trout are to be used for supplementing the stock in a river, experience has shown that putting in small fish is futile. Even if large fish are used, the return to the angler is likely to be poor unless two conditions are met: first, the river must be stable, that is neither shrunk by drought nor, especially, subject to flooding soon after the fish are introduced; second, fishing pressure must be adequate to remove most of the fish in a short time, since long-term survival of hatchery-reared fish in a stream is unlikely. In other words, the usual objective of stream stocking is to create a put-and-take fishery.

A very interesting innovation was introduced by Eric Brewer in the Transvaal in 1967. The owners of Santa Estate, near Dullstroom, wanted to have the best possible sport from their stream, so Eric suggested stocking with catchable-sized rainbows and then, instead of leaving them to grow lean and hungry, they were fed with a daily ration of trout pellets. Being used to taking the pellets in their hatchery ponds, the trout accepted them eagerly in the river. The results were spectacular, and now numerous other syndicates with streams (generally modified by putting in concrete weirs) use the system introduced by Brewer. A trout of 150 g can easily grow out to over a kilogram in less than a year, according to Brewer. "The growth of stream fish," says Brewer, "depends almost entirely on the rate of supplementary feeding." Despite being fed, the trout are not easy to catch on artificial fly.

Brewer himself runs a fishery for a syndicate on his own property where he has not resorted to artificial-looking structures to "improve" his stream, although he has put in weirs in places where the stream cannot carry trout. He relies on natural breeding, with some supplementary stocking of a variety of sizes to ensure a satisfactory catch-rate for his guests — an average of two trout per day, with the better anglers catching by far the larger proportion. Dam fishing is provided for inexperienced anglers.

Brewer operates a trout farm on which he produces 25 to 30 tonnes of fish annually, from which he sells about 10 000 live trout to about 20 fisheries. He lists his fishery management strategy (principles) as follows:

" (a) To provide angling, not just fish to be reeled in;
  (b) To keep the angling as natural as possible;
  (c) To provide a catch of assorted sizes of trout as in nature;
  (d) To provide only a few big ones of over a kilogram;
  (e) To keep the stream as natural as possible for anglers and others."

According to Brewer, stocking should depend on trout already in the stream and on the number being caught. "A point to remember is that overstocking is difficult when trout are fed on a supplement." This does not mean, however, that Brewer believes in masses of fishermen and daily stocking of trout. "I abhor that. My attitude to stocking water is that stocking should be kept to the minimum necessary to supply the anglers' needs. The fewer the stock the better the health and growth."

Intensive management is desirable on dams perhaps more than on streams, and I shall refer again to the man who has made his remarkable ability as a trout fishery manager available to an enterprise of considerable commercial as well as recreational value — the provision of weekend trouting in the Eastern Transvaal.

Some of Brewer's ideas are undoubtedly applicable to less intensively managed waters in Natal and the Cape. Intensified management is, however, more applicable to dams than to rivers in these provinces. In Natal, especially, the nature of our rivers and the low angling pressure which they draw, make such procedures as stocking large trout and feeding them in the stream unlikely to be practised, except in special cases.

There is also a strong feeling among many Natal fly fishers that river fishing should be kept as natural as possible. This means that the stock of fish that the natural food supply is capable of supporting has to be used to be best advantage.

Recent drought years have temporarily reduced the quantities of trout in many Natal streams to low levels. Stricter limits on anglers' catches are therefore being put into effect, with some stretches of river under Natal Parks Board control being declared "no-kill" fisheries, as an experiment.

On the more popular sections of river, limitations on the anglers' take will probably have to remain, in the interests of spreading the harvest among as many fishermen as possible. Catch records on the Bushman's, Mooi and Umzimkulu Rivers in the 1960s, when weather conditions were favourable, indicated that the better sections could be expected to yield about 10 to 15 kg per hectare per year, while electric shocker surveys and experimental poisoning showed that 30 to 40 kg per hectare was the weight of all the fish in the river. But this total was made up largely of yearling trout, whereas the anglers' harvest included a high proportion of two-year-old or older fish.

There is no doubt that anglers may remove a substantial, although unknown, percentage of the bigger fish. This would indicate that strict limits are beneficial, together with periodic closure of popular stretches of river — not, be it noted, to preserve the fish, but to give as many trout of an acceptable size to as many people as possible.

Survival of excess numbers of small trout in areas where breeding is prolific poses a threat as serious as overfishing. If we are looking at the objective of providing good sport it may, indeed, be a more serious threat, because, whereas angling pressure can be controlled, it is very difficult to improve the situation on an overstocked stream.

S.A. Hey, in his reports and in his book *The Rapture of the River*, states that rivers that are tending to become overstocked should be heavily fished to keep numbers down. My own research has shown quite conclusively, however, that the number of yearlings in a river does not depend on the size of the breeding stock, but on the physical conditions in the river. If conditions are favourable for spawning and for the survival of fry and fingerlings, a sparse population of adults produces as many as 1 000 yearlings per hectare, which is far more than can grow out to a satisfactory size.

Attempts to encourage anglers to remove small fish have no impact on the problem and the use of an electric shocker has only a local effect. Netting is entirely impractical in South African rivers.

Several experiments were conducted in 1963 and subsequent years to determine the results of complete eradication of trout from a section of river by means of rotenone. Much interesting information was obtained on the composition of these stocks in the affected areas, especially the finding that where anglers complained they could catch no big trout, there were, in fact, no big trout in the river. Competition from yearlings had reduced the growth rate of the older individuals and, apparently, put such stress on them that few had managed to survive to the age of three years.

After elimination of all the trout from a 5 km stretch of the Bungalow water on the Mooi, those trout that entered the poisoned stretch from up and downstream put on weight rapidly. For a couple of seasons some good sport was enjoyed, with fish of much better size and in much better condition than hitherto. Then the position reverted to an overstocked situation. In 1968 poisoning was carried out again, with temporary results similar to the first experiment. Smaller-scale experiments were tried elsewhere, with inconclusive results. One extensive section further upstream on the Mooi River was treated and restocked immediately with fish taken by electric shocker, but drought in the subsequent season prevented the expected improvement in growth of the fish taking place.

Experience in Natal has shown that manipulating trout populations to improve the quality of angling is generally an unprofitable exercise. Each section of river tends to develop a population determined by the physical characteristics of the aquatic environment. All we can do is to make the best use of what nature provides.

17. Trout in still waters

Dams are at once more difficult and easier to manage for trout production than rivers. Since still water is not a natural environment for trout to breed in, we have to introduce the fish ourselves. But that very fact may be advantageous: one never knows exactly how many fish a river is going to produce, but in a dam one can at least be sure that there are no more trout than the number introduced. Overstocking, if it occurs, is our own fault.

There are, of course, dams in which naturally bred trout are to be found, if there is a feeder-stream that has an adequate flow and gravel beds for spawning. The Dap Naudé Dam near Magoebaskloof is populated by wild-bred rainbow trout. Wemmershoek Reservoir in the Cape has ample breeding facilities. There are other examples, of which a particularly interesting one is a 12-hectare impoundment in the Dargle area of Natal, controlled by a syndicate headed by Col. P.C.A. Francis. The dam was built in 1959 across the Furth Stream, a tributary of the Umgeni, at an altitude of nearly 1 800 m above sea-level. Above the dam is about a kilometre of stream which supported a resident population of brown trout. Although the stream is narrow, only about 2 m in average width, it has adequate depth and volume to allow large trout to move up to a waterfall that bars further progress. After an initial stocking with 2 000 small rainbow fingerlings, the dam became self-sufficient due to breeding in the stream. After 26 years the dam is still providing excellent fishing, with rainbows of up to more than 3 kg being caught. Brown trout have gradually become rarer, with rainbows predominating. Minimal management has been required, apart from partial drainage to reduce weed growth. A consistent yield of about 20 kg of trout per hectare has been harvested by members of the syndicate and their guests each year.

A larger dam that is also self-sufficient is the man-made lake on the upper Umzimkulwana River, near Underberg, in which recruitment from the stream maintains a stock of vigorous, but not very fast-growing, rainbows. The moderate growth-rate indicates that perhaps more than the optimum number of young fish enter the dam each year.

Natural productivity of most Natal dams in which the trout depend on naturally produced food supplies is between 15 and 25 kg per hectare per year, although this may be increased considerably by heavy fishing and frequent restocking. The important point is to put in enough fish to utilise the available food supply, but not enough to compete with each other. A stock of about 40 kg per hectare is all one can expect a dam to carry, and if this figure is borne in mind it will give an indication of how many trout to put in. If there is no natural breeding, one's management policy can give satisfactory results, although initial expectations may have to be modified by trial and error.

Effective dam management depends, first of all, on the nature of the impoundment itself. A trout pond must be clear, cool and not too overgrown with weeds. Spring-fed dams, or those on small, clear mountain streams are the most favourable for trout.

Because coolness is so important, it is generally true to say that trout do better the higher the altitude. Trout thrive in the highlands of Lesotho and other parts of Southern Africa that lie above 1 500 m. Nevertheless, altitude alone is not a reliable criterion, since water temperature is not controlled entirely by height above sea-level. A shallow muddy dam, or one that lacks an adequate water supply to maintain its level, will never be worth stocking with trout however high up it may be. Conversely, a dam near the coast could have the necessary characteristics for a trout water. Of course the farther north one goes, the higher is the level generally required. Whereas trout occur at sea-level in both rivers and still waters near the Cape, most trout waters in Natal are over 1 200 m above sea-level.

The purpose of a dam is to conserve water and one of the main criteria in deciding on a dam site must be the relationship between the volume of water and the volume of earth or other material to make the wall. A good site is one where a relatively small wall will dam up a big volume of water. We have all remarked at one time or another on places that seem to invite the intervention of a bulldozer. A narrow neck along the course of a gently sloping valley may seem an ideal spot for a dam. But if the new pond or lake is going to be a good fishing water there are other features which must be considered as well as economy of construction. Even from the purely engineering aspect, the amateur often comes up against unexpected snags. Unless a good deep layer of soil overlies an impervious substrate, it may prove difficult to make a waterproof wall. Often an apparently less economical site may prove better than one that looks ideal.

First of all, should the dam be on a strong stream, or should it be fed by drainage from a relatively small catchment? Obviously if impoundment of water for irrigation is the primary object then the stronger the flow of the feeder stream the better, as long as silting is not a problem. And, of course, silting *is* a problem in the great majority of dams across the larger streams or rivers in this country. It is also a problem wherever soil conditions are unstable. A dam with the smallest catchment will soon fill with silt if there is wash from bare eroded earth.

Assuming that the land above the dam is well looked after, and that silt is not a major factor to be considered, a very strong feeder stream still has some important

Opposite above: The author fishes an Underberg dam.

Opposite below: Richard Pott watches for a rise on a small Eastern Transvaal trout dam.

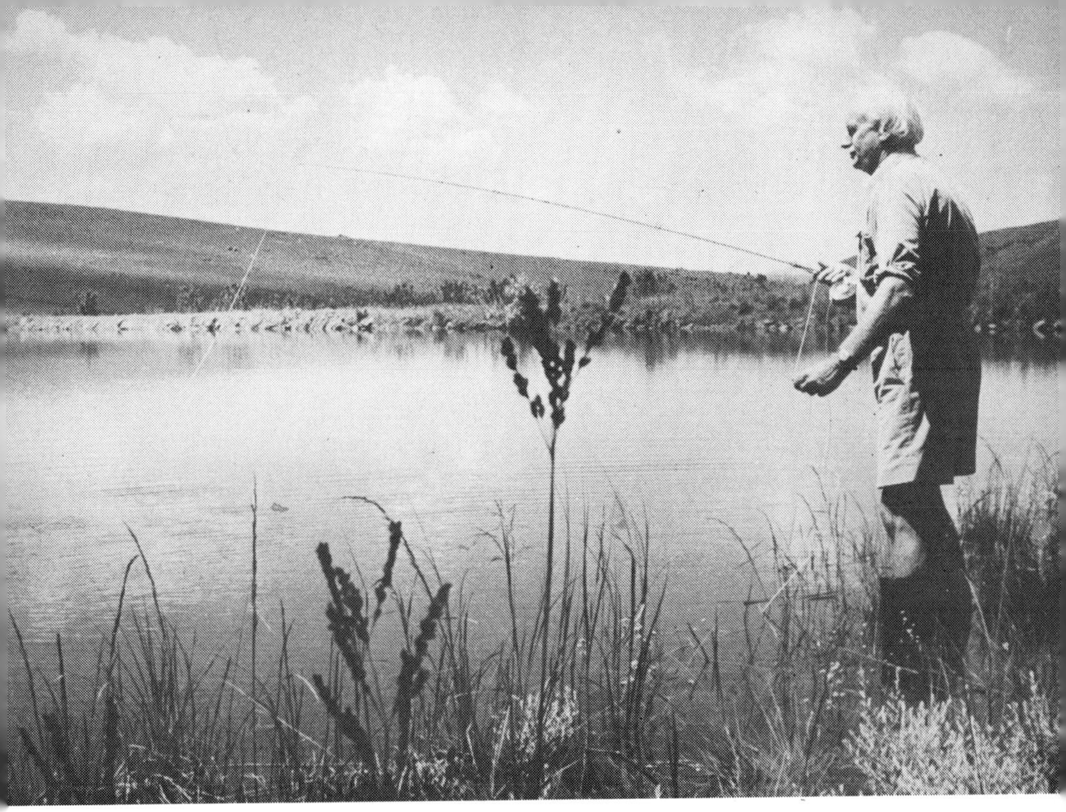

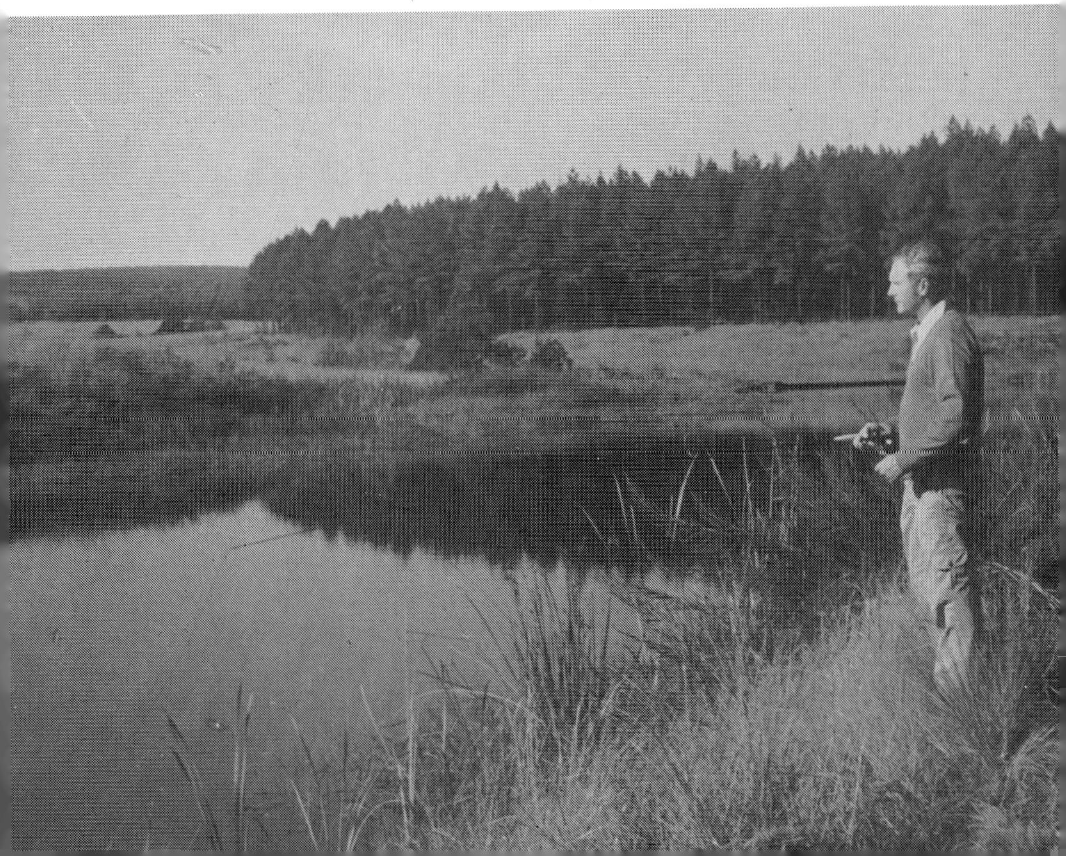

disadvantages. First of all, the spillway must be made wide enough to take the biggest flood, and adequate freeboard must be allowed on the wall. Engineers have a formula for working out maximum expected flows, according to the size of the catchment and recorded precipitation in that area. Spillway width and height of the wall above water level are designed accordingly. The bigger the volume of flow, the greater must be the margin of safety and the greater the expense of building the dam.

Secondly, fish are likely to be washed out of a dam when a lot of water flows through it.

Thirdly, fertility is reduced. Chemical substances, chiefly phosphate and nitrate, must be available if a rich development of plankton is to take place. Plankton is the name for all the minute plants and animals that grow in a stable body of water and that provide the basis for fish production. Both the necessary chemical nutrients and the plankton itself will be washed out if too much water passes through a dam.

One often hears a farmer say that he has a dam supplied by a good strong stream, and that there must therefore be plenty of food for fish. This is a misconception. A productive dam is one in which food is produced within the impoundment itself. Insects and other food brought down by the stream are of little importance.

A strong feeder stream is useful, indeed essential, if one wants to have trout breeding

Dangerous engineering! The eroding spillway of a dam on the Ndowana River, Natal.

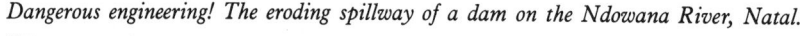

naturally in a dam. A strong stream may, therefore, be an advantage in a trout dam, but only if it provides spawning grounds. From the food aspect it is not good, as far more of the things fish eat will be washed out of the dam than will be washed in. For a fertile dam, the ideal is to have enough water to keep it full but not a big overflow.

Shallow water is generally more productive than deep water, but a shallow dam has widely fluctuating temperatures and will soon become full of weeds. The question of weeds is always cropping up among the problems that confront dam owners, but in a deep dam rooted plants are unlikely to be a real nuisance. A certain amount of weed growth and a reasonable area of shallow water are favourable for fish. One cannot expect much production from a flooded quarry that has vertical sides running straight into deep water. But the other extreme of a shallow basin that becomes choked with weed is also most unsatisfactory.

A good fishing dam should therefore have an area of water at least 4 m deep, shelving to the margins.

As far as actual construction is concerned, a farmer cannot go wrong if he follows the specifications laid down by the Department of Agricultural Technical Services. Many privately built dams would not meet these specifications, and yet prove satisfactory in practice. Other walls have been constructed on the cheap and either leak or have actually collapsed. Attempts at economy may prove costly in the long run.

One feature of great importance is an adequate spillway. Not only must it be wide enough to accommodate the biggest floods; it should be carefully levelled so that the overflow forms a broad, shallow stream. A relatively deep, narrow channel is likely to form a tempting escape route for fish from the dam. A lot of fish may be lost if they can swim easily down the outlet.

Another feature that is all too often neglected is a drainage pipe. It costs money to install a pipe and control valve, but generally the money is well spent. Effective management of an artificial pond or lake is made incomparably easier if control of the water level is possible. Sooner or later, perhaps after only five years, perhaps after 20, complete drainage will be desirable. Siphoning or pumping out the water may be feasible, but it is much easier to use a drainage system installed when the dam was built.

The standard outlet for a fish pond is commonly known as a monk's weir. This consists of a concrete or plastered brick tower, rectangular in cross section. Three sides are solid masonry and the fourth side is open but can be blocked by wooden boards which slide in grooves. Water level is controlled by the number of boards left in position. The tower stands on the inside of the dam, with a drainage pipe passing through the bottom of the wall.

This system does away with the likelihood of blockages which may affect drainage pipes controlled by a valve on the outside end. There is, however, a much easier system which does away with the need for either a monk's weir or an expensive valve. This system might be described as the upright, swivelling pipe outlet (see diagram). To install it, a galvanised T-piece is fixed to the end of the main drainage pipe that passes under the dam wall. The free end of the T is blocked with a plug that may be removed if necessary. To the side opening of the T is attached a barrel nipple and an elbow into which the upright, swivelling pipe is fixed. This should be the same length as the depth of water in the dam. When in the upright position the swivelling pipe serves as a trickle overflow.

The dam can be drained partially, or completely, by lowering the swivelling pipe to the desired level. To prevent debris clogging the outlet, a coarse mesh screen, preferably made of plastic which is non-corrosive, should be put over the inside end of the drainage pipe.

Temperature is a critical factor, and one may feel confident when putting trout into a dam if the water feels quite chilly, even on a hot summer's day. But, significantly, one always notices a contrast between the cool depths and the tepid shallows. There is often a layer of water near the bottom that is tolerable for trout. The value of that water to the fish depends, however, on its oxygen content. Trout require at least five parts per million of dissolved oxygen, and water that is out of contact with the air soon loses oxygen if any decaying matter is present.

Dead plants or organically rich silt have a high oxygen demand, which may easily make the lower layers of water unsuitable for fish. When a dam is first flooded, the grass and other herbage in the basin dies; in an older dam plant remains may accumulate, or mud that was once fertile soil in the catchment may be carried down by erosion. Any of this material is likely to have a high enough oxygen demand to make water near the bottom unhealthy for trout.

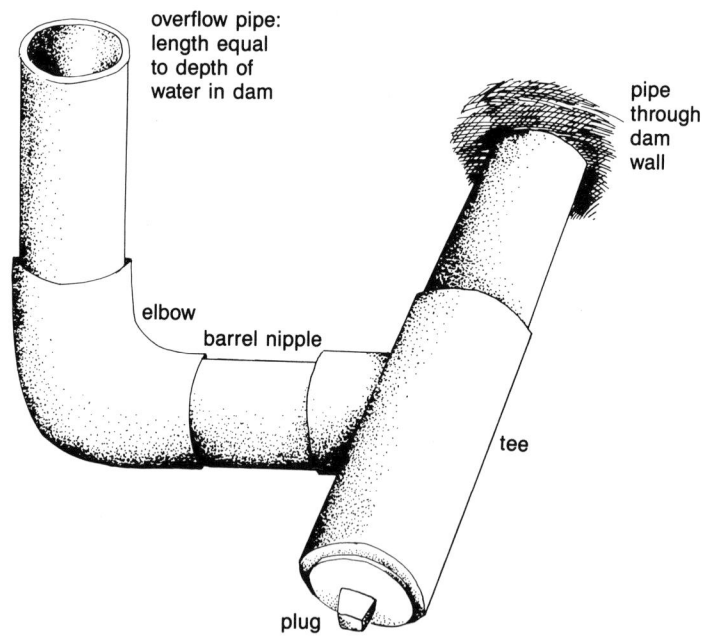

Swivelling pipe overflow system.

188

If the deeper, cool layers are short of oxygen the fish will be forced to live in the shallows and surface layers, where the temperature may become too high. A very shallow dam, of course, becomes warmed up all over during a spell of hot weather. Inadequate depth is therefore a serious shortcoming in a trout dam. A portion of the area must be deep and well oxygenated down to the bottom. Shallows are also necessary for a dam to be productive since food is found mainly where the depth is such that light can penetrate. Without light, the minute plant life that forms the basis for the food chain cannot exist. Light penetration depends on the clarity of the water, so turbidity tends to restrict the depth at which food production can take place.

A clear dam is much superior for trout to one that is discoloured. Not only is it likely to produce more food, but the trout can see better to catch their dinner. It is only with regard to temperature that turbid water may be better than transparent water. If there is poor light penetration, heat is also blanketed off and one will find that the main body of water stays cool, even though the top few inches may be heated by the sun.

Productivity of a dam depends largely on the constitution of the soil that forms the basin. A fertile loam contains mineral salts that go into solution when the dam is filled. This initial fertility inevitably declines as time passes but may be made good to some extent by adding fertiliser. The decline is accelerated if a large volume of water passes through, so the ideal is an inflow just large enough to keep the level constant. A dam that is built across a strong stream or small river is subject to another disadvantage in addition to loss of fertility. Unwanted fish are likely to gain access. Many an otherwise promising dam is ruined by fish which find their way in from the feeder stream.

It is impossible to exclude fish that may be living in the catchment above a dam. Many instances of bass coming into trout dams have been reported. One of the most unfortunate has been the invasion by largemouth bass of the Comrie Dam, belonging to SAPPI Forests at Donnybrook in Natal. This 70-hectare lake is a major amenity for the angling public, but its future as a trout water is now in jeopardy.

Rooted plants are commonly known as water weeds; and weeds, whether on land or under water, become a menace. A limited amount of submerged plants can be useful as a habitat for insects and as a refuge for fish, but extensive weed beds have several unfavourable effects. They reduce the volume of open water, they tend to push up temperatures in shallow water by restricting wave action, they use up oxygen at night (although during the day green plants produce oxygen) and they take much of the available nutrients out of circulation, so cutting down the production of plankton. More obviously, weeds are a confounded nuisance to the angler.

There are two useful ways of dealing with unwanted aquatic plants: draining the dam or introducing Chinese grass carp, which eat the weed. Trials in Natal by Tom Pike of the Natal Parks Board have proved encouraging and grass carp are also being used in the Transvaal. The Transvaal Fly Fishers' Club have obtained young fish with which to stock all their dams and the initial results are promising. When small, grass carp are subject to predation, especially by cormorants, so the TFFC are rearing them in a covered raceway and in cages to a size at which they should survive better.

Grass carp, being herbivorous, will not compete with trout for food supplies, although care must be taken not to overstock with grass carp. Bass, on the other hand, are direct competitors and if they are present in a trout dam the only hope of maintaining a stock of trout is to put in well-grown fish, preferably at least 30 cm in length.

Barbus minnows, especially the chubby-head minnow, is often found in trout dams. Sometimes they are introduced deliberately in the belief that they are valuable food for trout. This belief takes no account of the fact that the minnows eat the same types of food as trout and may not be easy for the trout to catch.

The dictum that "You can only eat whom you can meet" (Professor G. Hempel, quoted by R. Siegfried) is applicable to trout and minnows. The latter live mainly in the warm shallow water which trout do not frequent, and are, furthermore, adept at avoiding a meeting with trout. In winter, when they become less active, minnows may be taken by trout, but seldom in summer.

Stocking a dam correctly is, of course, a key to its successful management. In particular, it is worse to overstock than understock. Hugh Huntley, who looks after the stocking of Natal Fly Fishers' Club dams, is always resisting pressures put on him by other committee members to put in more fish than he reckons will grow to an acceptable size.

The first question to settle is what kind of trout to use. The answer may well depend on availability. Rainbow trout are far easier to come by than brown trout, which fish farmers find less amenable to propagation in a hatchery. If obtainable, however, and the possibility exists of obtaining some from an overstocked river, I recommend using a ratio of about one brown trout to five rainbows. The browns will be less easily caught and they also live longer than rainbows. Four or five years after they have been put in, they are therefore likely to be hooked as fish of 3 kg or more — an exciting catch for any fly fisher.

The next question is what size of fish to use. The general consensus is to use trout that are as large as possible. There are, however, exceptions to every rule and a new dam with good physical conditions may be stocked successfully with very small trout. Instances have been reported of good results even from eyed ova. In 1948, 1 000 eyed ova were sown in a gravel bed in the feeder stream of the municipal dam at Maclear. In May 1951, a trout of 2,75 kg was caught in the dam.

If the fish that are introduced do not survive, there will be nothing to show for the trouble and cost of putting them in. It is most important, therefore, to do one's best to see that a reasonable number do survive and grow to a size that will provide sport for the angler.

The most critical period is shortly after introduction. The young fish find themselves in strange surroundings with unfamiliar perils to contend with. Platanna frogs or cormorants may take their toll, or big trout may seek a cannibal feast on the new arrivals. More significant than attack by enemies, is the risk of high temperatures, lack of oxygen or starvation. Again, the inborn behaviour patterns of small trout may lead them to destruction although everything appears, to human eyes, ideal.

Let us remember that trout are by nature adapted to life in running water. Small trout, in particular, seek a place in the current. In a river, fry that have newly emerged from the gravel in which they hatched take up their station where the water is shallow and a constant flow brings them food. The still water of a dam is not, therefore, a natural habitat for young trout and they are likely to seek a way out of the impoundment if they can. Should they swim up the feeder stream, no harm will result since they will drop back into the dam later on, but if fish go out over the spillway they are lost. There is no way of knowing how many trout do escape from dams, but a recorded experiment was illuminating. At Highmoor State Forest in Natal a 0,3-hectare pond was built above a 12-hectare dam that has produced trout for a number of years. The pond was stocked with small trout and emptied again on two occasions, but each time the number of fish recovered was most disappointing. At the third stocking, Mr C.W. Wright, of the Natal Parks Board, and Mr Olivier of the Department of Forestry, installed a fine mesh trap at the outlet. Within a week of stocking with 500 fingerlings, 50 were found to have left the dam. This showed quite conclusively that small trout may go over the spillway of a dam in considerable numbers. An experiment at the Natal Parks Board's Himeville Nature Reserve proved, again, that mass emigration of newly stocked hatchery fingerlings may occur.

Disappearance of trout is not, of course, always due to emigration. There is bound to be a certain amount of mortality, and if conditions are unfavourable all the fish may die. When this happens it is important to know whether it is possible to change the unfavourable conditions or whether one must just accept that the dam is unsuitable for trout and try bass or other more hardy fish.

Large trout from a hatchery are obviously more expensive than small ones, but as Eric Brewer firmly believes, trout of 30 cm or more give a more reliable return than smaller fish. These are his comments about the cost of stocking: "You ask if the expense of stocking is justified and my reply to that is that if the anglers decide it is then there is no further discussion. What I do feel is that stocking with fingerlings in water with large trout is usually a nonsense economically and does not enable one to plan the fishing as the return is so erratic and poor. Another point of interest is that a dam could today cost R20 000 to build, which means the annual cost at 15 per cent is R3 000. The stocking of such a dam could cost R1 000, which is really quite small related to the R3 000. Nobody wants to wait a year before fishing a new dam. What we recommend in that case is a natural population with a stocking of all sizes, including some of over a kilogram, so that one can at once enjoy the unexpected catch, and not keep on catching a regular size."

With regard to the stocking rate, Brewer considers it should be the minimum to satisfy the requirements of the anglers. "I say to a prospective bailiff 'What do you want to catch in the coming season?' In other words, how many angler days do you expect and what do you want them to catch per day? I then suggest what in my experience is the best way of achieving the objective, bearing in mind any special circumstances and the cost. This generally entails one to four stockings per season; the heavier the fishing pressure the greater the number of stockings and the smaller the water the more the stockings. My preference is for one stocking a season as this results in the most challenging angling and also permits easier analysis of angling results."

As in a river, intensive management may involve feeding the trout in a dam. This is done by a number of syndicates who want the maximum return from a small area of water. The Transvaal Fly Fishers' Club do not distribute feed for their trout, once liberated, but they supply pellets regularly to the fish that are being grown out in cages. Peter Arderne believes that excess pellets, which drop through the bottom of a cage, may be eaten by fish outside, but the main effect of feeding in the dam is to increase the fertility of the water, with a consequent build-up in plankton.

The increase in fertility around the floating cages may reach undesirable proportions. At the end of November 1985, there was mortality of both rainbow trout and grass carp in the TFFC's No. 4 dam, into which a pipe was taking water from underneath the cages in No. 3. The fish evidently died from lack of oxygen due to the heavy load of organic material coming from the vicinity of the cages. One may push the fertility of water too far in an attempt to improve productivity.

A dam with high productivity, or any sort of productivity, is useless without sensible harvesting of the fish crop. If useful production is to take place, the standing crop must have room to grow. That means the total fish population must be kept below the maximum carrying capacity. If fish are continually being removed, production is likely to be higher than if harvesting is intermittent. Ideally, management should be aimed at keeping the fish population sufficiently large to make full use of available resources, but never allowing it to grow to the point where competition begins to limit production. Overfishing is obviously bad, because it cuts the stock down too low, but underfishing is wasteful — sometimes blatantly so.

A striking example was brought to my attention a few years ago in the Natal midlands, where a landowner had built a dam that covered more than 12 ha. It was high up near the source of a small, spring-fed stream nearly 1 550 m above sea-level in a well-conserved valley. Clear, cool water provided an ideal habitat for trout. The dam was duly stocked with small hatchery trout and the owner looked forward to some good sport.

He was a patient man who wanted to be sure that the fish grew big before he caught them. A year, two years, three years went by, but no one disturbed the blue waters. Finally, two fishermen arrived at the dam, put their rods together and began casting. The swirl of a rising trout near a weed-bed caught the eye of one of the anglers and straight away his fly was seized. The rod bent and an 18-inch rainbow broke the surface. What a thrill!

But instead of putting up a spectacular fight the fish soon came to the net. It was a male, with the long, hooked lower jaw of an aged trout. Others, males and femals, were caught in quick succession, some as much as 19 inches long. None weighed in proportion to their length and several of the females exuded loose eggs, although this was midsummer. The eggs were flaccid and opaque, long past the time when they should have been shed. Successful spawning is, of course, not possible for trout in still water, but the younger fish often seem to get rid of the ova. As they get older, trout in a dam are more prone to retain the eggs. This leads to their becoming spawn-bound.

By lunchtime a dozen fish were on the bank, and although they seemed an impressive catch when laid out in the shade of a tree, a closer look soon showed that they were all past their best. Their lack of fight when hooked had already indicated their poor condition and final confirmation came when they were cooked. They were not worth eating. Here was a crop that had gone too long unharvested to be of value for either sport or food.

A year or so later, the old trout had disappeared and the dam was restocked with young ones. This time fishing was started sooner and some fine sport was enjoyed. The owner had learnt his lesson.

One of the most important principles in getting the best possible production from fish is to catch them young. For sport fishing it is always interesting to have a few fish that are well above the average size. This adds to the angler's pleasure. But growth rate declines with age, and the key to good production is rapid growth. Look at it this way. If we have two one-acre dams each containing 20 lb of trout, one with 20 fish of 1 lb and the other with 10 fish of 2 lb, one might expect a similar total yield from the two dams. In fact, however, the smaller fish are likely to be putting on about as much weight each, per month, as the bigger ones. That means that if one wants to remove only the increase in weight, without reducing the standing crop, twice as much may be taken out of the dam containing small fish than out of the large-fish dam, over a given period.

Furthermore, losses of various sorts are going on all the time. The longer a fish is left uncaught by the angler, the more chance there is of its dying or disappearing. If one is particularly anxious to have large trout, and if only a few fish have been put into the dam, it is clear that no attempt should be made to pull them out too soon. As a means of utilising productivity, such a policy is inefficient. Assuming that enough fish survive for, say, three years ultimately to make up maximum carrying capacity for the dam, and assuming further (which is highly unlikely) that all the fish are then caught, average annual yield is only one-third of the carrying capacity. A more heavily stocked dam that is fished from the time the trout have reached a reasonable size may yield a weight equivalent to the carrying capacity each season. More wasteful than anything is to stock a dam successfully, let the fish grow until the standing crop reaches carrying capacity, and then to leave the crop unharvested in the hope that the fish will become bigger and bigger.

"No-kill" fishing may make sense on a river that has a limited number of trout, but it is wasteful or even counter-productive in a dam. In an experiment carried out at the Transvaal Fly Fishers' No. 1 dam, fishing was allowed, but all trout were returned to the water in the hope that they would reach trophy size. At first, things went well; the average size taken increased noticeably. Then the older fish simply vanished. In other TFFC dams, where the normal rule applied of three fish to be taken per angler per day, some of the trout did reach trophy proportions.

A dam can, of course, be overfished. If too many fish are removed, the survivors will not be able to maintain full production. Overfishing a dam is comparable with killing off too many livestock on a farm. This is well recognised, and precautions against overfishing are commonly put into practice.

A common bone of contention among anglers is the question of returning fish to the water. Some fishery managers insist that every fish must be taken and that as soon as an angler has reached his limit he must stop fishing. Others allow anglers to go on catching and returning trout after achieving their limit.

If handled carefully, a trout is unlikely to die from the effects of being caught, but as I mentioned in Chapter 11, I personally dislike the idea of trying to catch fish that I have no intention of keeping.

A dam that becomes choked with weed or that has undesirable fish — such as bass in a trout dam — may require complete drainage: hence the importance of the outlet pipe. If drainage is not feasible, one can kill off all the fish and start again, by using a chemical that exterminates the fish but does not poison other creatures. Rotenone, a natural plant product, is the most commonly used substance to remove unwanted fish. It is expensive, however, and may not be used without due authorisation.

Some dam owners take a lot of trouble over the management of their waters; others scarcely concern themselves about such matters at all. The hard workers deserve to have better fishing than their easy-going neighbours, and it is probably true to say that the better the management the better the results, provided other things are equal. But of course other things are not equal, since dams differ tremendously. A good dam will produce more and bigger fish with practically no management than an inferior dam that is looked after with the greatest care. Also, one must recognise that a dam, although of artificial origin, shares with natural waters a strong tendency to resist attempts to change its fish-producing capacity. This capacity is determined by the size, depth, stability and chemical composition of the water body as well as its clarity and temperature. To convert capacity into actual production depends primarily on correct stocking and harvesting. The harvest consists of a particular number of kilograms of fish per year, and the first principle of management is to balance this annual take-off with the actual production.

Effective management involves work, of which farmers have more than enough. This is where angling clubs enter the scene. If their members are willing to work for their pleasure, angler and landowner can happily co-operate.

Appendices

TROUT FOR THE GOURMET

Trout on the table may be superb, mediocre or downright disappointing. It all depends on the quality of the fish itself, how it is handled and the way it is cooked.

Fish from natural waters are generally considered superior to the product of a trout farm, but this is not necessarily true. An artificial pond with an adequate flow of clear, cool water provides a good environment for trout and, if the diet is correctly formulated, the resulting product is first class. On the other hand, an undernourished river trout may have soft flesh of poor flavour. This applies particularly to mature fish shortly before or after spawning.

I do not know whether the expression "in the pink" was derived from the observation that the flesh of trout that are fit and healthy is often coloured pink. A pink-fleshed trout is always in good condition, but one that has almost white flesh may be of equally excellent quality. Pinkness is associated with a nutritious diet, especially crustaceans, and a trout that is unusually pink tends to have a rich flavour that may appeal less to a gourmet's palate than the more delicate taste of a white-fleshed trout.

A trout that is brightly coloured when alive will have good-quality, firm flesh. An exception is the brilliantly hued male in nuptial dress. Despite its attractive appearance, such a fish will be scarcely worth cooking. The giveaway feature is the colour of the belly, which is blotchy grey in an out-of-condition trout. Lower surfaces that are bright silvery (or golden in the case of a brown trout) are a good sign.

Rapidly growing dam trout generally have softer, richer flesh than those that get more exercise swimming against the current in a river. This must be taken into account in deciding how to prepare a fish for the table.

As well as condition, size has a bearing on how a trout should be cooked. Recipes seldom indicate the size of the fish being dealt with. Perhaps the reason is that cooks usually handle farm-reared trout, which tend to be more or less uniform in size. An angler's catch, on the other hand, may range from less than a hundred grams to two or three kilograms. Different techniques are called for to make the best use of small and large trout.

The length of time that elapses after a fish is caught and the way it is handled are of vital importance. Everyone knows that the ideal is "out of the water, into the frying pan," but delays are inevitable in practice and one merely has to do one's best to avoid spoilage of a perishable commodity.

Killing and cleaning should be done as rapidly as possible. Fortunately one seldom sees a trout fisherman leave his quarry kicking about after landing it, as so many saltwater anglers seem to do. Not only is such action heartless: the more a fish exerts itself the more lactic acid builds up in its muscles, with subsequent deterioration in the quality of the flesh. A sharp tap with a weighted object at the point where the spine joins the skull is effective, but I prefer to hold the fish firmly and break its neck with a quick thrust of the thumb against its upper jaw. As well as being humane, this has the advantage of rupturing the main blood vessels behind the head to allow bleeding. Research in America has shown that bleeding improves the keeping quality of the flesh.

To leave a fish ungutted not only makes the job unpleasant (and I hope no one has the temerity to say that cleaning the catch can be left to the cook at home), but accelerates decomposition. An odd injunction that appears in older literature is against washing out the inside of a trout. I always make a point of carefully washing away all blood, especially near the head, after removing the gills. Unlike other types of fish, which need to be scaled, trout should not be scraped as their scales are minute. After washing, a trout merely has to be wiped dry — never allowed to soak in water. Thereafter, coolness and careful handling will enable the fish to keep for a day or two without appreciable loss of quality.

Trout are often deep frozen. This undoubtedly detracts from their culinary quality, although large fish keep better than small ones. If one wants to keep trout for consumption later on, smoking is an option that should be considered. Some trout farmers offer smoked trout for sale, but for an angler one of the small smokers, such as the ABU, produces excellent results. The ABU is a hot smoker, cooking as well as smoking, and is suitable for medium-sized fish. A big trout yields a product similar to smoked salmon if cold smoked by a butcher with the required facility. At a dinner party, you should have no difficulty in passing off local smoked rainbow trout, sliced thin, with brown bread, as the imported article if you want to impress your friends.

For small trout, up to about 300 grams (or 30 cm), the method of first choice is to fry them in butter, margarine, or cooking oil. Perhaps some people would look askance at the use of oil. Negley Farson, in his classic *Going Fishing*, records his horror at the action of his hostess who fried the trout he caught in the Caucasus in sunflower seed oil. To my palate, however, there is nothing obnoxious about any pure vegetable oil, or dripping, for that matter. Bennion (*The Angler in South Africa*) gives the following recipe taken from the cookery book of Mrs Jaffray of Balgowan:

> Small-sized trout are best fried. Clean them and wipe dry with a clean cloth. [It would seem that Mrs Jaffray's angling boarders did not gut their own fish!] A soft cloth and gentle handling are necessary. Then dredge them lightly with flour, or roll in fine oatmeal. Melt enough dripping in your frying pan just to cover the fish; when it is still [that is, presumably, not bubbling] and smoking put in the fish one at a time with a few seconds between each, so as to keep the heat

of the friture. Fry a golden brown, take up and sprinkle with salt, drain on thickly-folded kitchen paper in front of the fire and serve. A good appetite is the only sauce needed.

To do visual, as well as gustatory justice to the attraction of trout on the table, they should be cooked whole with head and fins attached. There is, incidentally, a lump of muscle in the cheek, which is worth digging out from a largish fish's head.

Crisp, brown skin is thoroughly edible and should not be left on one's plate. This applies particularly to small trout, which have a delicate flavour, superior in my wife's esteem to that of mature individuals. The 15 to 18 cm trout which anglers are encouraged to take from overstocked rivers are excellent eating and undoubtedly deserve a better fate than being fed to the cat.

Sizeable trout may be filleted if boneless flesh is desired. It is certainly hard to beat the taste of a fillet, suitably seasoned and fried for seven minutes skin-side down and then five minutes skin-side up. Served with a sprig of parsley and a slice of lemon, filleted trout are delicious, but one must be careful not to dry the flesh out. The flesh of a trout that is cooked whole remains moist and succulent, although it must be cooked until the bones are freely detachable. An underdone fish is most unappetising.

People sometimes seem puzzled when presented with a whole trout. If they adopt the wrong procedure, bones and meat may become hopelessly entangled. The secret is to slide the fish-knife down the side of the fish, using the natural divide between the back muscles and those of the lower flank to leave the spine exposed. Having dealt with the one side, the whole fish should be turned over and the operation repeated.

Trout of more than a kilogram (or about 45 cm) are best grilled, baked or simmered. In our household we generally eat them cold, with salad and a suitable sauce. Large trout, especially rainbows from dams, may seem over-rich when eaten hot, but if allowed to cool under a moist cloth such fish are a real treat. Either a lemon-flavoured white sauce, with chopped parsley, or mayonnaise is a good accompaniment. An excellent sauce may be made on the basis of a roux of butter, flour and milk cooked slowly with constant stirring, while fish paste, tobasco and mayonnaise or fresh cream are added, and finally a good squeeze of lemon juice.

When grilling a trout my wife puts seasoning, herbs, butter and slices of onion in the body cavity, with a little water and lemon juice in a baking dish. The trout should be placed about 15 cm below the grill, in an electric oven, and cooked for about ten minutes (or longer for a very large fish) on each side. The juice that remains in the baking dish should be added to the sauce.

Big trout taste good if simmered slowly in a pot large enough to hold the whole fish — curled round, unless you happen to own a fish kettle specially designed to cope with a salmon. The water should be about 50 cm deep, with two or three tablespoonfuls of vinegar or lemon juice and several bay leaves added, as well as salt. The fish is placed in the cold water, which is gradually brought to boiling point, but never allowed to boil hard. Gentle rocking of the trout shows that it is cooking. Allow 20 minutes plus 10 minutes extra for each 500 grams over a kilogram.

Serve, suitably garnished, either hot with new potatoes or chips, or cold with salad and parsley sauce.

Trout may, of course, be braaied on an open fire, either well rubbed with oil or butter, or wrapped in aluminium foil. Before foil was available, I remember many a delicious meal of trout wrapped in brown paper (newspaper will do as well) dipped in the river to wet the wrapping, and placed in the coals of a wood fire for 20 minutes or so. The paper stuck to the skin, which peeled off leaving succulent flesh with a slightly smoky taste.

Finally, here are four recipes published by Edith Combes in the *Newsletter* of the Natal Fly Fishers' Club.

STUFFED TROUT (FOR EIGHT)

8 small trout
3 + 1 tbs butter
½ tsp salt
500 g cooked, shelled prawns or shrimps
1 clove garlic, crushed
8 green olives   )
250 g mushrooms   )   finely chopped
4 anchovy fillets   )
2 tsp finely chopped parsley
slivered almonds

Fry together prawns, garlic, mushrooms, olives, anchovies and parsley in 3 tbs butter. Cool. Stuff trout firmly. Brush remaining melted butter and salt over trout. Sprinkle with almonds. Seal each in foil and bake at 180 °C for 20 minutes.

TROUT GRENOBLAISE

Clean and wash trout. Arrange on heavy foil in a baking tin and sprinkle with salt, pepper and mixed herbs. Add a tot of medium sherry and seal foil firmly with double fold to ensure that no steam escapes. Cook in hot oven (230 °C) for 25 minutes.

Sauce: While trout is cooking fry these sauce ingredients in butter for 15 minutes: 225 g mushrooms, 1 tsp capers, 115 g blanched almonds, juice of 1 lemon, 1 tsp chopped parsley.

Remove trout from oven and open out foil. Pour sauce over fish and return to oven for 5 minutes. Garnish with strips of red pepper and sprigs of parsley.

SHERRY BAKED TROUT

4 medium trout
2 tbs oil
2 tbs chopped parsley
1 clove garlic, crushed
½ cup (125 ml) breadcrumbs

¼ cup (65 ml) sherry
juice of ½ lemon
salt and pepper

Rub trout with salt and pepper. Heat oil, remove from heat and add parsley, garlic and breadcrumbs. Cover base of well-greased baking dish with half the crumb mixture. Place trout on top, and cover trout with rest of crumb mixture. Sprinkle lemon juice over. Bake at 180 °C for about 20 minutes, adding sherry after 10 minutes. Baste from time to time.

POTTED TROUT

500 g fresh trout
1½ tsp salt
½ tsp black pepper
½ tsp ground mace
pinch ground cloves
¾ teacup (about 170 ml) butter
4 peppercorns
4 bay leaves

Season the fish with half the salt and pepper and full quantity of mace and cloves. Place in ovenware dish and dot with 2 tbs of the measured butter, cut into small pieces. Sprinkle peppercorns over and lay bay leaves on top. Cover. Bake in moderate oven for about 40 minutes or until fish flakes easily. Remove fish from dish and flake. Strain and reserve any liquid.

Mix flaked fish, 4 tbs of remaining butter (melted) and the liquid and put through mincer. Mix in remaining salt and pepper. Pack into pots, set aside to cool. Melt remaining butter and pour over potted fish to seal. Serve with toast and lemon wedges.

NAMES AND ADDRESSES OF TROUT FISHING ORGANISATIONS

CAPE PROVINCE

Department of Nature and Environmental Conservation, Private Bag 9086, Cape Town 8000.
(Responsible for control of inland waters and legislation affecting freshwater fish.)

J.L.B. Smith Institute of Ichthyology, Private Bag 1015, Grahamstown 6140.
(Scientific and management interests in all types of fish and fishing.)

Albany Fresh Water Angling Association, P.O. Box 449, Grahamstown 6140.
(Members interested in trout, but no trout waters under their control.)

Barkly East Angling Society, B.E. Advertiser, Barkly East 5580.
(May assist visitors to obtain fishing in the district.)

Cape Piscatorial Society, Westminster House, 122 Longmarket Street, Cape Town 8001.
(Provides an excellent service on all aspects of trout fishing in the Western Cape; visitors welcome.)

Eastern Province Freshwater Fish Conservancy, P.O. Box 2544, Port Elizabeth 6000.
(The club has rights to fishing in dams within 100 km of Port Elizabeth.)

Federation of South African Flyfishers, c/o Cape Piscatorial Society, Westminster House, 122 Longmarket Street, Cape Town 8001.
(It is hoped to develop this as a co-ordinator for the activities of flyfishing bodies in South Africa.)

Frontier Acclimatisation Society, 39 Arthur Street, King William's Town 5600.
(Arranges fishing on Maden and Rooikrantz Dams.)

Hogsback Trout Angling Club, King's Lodge, Hogsback 5705.
(Trout fishing in Klipplaat River and dams.)

NATAL

Natal Parks Game and Fish Preservation Board, P.O. Box 662, Pietermaritzburg 3200.
(Provides public angling in seven game and nature reserves in the Drakensberg as well as being responsible for control of inland waters and legislation affecting freshwater fish.)

Directorate of Forestry, Department of Environment Affairs, Private Bag 9029, Pietermaritzburg 3200.
(Controls the well-known Highmoor dams, as well as a considerable amount of river fishing in Natal. Regional offices in the Western Cape and Eastern Transvaal control trout waters in their areas.)

Fly Fishers' Association, P.O. Box 37197, Overport 4067.
(Has fishing rights on trout waters in the Natal midlands.)

Hopewell Trout Angling Club, P.O. Box 40, Franklin 4610.
(Provides dam fishing for its members.)

Natal Fly Fishers' Club, P.O. Box 1535, Pietermaritzburg 3200.
(Provides facilities on a large variety of Natal trout waters.)

Natal Midlands Fly Fishing Club, P.O. Box 432, Estcourt 3310.
(Has fishing rights on several productive dams.)

Tswilika Trout Fishing Club, P.O. Swartberg 4710.
(Members fish local trout dams.)

Underberg-Himeville Trout Fishing Club, P.O. Box 7, Underberg 4590.
(Provides facilities for fishing on the well-known trout waters in the district.)

ORANGE FREE STATE

Nature Conservation Branch, P.O. Box 517, Bloemfontein 9300.
(Responsible for the management of Sterkfontein Dam.)

TRANSVAAL

Nature Conservation Division, Private Bag X209, Pretoria 0001.
(The controlling authority for the Transvaal.)

Haenertsburg Trout Association, P.O. Box 666, Tzaneen 0850.
(Provides facilities for fishing in the Magoebaskloof area.)

Machadodorp Trout Club, P.O. Machadodorp 1170.
(Visitors may obtain tickets to fish the Elands River and its tributaries.)

Sabie Trout Angling Club, P.O. Sabie 1260.
(Visitors wishing to fish the Sabie River are well catered for.)

South African Fly-Fishing Association, P.O. Box 82137, Southdale 2135.
(Club members fish small dams and a stretch of river near Dullstroom.)

Transvaal Fly Fishers' Club, P.O. Box 519, Edenvale 1610.
(Members enjoy excellent fishing on six dams in the Dullstroom area.)

SELECTED BIBLIOGRAPHY

Two club journals are devoted to fly fishing in South Africa: *Piscator,* of which the Editor's address is the Cape Piscatorial Society, 122 Longmarket Street, Cape Town; and *The Creel,* of which the Editor's address is Natal Fly Fishers' Club, PO Box 1535, Pietermaritzburg.

Newsletters are circulated to the members of several other clubs and associations.

The following are references to which I have had access:

Anonymous. "Trout fishing in Natal" in *Natal Province: Descriptive Guide and Official Handbook,* 1911, SA Railways Printing Works, Durban: pp. 359-373.

Perhaps understandably, as this is a Railways production, only those rivers accessible by rail are dealt with. Glowing descriptions are given of the fishing on the Umgeni, Mooi and Bushman's Rivers.

Anonymous. *South African Railways Official Illustrated Guide to Trout Fishing in South Africa,* 1916, Publicity Department, South African Railways: 124 + 6 pp.

This is an excellent guide book for all the trout areas. It mentions that the Natal Anglers' Association controlled all fishing in "Crown Native Trust Lands" and that the Transvaal Trout Acclimatisation Society was active and was giving pride of place to the Broederstroom near Haenertsburg in the north-eastern Transvaal.

Bachman, Robert A. "Foraging behaviour of free-ranging wild and hatchery brown trout in a stream", 1984, *Transactions of the American Fisheries Society,* vol. 113, pp. 1-32.

For anyone concerned with trout behaviour, this is of exceptional interest, as indicated in my text.

Beams, John. *Introducing Fly Fishing in South Africa,* 1974, Top Farmers Publication, Durban: 78 pp.

This was intended as an introductory section for a comprehensive book on fly fishing in Southern Africa, but the project was abandoned. The author came to South Africa in 1964 from the United Kingdom and for the next 20 years was an extraordinarily successful catcher of trout as well as a prolific writer, especially in the pages of *Piscator,* the journal of the Cape Piscatorial Society, which published *Trout in the Kloofs,* 1962, Reports of the Exploration Group of the Society: 119 pp. As well as factual information, much valuable comment is included.

Bennion, B. *The Angler in South Africa,* 1923, Hortors, Johannesburg: 190 pp.

The author also wrote an earlier book, *The Trout are Rising in England and South Africa.* He was a journalist with a pleasant anecdotal style, whose writing gives a good impression of conditions at that time.

Blackman, Jack. *Flies and Flyfishing in South Africa,* 1985, Acucut Books, Durban: 64 pp.

Useful information is provided by this well-known angler who has been associated with the tackle trade in recent years. The photography of Neil Hodges illustrates many of the flies used in South Africa.

Bowker, Fred. Using the pseudonym "Kingfisher," Bowker wrote three books: *A Trout Fisher in South Africa,* 1922, Flowers and Co., Cape Town; *Trout-Flies,* 1938, Heath Cranton Ltd, London; and *Shiny and Shiners,* 1946, Howard Timmins, Cape Town.

Bowker came from Cheshire to the Cape in 1902 and became adept at catching the large rainbows of the lower Eerste River. He did so through field craft, great patience and calculated control of his movements on the river. Strangely, he remained sceptical about the possibility that Eerste River rainbows migrated to sea and back again.

Crass, R.S. *Freshwater Fishes of Natal*, 1964, Shuter and Shooter, Pietermaritzburg: 167 pp.

This book has a section on trout as well as an historical summary. My second book, *Trout Fishing in Natal*, 1971, Daily News, Durban: 108 pp; deals with the rivers of Natal in a series of articles reprinted from a newspaper column together with some additional information.

Fling, Paul N. and D.L. Puterbaugh. *Fly Fisherman's Primer*, 1985, Sterling Publishing Co. Inc., New York: 160 pp.

Fling's writing and Puterbaugh's graphics make this an outstandingly informative work. Highly recommended.

Frost, W.E. and M.E. Brown. *The Trout*, 1967, Collins: 316 pp.

A superb compilation and explanation of the life history of the brown trout.

Goddard, John. *Trout Flies of Still Water*, 1972, Adam and Charles Black, London: 263 pp.

The close relationship between the natural insects and fly fishing techniques in Britain and South Africa is shown by the relevance of this book to angling in South African dams.

Goddard, John and Brian Clarke. *The Trout and the Fly*, 1981, Ernest Benn, London: 192 pp.

For clarity of exposition and superb illustrations this book is unsurpassed. The reader gains new insights into the underwater world of the trout, especially the effect of the "window".

Hey, S.A. *The Rapture of the River*, 1957, Balkema, Cape Town: 258 pp.

Without doubt, this is the most important contribution to South African trout fishing literature. Not only is the text evocative of the heyday of river angling; much of the comment on river management remains valid to this day. The only serious issue one might take up is his belief that heavy angling is the answer to the problem of overstocked streams. He shared with his contemporaries an exaggerated idea of the harmful effects of "poaching".

Hilliard, Helen B. *A Trout Rod in Natal*, no date (published about 1955), Central News Agency: 76 pp.

This little volume reflects the intense pleasure which Mrs Hilliard took in fishing the rivers of Underberg, the Umzimkulu in particular. Two quotations are worth recording: "Fishing is unique, almost in the annals of sport; you are not dependent on anyone else, you are complete in yourself" and "You need never lack interest in life so long as you can hold a rod in your hand."

Ivens, T.C. *Still Water Fly Fishing*, 1975, 4th Ed., André Deutsch, London: 319 pp.

Modern techniques of reservoir fishing in the English midlands owe much to Tom Ivens, whose angling skill is matched by his ability as a writer. South African anglers have benefitted from his excellent common-sense approach.

Jacques, David. *The Development of Modern Stillwater Fishing*, 1974, Adam and Charles Black, London: 237 pp.

Like Goddard's book, this is about English trout fishing; yet much is applicable to South Africa. It is particularly interesting to note the similarity in yield per hectare of United Kingdom and South African still waters.

Meintjes, Malcolm. *Trout on the Veld*, 1973, published privately: 96 pp.

This unpretentious book is a delightful addition to South African angling literature: it contains much common sense.

Nuttall, Neville. *Life in the Country*, 1973, The Star, Johannesburg: 136 pp.

This volume incorporates Nuttall's 1947 book, *Trout Streams of Natal*. Much of charm is to be found in his writing, including recipes for preparing trout. Nuttall produced a novel, *Proud River*, 1965, set in the Underberg district, published by Howard Timmins.

Proper, Datus C. *What the Trout Said*, 1982, Alfred Knopf: 273 pp.

Although based on the writer's experiences in America and Ireland, this book offers much of interest to the South African angler. Proper emphasises that design is what controls a fly's behaviour in the water and to a trout "his food's behaviour is more important that its tint".

Reid, Arthur H. *Trout and Angling in South Africa*, 1921, The Speciality Press of SA. Ltd: 101 pp.

Despite the wide coverage in a short book, a good insight is provided into conditions at that time, especially in the Cape.

Ritz, Charles. *A Fly Fisher's Life*, revised edition, 1972, Max Reinhardt, London: 280 pp.

Any angler unfamiliar with Ritz's classic should leave no library unraided until he can locate a copy.

No wonder the Ritz hotels were the world's finest. The Ritz dedication, insight and efficiency put Charles of that ilk at the top of world angling, as well as heading his catering empire. "Above all," he said, "do not begin fishing till you know how to cast."

Salomon, Michael G. *Freshwater Fishing in South Africa,* 1978, Chris van Rensburg Publications, Johannesburg: 156 pp.
    This is a well-produced book with a considerable coverage on trout, both by Salomon and other authors.
Sutcliffe, Tom. *My Way with a Trout,* 1985, Shuter and Shooter, Pietermaritzburg: 185 pp.
    This reprint of the delightful newspaper articles, familiar to readers of the *Natal Mercury,* has proved deservedly popular with the angling public. Sutcliffe is one of the leaders of the modern school of South African fly fishers.
Yates, J.H. *African Anglers Argosy,* 1956, Central News Agency Ltd: 167 pp.
    This book, together with his earlier (1950) *Angling Adventures in South Africa,* reflects the author's wide-ranging experiences with freshwater fish, including trout, mainly in the Transvaal.

GLOSSARY

Alevin — the first stage in a fish's life, after it has hatched from the egg; an alevin continues to subsist on the egg yolk attached to its belly (see *fry*).

Anadromous — migratory behaviour involving the movement of young fish from fresh to salt water and their subsequent return, as adults, to fresh water for breeding: characteristic of salmon, steelhead and sea trout.

Annulus — the break in the even pattern of a fish's scale, due to a check in growth at the end of summer; by counting the annuli on a magnified scale one can determine the fish's age.

Aquatic — refers to insects or other animals found in water; some aquatic insects spend only part of their lives in water.

Bait — edible material attached to a hook (see *fly* and *lure*).

Barbless hook — a fly hook on which the barb has been flattened with pliers, or which has been manufactured without a barb; used when the angler wishes to minimise damage to fish which are to be released.

Caddisfly — an insect with mothlike appearance and rapid flight, often seen flying over the water at dusk; caddis larva is the immature stage, which lives under water.

Cast — the act of moving a rod to deliver line, leader and fly onto the water; may also have the same meaning as *leader* (see definition).

Condition factor — a measure of the relative plumpness of a fish; trout in satisfactory condition should have a metric condition factor of 110 to 140, or a pounds/inches condition factor of 40 to 50.

Crustacean — a member of the group of invertebrate animals that includes shrimps, crabs and daphnia.

Damselfly — an insect of the order Odonata, suborder Zygoptera: slender, fluttering insects with aquatic nymphs.

Dead drift — allowing the fly to drift freely in the current, without any movement being imparted by the angler.

Double haul — pulling sharply on the line to impart extra speed of movement on both backward and forward cast; used to attain maximum distance.

Drag — unnatural movement of a fly caused by the action of a current of water pulling on the line.

Dragonfly — an insect of the order Odonata, suborder Anisoptera; large, colourful, swift-flying insects, with aquatic nymphs.

Dropper — a second fly attached to the leader between the tail (or end) fly and the line.

Dry fly — a fly that is designed to float on the water's surface.

False cast — a cast in which the fly is kept moving without being allowed to alight on the water; used for working out line to reach a desired spot.

Fibreglass — long fibres of glass embedded in a cementing compound; commonly used for constructing fishing rods.

Fly — an artificial arrangement of natural or synthetic materials tied to a hook; may include feathers, fur or processed silk, but not edible material (see *bait* and *lure*).

Fry — a young fish that has passed the alevin stage and has become active in finding its own food.

Gonad — male or female sexual organ; commonly known as soft or hard roe, respectively.

Graphite — a material consisting of carbon fibres used for the manufacture of fishing rods.

Imago — the fully adult stage of a mayfly; this group of insects has a nymph stage (aquatic), a subimago (or dun) and an imago (or spinner), all of which are imitated by fly tiers.

Leader — the thin, often tapered, length of nylon or other monofilament that connects the fly to the line; sometimes referred to as a *cast*.

Line — a fly line is woven from numerous fine filaments and coated with a smooth dressing; must have adequate weight to carry leader and fly when casting.

Loop — the curved shape assumed by a line in the act of casting; the loop may be broad or narrow and its form is of great importance for effective casting.

Lure — an artificial object with a hook, or hooks, attached; some lures may fall within the definition of a *fly*, but others (e.g. those that spin) do not.

Mayfly — an insect belonging to the order Ephemeroptera; after spending most of its life as an aquatic nymph, an adult mayfly lives for only a brief period; all stages are readily eaten by trout.

Ova — eggs: more specifically, fertilised trout eggs.

Ova, eyed — eggs in which the eyes of the embryo are visible through the transparent membrane.

Nymph — the immature aquatic stage of a mayfly, dragonfly, damselfly or stonefly; applied also to an artificial imitation of the natural insect.

Retrieve — the act of pulling in line with the hand to work a fly through the water.

Shooting — allowing a loop of line, held in the hand, to be pulled through the rod rings by the forward momentum of the leading section of the line.

Stonefly — an insect belonging to the order Plecoptera; adults have four wings which, in rest, are folded neatly along the insect's back.

Terrestrial — living on land: generally used to describe insects such as grasshoppers or ants that fall onto the water by accident; trout may eat large numbers of terrestrial insects at times.

Wet fly — a fly that is fished below the water surface: includes an artificial nymph.

Wind knot — a knot that appears in a leader owing to faulty casting technique; weakens the leader if allowed to tighten.

Index